THE FORM OF CITIES

URBAN AND SOCIAL GEOGRAPHY SERIES

General Editor
J. H. Johnson, M.A., Ph.D.,
Professor of Geography, University of Lancaster

THE FORM OF CITIES

D. I. SCARGILL

BELL & HYMAN
LONDON

First published in 1979 by
BELL & HYMAN LIMITED
Denmark House
37-39 Queen Elizabeth Street
London SE1 2QB

© D. I. Scargill 1979

ISBN 0 7135 0269 X

Printed in Great Britain by
Holmes McDougall
137-141 Leith Walk
Edinburgh EH6 8NS

To
C. F. W. R. Gullick

Acknowledgments

All the figures have been drawn in the Oxford School of Geography, but many of them are based closely on the research of others. I wish to record my thanks to those authors who have kindly given me permission to reproduce their maps or diagrams in this way. Acknowledgment has been made in the titles accompanying the figures and fuller particulars, including the names of the publishers concerned, will be found in the bibliography. I am grateful to Penny Timms and her colleagues at Oxford for the care which they devoted to the drawing of these illustrations during a long, hot summer.

D.I.S.

Preface

About ten years ago the Oxford School of Geography introduced a final-year option in urban geography which took as its theme, the internal structure of the city. This book arises from my attempts to teach that option over the last decade. It does not offer any new research; rather it seeks to review the existing literature and draw together strands which, in the author's opinion, have too long remained disparate in their treatment. Research into contemporary social and economic patterns, for example, frequently ignores the influence of the pre-urban cadaster, whilst cross-cultural studies are rare at anything more than a superficial level. Thus the book opens with an exploration of the historical background to urban growth, and later chapters look at the city in the Third World and the Socialist World as well as the West. Recognition is also given to the influence of planning decisions in the creation of modern urban forms. The work is not aimed at any one kind of reader; it is hoped that what has been brought together will be of interest and value, not only to school and university students, but possibly also to those who, like planners, have the responsibility of putting theory into practice.

A review which takes such a wide canvas could never claim to be complete. Selection has been inevitable but not, it is hoped, at the expense of presenting that balanced view of the city which has always been my aim. I am indebted, of course, to all those authors whose original work provides the research foundations on which the book is based. If I were to single out anyone else, for special thanks, it would be my former tutor, Rowley Gullick, whose vision of geography as a single discipline has survived the years when narrowly-based research has often appeared to fragment it. Finally I must express my gratitude to the University of Oxford for granting me two terms of leave in order to write the book.

St. Edmund Hall, Oxford

Contents

List of Figures

1

Processes Shaping the City

What is meant by the *form* of cities? To some the word may suggest involvement only with the morphology of the city, i.e. its physical fabric, dwellings and the more specialized structures that house retail, office and manufacturing functions. Interest in buildings is a legitimate part of the urban geographer's concern. Study of housing types, for example, is reviving as more attention is now paid to the housing market as a variable in the social patterning of cities. House types also serve as a mirror to cultural traditions and one of the objects of the present work is to explore the role which such traditions play in urban growth in different parts of the world. But assemblages of structures also have a spatial form and our concern in what follows is principally with the spatial expression of urban phenomena and with the many different kinds of process which underlie this patterning, this urban form. Such processes are economic, social and political. Some, especially the economic ones, are international in character; others are much more culture-specific. And underlying all are the inherited effects of the past.

Despite an already voluminous literature, urban geography is continually benefiting from new forms of research. Studies of human behaviour, for example, bring new understanding to the nature of such phenomena as population segregation and the use and distribution of urban retail centres. But research on a wide front also carries with it the danger of fragmentation and, worse still, of attempts to apply universally conclusions derived from a narrowly-defined field of enquiry in a single city or group of closely related towns. A major objective of the present work, therefore, has been to draw together strands of research, exploring the degree to which problems observed in one place are generally applicable or not. In particular an attempt has been made to bridge the literature relating to the cities of the industrialized West and the growing number of works devoted to cities in what, for convenience, we may call the Third World and the Socialist World. There are obvious pitfalls in approaching the subject in so comprehensive a fashion, not least those of over-generalization, but the paucity of comparative studies of this kind would seem to justify some attempt at what is here proposed: an overview of urban form, planned and unplanned, in different parts of the world.

The remainder of this largely introductory chapter looks at processes shaping the city, two principal categories of which are examined. The first of these may be termed the historical process, and attention is here given to the manner in which former patterns of land-ownership have fashioned the growing city. This kind of investigation has been a popular one with historical geographers and economic historians but it is one which rarely receives more than passing reference by those urban geographers whose interest lies primarily in the social forces of the contemporary world. The second set of processes examined are the political ones. The role of politicians and planners in shaping the modern city cannot be denied, but it must be remembered that planning is not a new phenomenon, and the power of the planner to direct urban growth varies from country to country, in turn being influenced by concepts of the role which the city is called upon to perform. Subsequent chapters are devoted to the forces which affect the form, firstly of the western city, then of cities in other parts of the world. An aim throughout is to observe the distinction, however blurred, between urban growth that is planned and that which is of a more spontaneous nature.

The pre-urban cadaster

The physical expansion of a city is rarely haphazard. Even when it is not planned, the outward growth of a town or city is constrained or directed by existing forms of land use and land ownership. In applying the analogue of wave movement to urban growth, Blumenfeld (1954) has used the term 'precession wave' to describe the forces operating in the fringe zone beyond the built-up limits of the city. Pressure to develop open space is less here than it is within the city where a stronger, 'tidal wave' of change can be observed, and because it is weaker the precession wave is more likely to be affected by obstacles in its path. As the waves at the head of the beach are halted or channelled by natural and man-made obstacles, so is the spread of the city checked by such diverse barriers as Green Belts, land reserved for gravel extraction, or estate villages. Elsewhere it is directed to categories of land which, for various reasons, are more open or attractive to development.

Models of urban structure like those of Burgess, Hoyt and Harris and Ullman make little allowance for the effect of pre-urban patterns of land use, although the generalization of Harris and Ullman recognizes that there is a unique element in the form of every city, in part a legacy of its history. It is salutary, therefore, before embarking on an analysis of city form and of the factors which bring about urban growth to remind oneself that the city is successor to some pre-existing land use and that its present structure owes something to the past. It is worth stressing also that certain land uses resist change and become fossilised, as it were, within the otherwise largely built-up area of the city. Certain land uses are typical of the city fringe, for example sewage disposal works, golf courses, cemeteries, certain industries and, more recent phenomena, Country Parks, hypermarkets, and drive-in garden centres. As the city spreads outwards to engulf them, certain of these peri-urban land uses remain embedded in the urban fabric of the city like porphyritic crystals in a sample of volcanic rock. Whitehand (1967) has drawn attention to the presence of such relict features within the Tyneside conurbation of North-East England. The fact that one can distinguish pre-urban land uses typical of particular periods in the conurbation's history, further serves as a reminder that the growth of cities is irregular in time as well as in space, related as it is to building cycles and to phases of economic prosperity.

Enclosure

Despite the increasing control exercised by government and by local planning authorities, the conversion of land from rural to urban uses is still governed by its existing use and ownership. Certain types of farmer are more inclined to sell up than others: the joint or absentee owner, the farmer nearing retirement or the one whose land has already been affected by urban encroachment, for example by the building of a ring road (Gasson, 1966). In contrast the estate-owner is likely to resist development, and Mortimore (1969) has shown how the preservation of tracts of farmland within the West Yorkshire conurbation is closely related to the distribution of estates. Owners, who in later life may have been tempted to sell, have ensured that the estate is passed on intact by entailing it to the benefit of their eldest son. Emery (1974) has used the terms 'closed' and 'open' villages to describe those settlements in Oxfordshire that have repelled or attracted the developer, the former coinciding closely with estates over which the policy of the 'big house' is still exercised. These days the estate-owner may be a company or institution. Thus Wytham, on the western fringes of Oxford, has resisted change because it is owned by the University which maintains farmland for teaching purposes and woodland for research. When eventually a farm or estate is sold it may retain its identity as a town park. Many such examples can be found in the cities of industrial Britain, the former owner's mansion serving as museum, library or art gallery. The need to pay death duties has compelled more estate-owners to sell in recent years and the availability of a large estate on the fringe of a city has proved attractive to local authorities seeking to build large-scale municipal housing using industrialized building methods in order to achieve economies of scale. Ward (1962) has demonstrated how, in Leeds, the distribution of such municipal housing projects is closely related to the former land-ownership pattern.

Enclosure, or failure to enclose, the open fields affected the growth of cities in several ways. Nottingham, which in the 1840s had some of the worst slums in Britain, is a classic example (Hoskins, 1955). Despite the fact that the rights to common grazing were held by only a small minority of the citizens, it was not possible to obtain an Act to enclose the open fields which girdled Nottingham until as late as 1845. By this date the population of the town had grown to over 53 000 and insanitary, closed courts were built to house workers in the rapidly expanding lace and other industries. When eventually enclosure took place, expansion of the built-up area was immediate and rapid, so that the network of paths which had formerly served the open fields became fossilised beneath road patterns of Nottingham's later nineteenth century suburbs. Enclosure rarely affected the whole of a town's fields at the same time, and some common lands were never enclosed. These have afforded valuable areas of recreational open space as the city has grown. Southampton's commons and the Town Moor at Newcastle upon Tyne are well-known, but many other cities possess a similiar lung, if not of the same extent.

Early piecemeal enclosure tended to impart the shape of the original holding on the newly built-up area and the sinuous inverted S-shaped plot, readily recognized in the shape of the fields which surround an early-enclosed village, can similarly be picked out with careful observation of certain town streets. In his work on West Yorkshire, Mortimore contrasts the small town of Heckmondwike, where early enclosure produced long curving streets, with Cleckheaton, higher up the Spen Valley, where late enclosure under Parliamentary Act resulted in a more regular, geometrical layout.

Size and shape of plot

Although enclosure was sometimes followed directly by house building, as in mid-nineteenth century Nottingham, the more usual reason for enclosing open fields has, of course, been to create individual farm holdings. These holdings may subsequently have changed hands several times, experiencing changes of boundary or subdivision, so that in time the pre-urban cadaster becomes a highly irregular one. Plots of varying size and, possibly, highly irregular shape, make up a kind of tapestry in which the different strands of the building process weave an even more complicated pattern.

It is possible to reconstruct the pre-urban map of land-holding by reference to such sources as enclosure awards, tithe and estate maps, sale plans, and surveys of farm holdings carried out by the Ministry of Agriculture. Relating this map to large-scale town plans reveals the high degree of control which the inherited pattern of land occupance has exercised over the layout of streets and even over the shape of individual buildings (Fig. 1). In their work on Leeds and Bradford, Ward (1962) and Mortimore (1969) demonstrated the closeness of connection between plot size and shape and the complicated street pattern of the city as it really is. This is brought out in detail in the study of the growth of Camberwell by Dyos (1961): '. . . innumerable tiny variations in the style of construction of the houses, even when these are terraced, the numerous breaks in the lines of eaves, the restless changes in the treatment of windows, doors, bays, and so on. That the Victorian suburb was no consciously made artefact is evident enough from a walk along its disjointed streets and from the attempt to find reasonable explanations for the directions some of them took.'

Small irregularly-shaped plots were typical of those parts of West Yorkshire where the domestic textile industry had flourished, and the pattern of streets and terraced housing which succeeded them reflect in their intricacy the fragmented layout of holdings. Successive rows are reduced in length to fit into a triangular plot, streets acquire abrupt changes in direction as attempts are made to join up adjacent developments at their boundaries, and oddly-shaped houses are built at the ends of terraces to make maximum use of the amount of building land available. Such a house type, common in Leeds, was the 'salt pie', one half of a back-to-back pair, the blank rear wall built up against the property boundary having no window openings. The back-to-back type as a whole probably evolved from the constraints imposed by the shape

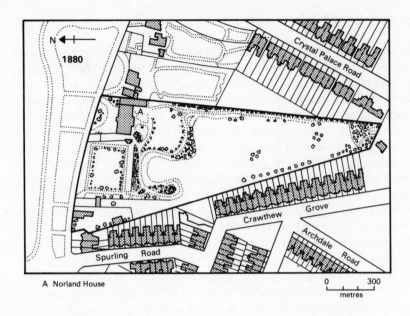

A Norland House

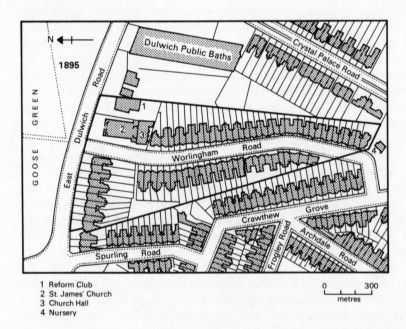

1 Reform Club
2 St. James' Church
3 Church Hall
4 Nursery

1   Effect of the pre-urban cadaster on the form of the built-up area.
      Worlingham Road estate, Camberwell. After Dyos, 1961. (Cour-
      tesy Leicester University Press)

of building plots. Long strips of land, formerly used as tenter crofts for stretching and drying cloth, encouraged developers to build houses around a narrow yard. What more natural, when the rows backed up against those of adjacent properties, than to join the houses physically, creating back-to-backs and avoiding waste? Similarly Mortimore sees the tenement pairs, typical of Tyneside — one downstairs and one above served by an external stair — as a response to divided ownership of land.

The role of the speculator must not be overlooked in this process of converting land from rural to urban uses. Sale, or leasing of land for building, may have been preceded by speculative purchase and sub-division of former agricultural land. This has been common in the United States, assisted by the division of land into lots for taxation purposes by city assessors anxious to raise revenues. Fellmann (1957) has described the process for Chicago, distinguishing between the initial, speculative subdivision of land and the later sale of building plots when re-subdivision was often involved. Saleability of individual plots is related to such obvious controls as accessibility, the presence of parks and of pre-existing settlement nuclei, but the earlier process of subdivision reflects the speculator's anticipation of where such demand is likely to arise. The two may not coincide, a fact worth keeping in mind in assessing the merits of models of city growth (Chapter 2).

In Camberwell, Dyos observed a tendency, not only for the layout of streets to reflect the pre-urban pattern of ownership, but for these in turn to dictate the social character of the locality. 'The geometry of the ground plan tended to settle some of the social issues from the outset, for the longer and straighter and flatter the street the fewer pretensions it normally had.' Although allowance must be made for changes that take place over the course of time, this statement has an interesting bearing on attempts that have been made to define social areas in towns, a subject explored more fully in Chapter 3.

Land tenure

In their studies of English towns, urban historians have emphasized the distinction between freehold and leasehold tenure, the latter system being one under which the landowner retained ownership of the land on which property was built, receiving a ground rent from it. At the expiry of the lease, the property became his. It is a subject which geographers have tended to neglect, surprisingly in view of the degree to which property development was affected by the legal conditions that were, or were not, imposed upon it. In general it may be said that the leasehold system brought about some of the worst, but also some of the best, building in English nineteenth-century towns. Furthermore, through covenants that were written into the leases, it has influenced the subsequent use of this property, a fact which makes the study of land tenure of more than historical concern.

The builder of freehold property was required to buy the land on which his development took place and this requirement tended to exclude from freehold operations the small speculator without any source of capital. Although the building society movement came into being to help the small house-buyer and was associated especially with the freehold situation, it remained difficult for the impoverished speculator to get into business because of the problem of acquiring land on which to build houses for purchase. Housing built under conditions of freehold tenure thus tended to avoid some of the worst problems encountered where leasehold was more common. This latter system, by contrast, attracted the speculator because there was no initial outlay on land. Unskilled builders with no previous experience were able to get into business by raising a small amount of credit, sub-contracting the actual construction work, and mortgaging the property as they went along. Such practice was impossible when stringent conditions were imposed on the lessee, but many leases were vaguely drafted, imposing few restrictions, and shoddy building would often result. The worst kind of builder was unimpressed by the fact that on the termination of the lease — often as short as 60 years in London — the property was required to be handed over in good order. Long before this it would have been sub-leased, or assigned to others.

In marked contrast with the worst products of speculative building were the developments which took place under carefully specified leasehold conditions. Covenants contained in the leases could regulate such matters as the width of streets, the materials used for house construction, the depth of front gardens, and the present and future use to which any of the buildings could be put. Some leasehold estates engaged architects to draw up plans and to supervise the actual building. Regulations were not always absent under conditions of freehold development — some were imposed by the building societies — but they were of a limited nature before legislation in the 1870s introduced building byelaws. The covenants were important, therefore, in determining the physical and social character of whole areas of towns, protecting them also from both delapidation and from the loss of social status which frequently overtook other districts where there was no such control. Edgbaston, close to the centre of Birmingham, affords a good example of a spacious suburb which has retained its appearance and its status as a result of the covenants that were imposed by Sir Henry Calthorpe, owner of the Edgbaston Estate. The nature of Dulwich in south London similarly owes much to management exercised by the Dulwich College Estates Governors (Dyos, 1961). In Oxford, St. John's College maintained a watchful control over the development of their Norham Manor and Walton Manor estates from the 1860s. Though built for individual clients, most of the houses on the Norham Manor estate were designed by the same architects, Wilkinson and Moore, under regulations intended to preserve the suburb's parklike appearance. Rows of artisan cottages were built on the neighbouring Walton Manor estate but these were also architect-designed (Hinton, 1974).

Most English towns are a patchwork of leasehold and freehold tenure but in some of them one particular form has dominated to the extent that they may be described as leasehold or freehold towns. The former include the Sussex resort of Eastbourne where the Dukes of Devonshire built parades of houses of an elegance equal to those of the great ducal estates of central London. In West Yorkshire, Huddersfield was a leasehold town in contrast with the other large towns of the textile belt where freehold tenure was typical. As a result of interest taken in the quality of workmen's housing by the Ramsden family, Huddersfield acquired very few of the back-to-back houses that were so typical in nearby Leeds, Bradford and Halifax.

In total contrast with the spacious suburbs that have been protected by covenants are those localities, usually close to the city centre in what Burgess described as the 'zone in transition', where residential property has undergone change of use in part because of the absence of any such restrictions. As population moves out the houses are taken over by light industry or converted for storage or office use. Describing the evolution of the jewellery and gun-making industries of Birmingham, Wise (1949) has shown how these became localized in distinctive 'quarters' to the north of the city centre, because of the absence there of restrictive covenants. Both industries were made up of close-knit but small-scale trades which were attracted to property that could be rented cheaply. Once-elegant three-storeyed houses in Vyse Street and adjacent roads were converted into jewellery workshops in the mid-nineteenth century and the industry has remained there although the old dwellings are now being replaced by Council-built flatted factories. The clothing industry in other cities provides similar histories of property conversion, an added attraction being access to sources of female labour wishing to work at home.

The industrial colony

Model townships such as Saltaire or Bournville (Chapter 6) were exceptional features in the general evolution of British industrial towns and Marshall (1968) argues that preoccupation with these few, well-known examples has diverted attention from the part played in the growth and spatial arrangement of nineteenth century towns by what he calls the 'industrial colony'. The latter grew up around mills or factories, usually established beyond the contemporary built-up area of the town because of the need to seek out water-power sites or cheap land. Absorbed later into the fabric of the expanding town, they have not only affected the physical growth of that town through their influence on the direction of house-building or layout of its streets, but they have also retained sufficient architectural and social identity to enable them to remain distinctive districts within the now larger town. Marshall uses, for illustration, the cotton manufacturing towns of Lancashire — quoting the examples of Freetown (Bury), Brookhouse (Blackburn), Belmont (Bolton) — and the iron-making settlements of Furness. The architectural whims of the mill- or factory-owner gave the colony some visual identity and for the local population a sense of place was heightened by the close-knit nature of a community engaged in the same occupation and by independence in matters of local government which, for a time, survived the physical absorption of the district by the parent town.

Influence of the railway

Pre-urban patterns of land-ownership help to explain the routes selected for entry into cities by nineteenth-century railway companies, and also the sites chosen for their stations and marshalling yards, the companies preferring to negotiate with a few major owners rather than with many small ones (Fig. 2). When it was necessary to demolish property, it was usually areas of working class housing that suffered since tenants had no legal basis on which to object (Kellett, 1969). Like the industrial colonies, the railways, once built, affected the subsequent alignment of streets which had to be fitted into the shapes created by straight or broadly curving

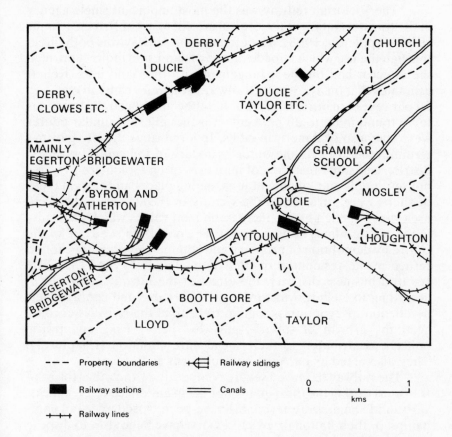

2 Effect of landownership patterns on the location of railway lines and terminals in Manchester. After Kellett, 1969. (Courtesy Routledge and Kegan Paul)

approach lines and an older road pattern. This effect was most marked where 'islands' were created by the intersection of lines, the most common form being the triangular junction. Sometimes these sequestered areas were used for housing, more often they attracted industrial land uses or were left to become overgrown and derelict. Some have since provided a site for allotment gardens.

'The Victorian railway was the most important single agency in the transformation of the central area of many of Britain's major cities' (Appleton, 1968). The effect of the railway was both direct through the use which it made of its own land, and indirect through the effect it had on the arrangement of other land uses. Kellett estimates that on average the railway companies came to own 8 to 10 per cent of 'central land' and that they influenced the functions to be found in up to 20 per cent. It is thought that similar figures were true also of American cities. In large cities the siting of rail termini tended to fix the outer boundary of the central business district, and some resorting of land uses often took place as warehouses, hotels and lodging houses, eating places and certain types of shops were attracted to the vicinity of the station. Other land uses were repelled by the increase in land values which proximity to the rail terminals brought about. The poor, 'elbowed out' of the centre by demolition of property and commercial pressures, found refuge in the residential districts immediately beyond the CBD [central business district], the effect of the railway upon which, according to Kellett, was to 'freeze their value and confirm their dereliction'. Beyond this 'zone in transition' the railways encouraged the growth of suburbs and, by their pricing and traffic policies, contributed to their social differentiation (Chapter 3). They also acted as barriers, both physical and social.

The railway has faced severe competition from other forms of transport during the third quarter of the twentieth century. Tracks, yards and some entire terminals have been closed. Yet rail companies, or their nationalized successors, have been slow to dispose of land which they no longer require for their operations. At the same time, financial constraints have acted as a brake on the companies redeveloping their sites themselves. In the future, however, one may expect to see greater re-use of railway land and property and in this manner the railway will continue to play some part in directing urban land use.

Constraints of the housing market

The pre-urban cadaster provides the foundation on which urban growth takes place and the layout of the contemporary city cannot be fully understood without some reference to the past. But urban growth is also directed and constrained by processes — economic, social and political — that operate in the present. Of these, the economic processes have hitherto received most attention and theories of urban spatial structure have relied to a disproportionate extent on the relationship between land rent and accessibility (Chapter 2). Interest in recent years, however, has shifted towards the social and political forces that underlie the spatial structure of the city. Typical of this trend is the emphasis now placed on the operation of the housing market, particularly as it operates to affect the social patterning of the city.

Concern for the housing market arises from the fact that a household's choice of place to live is determined not only by income and personal preferences but by a range of institutional constraints that act as a filter to these preferences. Households of different characteristics have differing degrees of access to housing which are related to policies pursued by central and local government, by financial organizations and by the property and construction industries. These policies operate through three distinct housing sectors — the owner-occupier, private rental and public sectors — with the proportion of the total housing stock belonging to each varying from city to city. The fact that policies change over the course of time is an additional complication in seeking to generalize about the role of institutions operating in the housing market. Reference will be made to three institutions: the building society, the estate agent and the housing department of the local authority. Each pursues distinct policies but their activities are not wholly independent of each other, all, for example, being affected by trends in the national economy and by government actions.

The building society movement dates from the final quarter of the eighteenth century when small societies were set up with limited objectives, usually to build a specific number of dwellings for their members. When they had done this, they were wound up, and societies that operated on a permanent basis became common only towards the middle of the nineteenth century. Paralleling the work of the building societies for a time were the freehold land societies. These often had a political as well as a social motive, municipal reform in 1832 extending the franchise to all who owned a forty shilling freehold. Coupled with the less worthy political or economic motives, however, was often a strong wish to better the lot of the working man and both forms of society played a positive role in the evolution of the nineteenth-century town. This was specially true of the industrial North where, for example, the largest of the present permanent societies in Britain — the Halifax — originated in a town that was fortunate to have one or two manufacturing families of strong religious conviction who, in a well-meaning way, tried to rival each other in good works (Scargill, 1963).

Building societies are now responsible for 78 per cent of the funds loaned for home purchase in Britain (Boddy, 1976). The significance of this figure must be measured against the increase in home ownership that has taken place during the present century, from under 11 per cent in 1914 to 28 per cent in 1953 and 52 per cent in 1973. The steep rise in owner-occupation that has taken place since the early 1950s has been partly in response to government policy, but this is in many respects only a permissive factor and an active part in bringing about home ownership has been played by the building societies. The geographer's interest in this work of building societies arises principally from the rules which they operate in allocating funds to intending house buyers and the spatial implications of such selectivity. In determining whether or not to grant a loan, account is taken by the society both of the nature of the dwelling—including its age and state of repair, the tenure under which it is held and its location within the city — and of the socio-economic characteristics of the intending borrower. They will take into account in their assessment not only the latter's age and income but also his credit-worthiness based on the stability of that income. Thus a salaried person with an expectation of regular increments is more likely to obtain a loan than a wage earner in some insecure form of employment.

The procedures and guidelines under which they operate vary to a certain extent from one society to another. The small, locally-based building society is likely to be rather more sympathetic to a request for a loan in its own area than is the national society which has little knowledge of that particular district. All, however, are selective in order to protect their lenders' funds and the consequence is a concentration of loans in those parts of the city that are considered safe, where property values will be maintained or rise. This being the case it is difficult to avoid the conclusion that the building societies are influential in maintaining existing social distinctions between one part of the city and another and in extending these differences to areas of new housing development. Boddy also considers that they contribute to urban decay in the inner city by denying funds to all but the most stable of these areas, namely the 'upper class' enclaves. Depending on its redevelopment plans, the local authority may be rather more willing to make loans for house-purchase in the inner city, but the role of the council in granting mortgages is very much smaller overall than that of the building societies.

The activities of estate agents are governed by a code of ethics but this does not mean that their role in the housing market is a wholly passive one. The contribution of realtors to the spread of the negro ghetto in the United States is examined in Chapter 3. In a study of Islington, Williams (1976) has examined the part played by both estate agents and building societies in the 'gentrification' which has taken place in that inner London suburb since the mid-1960s. From being concerned primarily with the management of property, the agents turned their attention to sales and sought to encourage these by advertising in the press and by the distribution of circulars offering their services. Some entered the property market themselves; others took on a role as advisers to owners, development companies and building societies. In an American study, Palm (1976) demonstrates how the estate agent may influence the choice of place of residence, intentionally or otherwise, because he possesses knowledge of the housing market which is limited and biased in favour of certain areas.

Public involvement in the housing market arose in Britain in response to the insanitary conditions prevailing in many towns that had experienced rapid nineteenth-century growth. At first the role of local authorities was indirect, confined to the making of byelaws in order to control standards of housing and street layout, and the earlier attempts to build housing of an improved kind were made by philanthropic housing associations such as the Peabody Trust founded in 1862. It was the Public Health Act of 1875 that gave to all local authorities the right to enforce byelaws. Although there was much variation throughout the country in the extent to which these new powers were used, the adoption of byelaws did have a considerable impact on the townscape of late nineteenth-century Britain, monotonous rows of terraced dwellings reflecting the newly-imposed regulations. The need for something more than byelaws, however, was recognised in the appointment of the Royal Commission on the Housing of the Poor in 1884. The reports of this Commission led to the Housing of the Working Classes Act of 1890 which gave to local authorities the power not only to demolish unfit dwellings but to build new ones out of public funds. The opportunity of building such housing had, in fact, existed since 1851 under the Labouring Classes Lodging House Act, but few local authorities had taken advantage of this permissive legislation.

The Act of 1890, too, was permissive rather than mandatory and since they were not compelled to build houses, local authorities were often content to leave the initiative to private enterprise. But change came with the First World War and a new sense of social responsibility. The report of the Tudor Walters Committee was published in 1918, setting out standards for working class housing that were wholly without precedent for this kind of dwelling. A density of not more than 12 houses to the acre (30 per hectare) was proposed, together with suggestions about layout and the use of gardens and open space that owed much to the inspiration of the Garden City Movement (Chapter 6). The legislation necessary to enable local authorities to build on a large scale and to these standards followed in the form of the Housing Acts of 1919 and 1924. Subsequently low-density housing estates were built by almost all local authorities, their spacious layout with a predominance of semi-detached (duplex) houses and geometrical patterns of curving streets and cul-de-sacs contrasting sharply with the compressed rows of byelaw housing that had preceded them (Fig. 3). Cherry (1972) comments: 'the inter-War Council estate became a highly distinctive element in any urban landscape: low density with blocks of houses arranged along streets following geometric layouts; dwellings set back behind front gardens; building lines splayed at all road junctions and, noticeably, at roundabouts; incidental green spaces to complement garden space; and with a deadening similarity of house styles and materials over vast areas, monotony was reinforced by occupancy largely from one social class.'

Local authority housing has continued to be built since the Second World War, employing new legislation, such as the Housing Repairs and Rent Act of 1954 which encouraged councils to undertake slum clearance and redevelopment programmes, and adopting new standards such as those set out in the Parker-Morris Report of 1961. Blocks of flats and a return to terrace construction have been a response to the wish to save land and to postwar planning regulations. At the same time more imaginative layouts have been achieved, with attempts to create a sense of neighbourhood. Since 1969, when the Housing Act of that year gave councils the opportunity to designate General Improvement Areas, there has been a shift in emphasis from the wholesale redevelopment of slum clearance areas that characterized the 1950s and early 1960s, towards piecemeal renovation of existing housing areas. The changes can be seen as a product of more-informed social attitudes towards the community and it carries with it important implications for the future of the city, involving as it does the preservation of the inner city housing areas as well as a possible slowdown in the consumption of land on the urban fringe for large-scale estates.

Local authority housing now accounts for a quarter of the stock of dwellings in Great Britain. The comparable figure in the

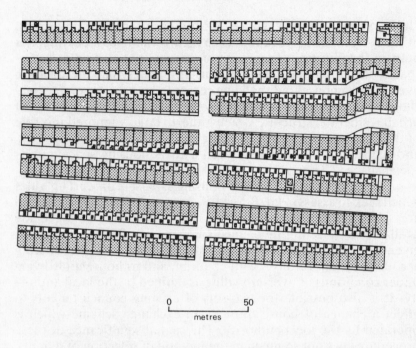

0   50
metres

School

3   Contrasted forms of bye-law and local authority housing. After McCulloch et al., 1961. (Courtesy the Editor of the *Town Planning Review,* vol. 32, nos. 3 and 4)

United States is 1½ per cent (B. S. Morgan, 1976). The proportion of the total housing stock that is council-owned has a bearing, not only on the physical appearance of the city, but also on its socio-spatial structure since council housing implies that the decision over where a household shall live ceases to be a matter of personal choice and is determined instead by the local authority. Theories of urban residential structure which hitherto largely ignored this role of the local authority are now being modified to take account of it, and a distinction is made between a city's housing space and its social space (Chapter 3).

The allocation of council housing is based on certain rules which seek to assess need. Priority is given to families whose homes are scheduled for slum clearance, after which houses are made available to those on the council's waiting list. Preference here is given to householders without a separate home; i.e. ones sharing accommodation, to those with children, and to households living under conditions of over-crowding as defined by the local author-ity. It is also possible for two sets of existing council tenants to effect a change of house through an exchange scheme which is operated by the local authority. The spatial significance of these procedures lies not so much in the method of selection of tenants, however, as in the policies which underlie the actual allocation of dwellings to them. These are based on an assessment of the suita-bility of tenants, not only for a particular kind of dwelling, but often also for a particular estate. In his study of Hull, Gray (1976) found a correlation between type of tenant and characteristics of the dwelling and area which he described as 'not a natural coincidence' and suggested that a similar situation was to be found in other cities. Local authorities justify the concentration of 'low-status' (problem) tenants in certain areas and 'respectable' ones in others in terms of management objectives, but Gray sees the system of allocation as tending 'to perpetuate and perhaps accentuate exist-ing socio-spatial patterns within the council sector'. He fears the substitution of the 'corporation slum' for that which the council is endeavouring to erase from the private sector.

The influence of government in the housing market is not confined to the publicly-owned sector but affects also the private one. The effect of rent control measures, for example, has been to reduce the scale of the private rental sub-sector in many towns, landlords of property preferring to sell rather than pay large repair bills on rent-controlled dwellings. Williams considers that, by encouraging landlords to sell, rent control measures have con-tributed to the 'gentrification' of such places as Islington. Other government measures, however, were intended to help low-income people themselves to become owner-occupiers. Such was the Option Mortgage Scheme and the Leasehold Reform Act, both introduced in 1967. The latter was intended to help leasehold tenants to acquire the freehold of their accommodation at modest prices. Grants can also be obtained from local authorities towards the cost of undertaking certain improvements to property, e.g. for installing a bathroom. The introduction of such measures is consistent with the shift in planning policy generally from redevelopment to rehabilitation and to the stabilization of the existing population in inner city areas.

Planning control

The Town Planning Act of 1909, which gave to local authorities the power to authorize town planning schemes, represented a first attempt by government to exercise control over urban development in Britain, but the powers were permissive only. So very largely were those provided under later Acts in 1919 and 1932, and it was not until after the Second World War that effective powers of development control and of plan making were introduced under the Town and Country Planning Act (1947).

The inter-war years were marked by a greatly accelerated loss of agricultural land to urban uses as housing estates were built at the fashionable density of 12 or fewer houses to the acre and as growth in the number of motor vehicles created a demand for new roads. Building took place alongside these roads, adding to the urbanized appearance of the approaches to many towns. The Restriction of Ribbon Development Act (1935) was an attempt to control this particular form of sprawl but too many loopholes were found in the Act to make it really effective. Problems of a different nature were created by the drift of population from the traditional coalfield industrial regions of northern Britain and South Wales to London and other parts of the South-East and Midlands. Attention was drawn to these in the Report of the Barlow Commission (on the distribution of the industrial population) in 1940 which considered the social, economic and strategic disadvantages that may arise from permitting the concentration of industry or of the industrial population in a few large towns and in particular areas of the country. The Commission recommended that a balance of industrial employment be maintained throughout the country and that congested urban areas be redeveloped. Together, the Barlow Report and Abercrombie's Greater London Plan (1944) were influential in the formulation of postwar planning legislation. Useful guidelines were also provided in the reports published in 1941 of the Uthwatt Committee which looked into the matter of payment of compensation and recovery of betterment, a major prop of postwar land use control, and of the Scott Committee which was concerned with land utilization in rural areas.

Under the 1947 Act, County and major city (County Borough) authorities were required to produce a Development Plan. These plans looked forward for a period of 20 years but were subject to a five-yearly review. Once approved they also acted as a means of development control since the Act established that all forms of development be subject to the permission of the relevant planning authority. Permission could be withheld if it did not accord with the Development Plan. There was a right of appeal, but in general the system worked well and since 1947 the annual loss of agricultural land to urban uses has been reduced from inter-war levels and the excesses of urban sprawl have been largely avoided. The Development Plan remained the key to British planning legislation until the mid-1970s but has now been superseded by the Structure Plan, provision for which was made in the Town and Country Planning Act of 1968. The Structure Plan is a more flexible instrument of planning, better suited, it is claimed, to conditions of continual change. Prepared by the (post-1974) county authorities, it examines likely trends in population and employment growth and sets out a broad strategy selected from a number of stated alternatives. The Structure Plan for Oxfordshire, for example, published in 1976, was faced with the problem of accommodating an expected increase in population of 116 000 between 1971 and 1991. Two strategies were proposed: a preferred strategy dispersing most of the expected growth amongst the smaller towns of the county; and an alternative strategy which concentrates a larger proportion of it on the edge of the city of Oxford. The proposals contained in a Structure Plan are subject to public discussion and possible modification, after which the approval of the government (Secretary of State for the Environment) must be sought. Once a strategy has been accepted it becomes the responsibility of local authorities (District Councils) to prepare detailed 'local plans' which accord with the broad objectives contained in the Structure Plan.

The change in approach to planning represented by the 1968 Act owes much to ideas formulated in the 1960s. These included a new awareness of the importance of regional planning (Chapter 11), and a realization of the necessity for traffic management if cities were not to be overwhelmed by uncontrolled use of the motor vehicle. The Buchanan Report, *Traffic in Towns,* published in 1963, stimulated considerable interest in this problem and was influential in awakening a latent concern with the quality of the environment. Buchanan's method of classifying roads into primary, district and local distributors and access roads, provided a means of assessing the role of city roads and a basis for the traffic planning measures that have been widely adopted by local authorities since the early 1960s. More recently the attention of government has been focused on the financial aspects of urban development, particularly those arising from the continued demand for office space, and the Community Land Act of 1975 represents an attempt to bring about the return of development values to the urban community.

A variety of planning strategies have been evolved in other countries of Western Europe in order to deal with problems that range from the preservation of historic city centres, to the need for urban renewal in industrial agglomerations, and the peculiar difficulties that arise in areas of closely associated cities such as that of Randstad, Holland. These have been examined by Hall (1975) and attention will be concentrated here, by way of example, on French experience. The city has been used as a vehicle of regional planning strategy in France since 1965 when eight *métropoles d'équilibre* — major provincial cities or groups of cities — were selected as foci of regional development. Complementing these in the 1970s has been the designation of *villes moyennes* and a policy involving *contrats de pays,* both aimed at helping small and medium-sized towns to share in regional investment, avoiding over-concentration of people and activity in a few leading centres. Several New Towns are also being built (Chapter 6).

Paralleling this form of planning in France, there was legislation aimed at improving the quality of the urban environment, and especially the standard of housing. From 1958 local authorities were authorized to set aside priority housing areas (*zones à urbaniser en priorité* – Z.U.P.). In many cases the local authority was responsible only for providing public utilities and essential services, but sometimes subsidised housing *(habitations à loyer modéré* – H.L.M.) was grouped on the estates. The policy was not an unqualified success, the massing of dwellings in *grands ensembles* leading to much criticism. A greater variety of housing types, and hopefully therefore a greater population mix, is now achieved through the system of *zones d'aménagement concerté* (Z.A.C.) which has succeeded the Z.U.P.s. Since 1973 their size has been limited to 1000 dwelling units and in these projects, which are part local authority and part private developments, an agreed proportion of the housing must be for letting. In order to avoid speculation in an area where development is proposed it has been possible since 1971 for local authorities to designate *zones d'aménagement différé* (Z.A.D.), within which land values are stabilized. The government may also give financial assistance to local authorities in order to acquire land which is included in the area of the town plan (*schéma directeur*). The first financial agreement of this kind was signed between the government and the city of Angers in 1974. Government powers over the disposal and use of land have been further increased under the *Loi Foncière* of 1975 which also establishes rules over housing density. Finally reference may be made to a law of 1971 which makes the merger of communes not only permissible, but in circumstances where such amalgamation is necessary for urban planning, obligatory. Under this legislation a voluntary grouping of 17 communes which had been in existence at Nancy since 1959 was increased by order of the *préfet* to 24 in 1974.

In the United States the planning powers of both central and local government are weaker than in Britain. A degree of land use control is, however, exercised through the system of zoning. Responsibility for drawing up zoning maps lies with local authorities, the earliest zoning ordinance being that produced for New York City in 1916. The zoning map can be said to establish planning goals, but it is subject to amendment if the local authority is prepared to accede to the petitions of corporate bodies or of individuals. Hall (1975) sees zoning as a device for segregating land uses on a coarse basis and this view is supported by Natoli's (1971) study of rezoning in Worcester, Massachusetts. There was most opposition on the part of the local authority here to 'spot rezoning', land use changes on a small scale, which Natoli considers to be consistent with the 'primary goals of zoning — the creation of homogeneous use-areas'. The extent to which rezoning requests were approved was also shown, however, to be related to the distribution of ethnic groups in the city and to that of political pressure groups. As a planning device, zoning is further weakened by the lack of powers of compensation comparable with those possessed by planning authorities in the United Kingdom. Overall the local authority's zoning commission must be considered to possess only limited power, either to control land use change within the city, or to prevent the encroachment of the city over the surrounding country.

Despite the weakness of planning powers in the United States it is clear that in many countries these now constitute a powerful influence on the nature of urban growth. But concern with planning must not be allowed to obscure the wider economic and social factors which underlie urban form. Some of the latter are so deeply embedded in western culture that there is a danger they may be taken for granted, e.g. social aspirations expressing themselves in where different groups of people choose to live. It is intended that these factors will emerge in the chapters which follow.

2

Models of City Structure

Spatial models present a generalized picture of reality and it would clearly be wrong to judge them by reference to particular situations, in this case cities, where, for a variety of reasons, the local arrangement of land uses may depart substantially from that presented in the model. Equally it must be remembered that models like that of Burgess are very often derived from observations limited in terms of both space and time. His ideas were based to a large extent on experience of American Mid-Western cities, and above all Chicago, in the early 1920s. This must be borne in mind in seeking to apply the models to situations in which the level of technology or the nature of society differ significantly from those which relate to the model. Students of the city have devoted so much attention to the ideas of Burgess and Hoyt that these cannot lightly be dismissed, but there is a danger in pursuing the Chicago model so zealously that one fails to observe patterns elsewhere which are equally worthy of the attention of the model-builder.

The concentric zone theory

The City, a collection of essays by Park, Burgess and McKenzie, was published in 1925, an introduction to the research into social behaviour taking place in Chicago at that time. The familiar zonal diagram (Fig. 4) appeared in a short chapter by Burgess entitled 'The Growth of the City' and subtitled 'An Introduction to a Research Project', in which the physical expansion of the city is seen as a framework against which the relationship between population mobility. and social organization can be studied.

Drawing his ideas from the study of plant and animal ecology, Burgess envisaged the outward growth of the city taking place by invasion and succession, each of his concentric zones expanding at the expense of the one beyond it. Invasion and succession did not, however, preclude concentration which is regarded as a com-

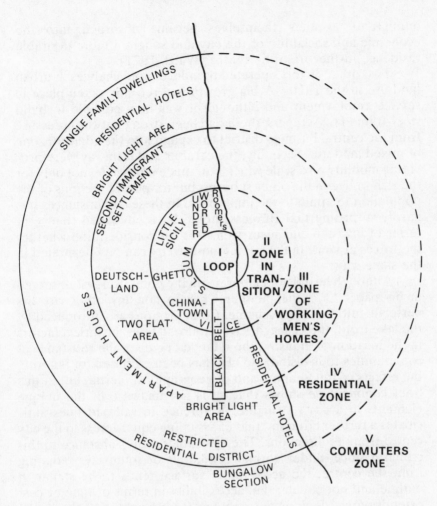

4 The concentric zone model of E. W. Burgess. (Courtesy University of Chicago Press)

plementary process, business activities clustering in the central business district or in 'satellite loops', and first-generation immigrants in their Little Sicilies, Greek-towns, etc. To appreciate the emphasis which Burgess put on mobility and replacement it is necessary to recall that in the early 1920s the cities of the American Mid-West were only just reaching the end of a period of fifty years or so, in the course of which they had absorbed a great variety of immigrant groups from Europe. During this period it had been common for the immigrants first to find cheap housing in inner-city tenements, later to abandon these in favour of the next colony of immigrants as they themselves became absorbed into the economic and social life of the city and sought a more desirable residence further from the centre (Ward, 1971).

Two other factors operated to induce rapid changes in urban land use in the 1920s. A big growth had recently taken place in service employment and although it was now possible to build steel-framed skyscrapers, there had been strong outward pressure from the central business district to expand into the adjacent zone of mixed land use. Secondly, the car, bus and tramway were providing mobility on a scale which now made it possible, not only for the rich to live in the outer suburbs, but for poorer sections of the population to attain to the inner ones. In these circumstances it is hardly surprising that Burgess should have envisaged change in terms of invasion and succession. It is for consideration whether the forces at work in the contemporary city can be interpreted in the same way.

Although he did not elaborate on the point, Burgess observed in his paper '. . . that neither Chicago nor any other city fits perfectly into this ideal scheme. Complications are introduced by the lake front, the Chicago River, railroad lines, historical factors in the location of industry, the relative degree of the resistance of communities to invasion, etc.' He has been criticised for ignoring the effects of topography, and of geographical inertia, but in this brief comment he shows that he is not unaware of the unique elements in a city's structure. Reference to railroad lines anticipates a further criticism, that of assuming equal access to the city centre from all directions. There is rather more substance to this criticism since, under normal conditions of routeways radiating from the centre, the accessibility surface tends to be stellar in outline and not circular, i.e. accessibility in terms of time or cost extends outwards along these routes. It is arguable that the model could have been stellate without losing its qualities of universality, whereas any attempt to allow for relief or history is bound to result in the loss of the generalised pattern that is the great attraction of the Burgess model and to produce a diagram of the multiple nuclei type.

Urban land rent

The concentric zone model derives support from the theory of urban land rent (Alonso, 1964; Richardson, 1971; Goodall, 1972). This assumes that the centre of the city is a highly desirable location, that land here is in short supply, and that users of urban

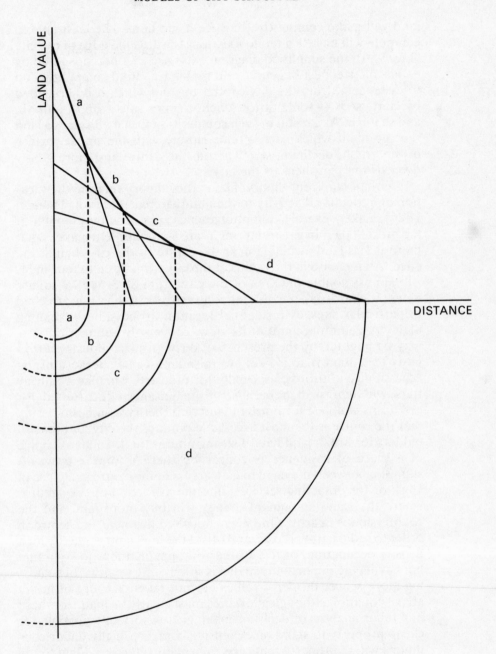

5   Urban land rent theory. Concentric zones are determined by the
     respective ability of land uses **a-d** to pay the higher costs of a central
     location.

land will make competitive bids for a site here. The least able to compete will be relegated to locations towards the edge of the city (Fig. 5). In the simplified diagram, land use a — perhaps retailing — has the steepest bid curve and is able to outbid competitors up to distance a, from the city centre, beyond which it is succeeded by land use b — some office function let us say — up to point b, and so forth. As a result of such competition the city displays a land rent gradient which corresponds closely with the upper surface of the graph, declining steeply from the centre and more gently towards the periphery of the city.

Urban land rent theory, like earlier theory relating the location of agricultural activity to the ability to pay rent (von Thünen, 1826), makes several assumptions which are not equally tenable at the present day. In general terms a safe assumption to make is that there is less land available near the centre of the city than at the edge. An increase in the radius of the city from three to four miles will almost double the area of the city, from 28.3 to 50.2 square miles (Richardson). Yet this takes no account of the value attached to particular sites. A residential location in the suburbs may be highly prized on account of its view; conversely an inner city site may be blighted by the presence of dirty or noisy industry. Proximity to a main road is likely to raise land values because of the accessibility it affords, especially for industry, whereas a railway track will depress them because of the nuisance effect (Goodall).

In its simplest form urban land rent theory assumes not only that the centre is the most accessible point of the city, but that all bidders for urban land have a strong interest in it. So far as choice of a place of residence is concerned there is thus a trade-off situation between the need to gain access to the centre as a place of work or for obtaining services, and the attraction of the suburbs where the same amount of money will buy more land and the countryside is nearby. One may choose to live near the centre in order to reduce travel costs, and offset the high land values by high density occupation, or live further out, paying more to commute but having the opportunity, if one is sufficiently wealthy, of acquiring more space. Property values are not taken account of in the above equation although allowance must clearly be made for these in a fuller analysis of decision-making. It is perfectly possible for cheap property to stand on expensive land, especially under conditions where property rents are controlled, a factor adding to the immobility of the poorer sections of the population, as any Scottish planner will confirm.

In a modern city, plagued by traffic congestion and with

restrictions on vehicular access and parking, the centre has lost some of the accessibility it formerly possessed. It is quite likely that in terms of time taken to get there, a location on the outer ring road is now the most accessible point, at least for the car-borne population of the city, a fact with obvious bearing on commercial applications for sites in this kind of position and therefore on land values. On the other hand the centre may retain its land values because of prestige, important for office location. A distinction must also be made between access to the centre from within the city itself, and access from the city region. To the commuter travelling into the city by train from a dormitory town outside it, the centre, being close to the railway station, is far more accessible than any point in the suburbs. Despite these and other factors which maintain high values at the centre (page 83), some allowance must be made for nodes of secondary accessibility within the city, perhaps where a radial route is intersected by an inner link road. The curve of declining land values displays local peaks as it encounters these, whilst they in turn invite competitive bids for sites (Fig. 6).

To the urban resident accessibility means not only the journey to work but also access to schools, shops and neighbourhood facilities such as parks and recreation grounds. For some it involves access to place of worship. In addition the individual's or family's choice of place to live is influenced by factors relating to the actual house and to the physical and social characteristics of the neighbourhood. Investigation in California revealed these latter considerations to be more important in decisions over residential location than ones concerned with accessibility, the exception being access to school (Weiss, Kenney and Steffens, 1966). Other research in western industrial cities tends to confirm the relatively minor role of access to place of work in decision-making, except amongst small groups of the working population. In these circumstances it becomes somewhat unrealistic to interpret residential location as the product of a trade-off situation between travel costs and land costs. Allowance must be made for the behavioural, or 'satisficer', factor. In turn, it is evident that residential land values are determined by other factors than accessibility (Brigham, 1965).

The concentric zone model assumes competition for central sites, but changes in the nature of manufacturing or retailing make suburban or urban fringe locations more attractive to many forms of economic activity than congested urban centres. Such decentralization, with its further implication for the other forms of accessibility considered above, distorts still further the theoreti-

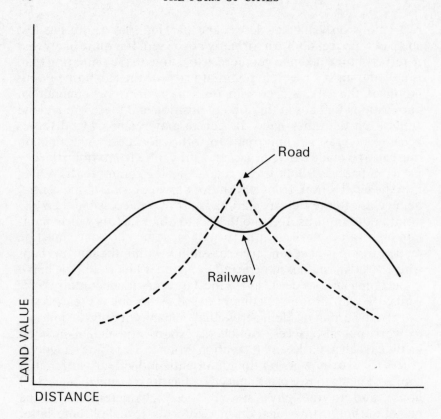

6   The contrasted effect of radial road and railway on land values. After
     Goodall, 1972. (Courtesy Pergamon Press)

cally smooth curve of land values. Allowance must also be made
for non-economic controls on land use exercised by local government and for the distortions introduced through, for example,
leases (Chapter 1). Yet if study of the city is not to become lost in
detail, there is merit in retaining in as simple a spatial form as
possible the idea of a relationship between accessibility, land values and land use. It is for this reason that the Burgess model
remains a valuable tool.

Hoyt's sector theory

Hoyt's sector model (Fig. 7) is as familiar to students of the city as is
the concentric zone diagram of Burgess, and they should be seen as
essentially complementary rather than mutually exclusive (page

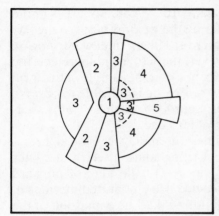 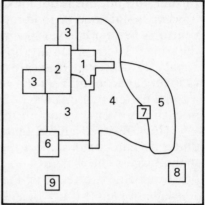

1 Central business district   4 Medium-class residential   7 Outlying business district
2 Wholesale light manufacturing   5 High-class residential   8 Residential suburb
3 Low-class residential   6 Heavy manufacturing   9 Industrial suburb

7   Hoyt's sector model and the multiple nuclei diagram of Harris and Ullman. (Courtesy *Annals of the American Academy of Political and Social Science*)

53). The two men approached their study of the city from different viewpoints. For Burgess, the sociologist, the city was a laboratory for observing social behaviour, whereas Hoyt, an economist, was concerned with discovering how the housing market operated in order to advise the American government on mortgage policy (Hoyt, 1939). Using rental value as a surrogate of housing quality, Hoyt demonstrated how residential land uses tended to be arranged in sectoral fashion, radiating outwards from the city centre along transport routes. High quality development was drawn in a particular direction because of the view and other physical or social attractions; housing of intermediate quality flanked the expensive sector on one or both sides in order to take advantage of the latter's reputation, whilst cheap housing was confined to the least favoured sectors. The economic status of the different sectors was perpetuated as they grew outwards.

Hoyt's work can be said to have added a directional element to the earlier ideas of city growth put forward by Burgess. But Hoyt also criticizes Burgess for implying that there is a progression from run-down property occupied by the poor near the city centre to expensive new housing for the wealthy on the fringe. It is not denied that property frequently becomes dilapidated over time or that housing tends to filter down the social scale as people move further out, but this is not universally true. There are areas of old housing maintained in good repair by the wealthy close to the city centre as there are lower income groups living in new housing on the fringe. This is not to say, however, that Hoyt wholly rejects the zonal idea. Although there are exceptions, for example in the form of luxury apartments near the city centre, he is still able to observe a zonal pattern within each of his sectors, the highest-status areas in each case being found on the outer edge.

Hoyt also recognised that invasion and succession operates under certain circumstances, but writing some fifteen years later than Burgess, he was less ready to accept the idea of outward pressure being exerted from the centre. He elaborated this idea in subsequent papers (Hoyt, 1964), noting that the expansion of the central business district has been limited by building upwards and by the movement to the suburbs of shopping, hotels, wholesalers, industry and certain categories of office work. Where outward expansion of the CBD is taking place it tends to be directional, being drawn towards the higher income sector. Hoyt also stressed the need to take account of zoning ordinances and of slum clearance and redevelopment laws. He drew attention to the presence now of a large negro population in those areas that had not been cleared, observing at the same time that some inner residential districts had undergone rehabilitation and become fashionable (1964). His general view expressed in the early 1960s was that, principally because of the use of the private car, 'future high grade residential growth will probably not be confined entirely to rigidly defined sectors'. A number of differences between American and foreign cities were also noted.

Multiple nuclei

The cellular diagram of city structure presented by Harris and Ullman (1945) cannot be regarded as an alternative to the models of Burgess and Hoyt since it lacks a basic pattern common to most cities, the spatial arrangement of the nuclei proposed varying widely from place to place (Fig. 7). Yet it serves as a useful reminder, firstly of the role of pre-existing settlement nuclei in the evolution of the city, and secondly of the tendency of urban functions to cluster and to segregate, especially under conditions of decentralization. Activities concentrate so as to exploit certain site advantages and to achieve economies of scale; some are mutually repulsive, whilst others are prevented from establishing themselves in particular locations by, for example, high land values. As a city grows it absorbs existing nuclei and others are created, increase in the number of nuclei usually involving greater specialization.

Urban profiles

Far less attention has been given by urban geographers to the cross-sectional analysis of city structure than to spatial layout; yet the two approaches are essentially complementary. Early work was concerned with the townscape—buildings and the skyline which they created—a subject notoriously difficult to quantify, but more recent studies involve the analysis of population density gradients: 'The town is not merely a street pattern or disposition of filled and open spaces in two dimensions, but is first and foremost an arrangement of structures that rise from the ground in different shapes . . . The panorama and sky-line present aspects of the urban ensemble, wherein the diversity of the human contribution is associated with the physical setting' (Smailes, 1955).

In what was then largely an exploratory work, Smailes in 1955 called for the study of townscapes as an aid both to the classification of towns and to more detailed analysis of their internal structure. The urban profile has a generic association, individual buildings or groups of buildings providing evidence of the town's functional role, even of its regional identity. Stages in the growth of the individual town can also be recognized by reference to types of building characteristic of particular periods. Smailes distinguished the terrace, villa and block, associated respectively in the townscape with 'ribbing', 'studding', and 'clumping'. Others have utilized a wider range of house types as an aid to town plan analysis (Haughton, 1949; Conzen, 1958), but these detailed schemes have less value as tools for comparison or for deriving generalized models. Nevertheless, on the basis of work in Melbourne, Johnston (1969) was able to put forward a diffusion model of townscape development based on the idea that new styles in building are adopted first in high status areas; by the time these have become fashionable in low status districts, the former have already begun to build in a still newer style.

Such a diffusion model is valid if it can be shown that there is a close correlation between house types and social areas of the city based on population characteristics. A problem which inevitably arises when the correlation is sought and which Johnston recognizes, is that houses are often occupied by sections of the population for whom they were not built. This difficulty, coupled with that of arriving at a categorization of house types of sufficient validity to permit comparisons, has restricted the use of the townscape method in urban studies at the national scale. At an international level, however, where interest is in cross-cultural comparisons, the method possesses greater potential as an analytical tool. Social and cultural characteristics of the population are betrayed in the style of houses and institutional buildings, whilst levels of technology, particularly those relating to transport, are reflected in the overall arrangement of structures and open spaces which constitutes the urban profile. Writing about the contemporary Japanese townscape, Yasuo Masai (1970) looks at this in the context of what are described as townscapes of the major culture regions (Fig. 8). It becomes possible to quantify the study of these by reference to certain visible traits relating not only to the nature of the buildings, height, materials, etc., but to the presence or absence of such recognizable features as a CBD, markets and industry.

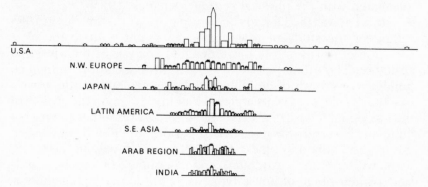

8   Townscapes of the 'major culture regions' according to Masai, 1970. (Courtesy Association of Japanese Geographers)

The population density profile affords a more statistically rigorous method of examining the city in cross-section. It also possesses considerable value for urban studies if it can be shown that there is a connection, not only between land values and density, but also between population density and social behaviour.

In general the population density of western industrial cities declines exponentially with distance from the edge of the central business district to the urban fringe (Clark, 1951), a function of competition for land (above). Further, this density gradient itself tends to flatten out over the course of time, also declining in a negative exponential manner, largely in response to improved transport facilities. From these observations it is possible to derive density profiles (Fig. 9) representing the city at successive stages in its growth (Newling, 1969). A 'density crater' develops in the city centre in response to the emergence of the central business district and a 'crest' of maximum population density moves outwards over time. Blumenfeld (1954) described the crest as a tidal wave, observing that it moved through the city of Philadelphia at the rate of approximately one mile per decade.

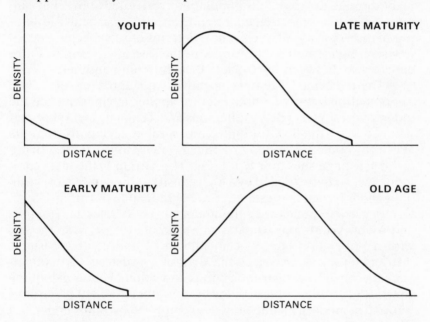

9   Population density profiles at successive stages of city development according to Newling, 1969. (Courtesy the Editor of *The Geographical Review*)

The idea of stages in the development of a density profile has obvious attraction as a tool for purposes of comparison, but it raises a number of questions, not least ones relating to the calculation of density. Gross residential density is easy to work out and, bearing in mind the availability of data, is probably the only figure that can be widely used in comparative studies. Furthermore as a measure of the overall use of urban space it is likely to bring out contrasts of the kind revealed in the cultural townscapes of Fig. 8. Net residential density, which relates numbers of people to the amount of residential floor space available, may be of greater value in studies which seek to explore the social response to population pressure, although it does not take into account such factors as the absence of recreational open space which bear on social problems. According to Newling (1966) there is a critical density— represented for North American cities by the gross figure of 30 000 persons per square mile—above which delinquency, mental disorders and other social costs are incurred. The response is outward migration on the part of the more mobile sections of the population. This observation has an obvious bearing on the movement through the city of the population crest noted above, but care must be exercised in attaching significance to a particular level of population density. The relevance, in terms of social behaviour, of any such figure is likely to vary with the size of city and to differ enormously between one society or culture and another.

There is evidence that the negative exponential rate of decline in population density from the centre applies in cities outside the industrialized West (Berry, Simmons and Tennant, 1963) but that it is necessary to allow for quite considerable deviations from the Western model. In a study of Indian cities, for example, Brush (1968) distinguishes four types (Fig. 10). Group 1, the most common type, is characterized by a high density at the centre close to an indigenous bazaar and a steep, convex gradient to the urban fringe; Group 2 corresponds with the major ports of Calcutta, Bombay and Madras and approximates most closely to the western type with a population 'crater' coinciding with the central business district; Group 3 embraces the dual cities such as Hyderabad-Secunderabad with their indigenous and colonial cores exhibiting contrasted profiles; whilst the lower, smoother gradient of Group 4 is found in modern planned towns exemplified by Jamshedpur and Chandigarh. High rates of population increase mean that densities are continuing to grow even in the centres of many of these cities. It is to be hoped that work in other parts of the world will permit comparisons with the findings of Brush and assist the search for a more general model or set of models.

Density profiles, like spatial models, provide a useful means of expressing generalizations about the form of cities. But the success of both requires that attention be paid to the passage of time. The fact that higher densities are associated with older buildings, the latter being more common in the inner city than in the suburbs, may suffice as reminder of the importance of the time dimension in the interpretation of gross residential densities.

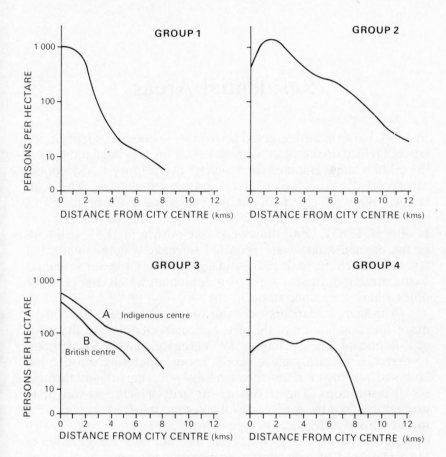

10 Population density profiles of Indian cities according to Brush, 1968.
(Courtesy the Editor of *The Geographical Review*)

3

Residential Areas

In 1934, barriers were erected across two residential streets in the city of Oxford. Brick-built, with spikes on the top and a red light in the middle, they remained for a quarter of a century as a symbol of the social divisions which divide urban populations. The Cutteslowe Walls were, in fact, put up in response to the building of a municipal housing estate adjacent to a privately-developed one (Collison, 1963). Until they were taken down in 1959, residents of the council estate were required to make a detour via other streets to reach the main road, and a reminder of the walls remains to the present day in the form of street names which change at the point where they once stood.

Although as barriers between residential areas, walls are a more common feature of the 'pre-industrial city' than of the western, industrial cities (Chapter 7), segregation in the latter takes powerful, if generally more subtle, forms, operating through the land and housing markets, through local government, and through social institutions. The territorial integrity which it is sought to protect may not be apparent to the casual observer except in the form of broad differences in type of housing, and the graffiti which demarcate one area of Belfast from another must be regarded as the same kind of exaggerated expression of segregation as the Cutteslowe Walls. Evidence may be found in the form of zoning plans or conservation areas but, for an understanding of the behavioural and perceptual traits which underlie the sense of territory, it may well be necessary to construct some form of mental map (Gould and White, 1974).

Urbanism as a way of life

Louis Wirth's classic study of 'Urbanism as a Way of Life' (1938) has attracted in recent years the same kind of criticism that has been levelled at Burgess. He is accused of deducing a theory meant to be applicable to all cities from evidence drawn only from the North American industrial city of the 1930s. The later work of sociologists and others has suggested that, as well as having little relevance to the 'pre-industrial city', Wirth's generalizations tend to obscure the presence within western industrial cities of 'primary' (e.g. extended family) groups lacking the very qualities of urbanism on which his theory is based. Nevertheless, Wirth's ideas cannot be ignored since they form part of the theoretical structure on which social area analysts have based their assumptions.

Associated with urbanization, involving, according to Wirth, an increase in the numbers, density and heterogeneity of urban populations, certain changes are seen to take place in both the economic and social structure of these same city populations. Economic changes take the form of a highly developed division of labour, specialization in production, and growth in indirect means of communication. Standardization of products and services gives rise to elements of a common culture, but offsetting this are changes of a social nature which include the impersonalization of social relationships and weakening of emotional ties, categorization of people according to their material possessions, and membership of a variety of social groups within the city which makes the city-dweller socially and geographically more mobile than his rural counterpart. In addition Wirth recognizes two forces which operate directly on the residential structure of the city. Firstly, city-dwellers tend to react to the great diversity of population they encounter there by withdrawing from those with characteristics different from their own. 'In this way relatively homogeneous areas will form within the city, and within these areas stronger bonds may be maintained.' Secondly, since the desirability of a particular part of the city for residential purposes is affected by a group's social make-up, 'people with similar backgrounds and needs select, drift, or are forced by circumstances, into the same section of the city.' Different parts of the city thus come to be identified with a particular social class or occupational group.

Social area analysis

The delimitation and analysis of urban social areas follows largely from the pioneering work on Californian cities by Shevky, Williams and Bell (Shevky and Williams, 1949; Shevky and Bell, 1955). Setting out the theoretical background to their method in the later of these publications, Shevky and Bell accept Wirth's ideas relating to the structure of urban society, but differ from him in seeing these as a product of changes in the *scale* of society rather than of density and heterogeneity. Fundamental to their work is the belief that there are three elements in its social composition which determine the differentiation and stratification of urban society: social rank, urbanization and segregation. For these Bell preferred the terms economic status, family status and ethnic status.

As a measure of *social rank,* Shevky and Bell used data relating to occupation and to the length of full-time education. The choice of the occupation measure can be justified by reference to functionalist theory which states that a person's social standing is related to the functional importance, and usually therefore the rewards, that society attributes to his/her occupation (Johnston, 1971, p.25). Care must be exercised over terminology, however. The word 'class' is commonly used in the sense of social rank, i.e. of position in the economic system (Johnston, p.24), but this should not be confused with 'power' or 'status', the latter implying the attachment of prestige to an occupation that may be independent of class. There is usually a close correlation between length of full-time education and the occupational groupings recognized in the Census but problems are likely to be encountered if income is employed as a measure of social rank. A sudden increase in the demand for a particular good or service may bring substantial rewards to a manual category of occupation, but without an equally rapid change in how that income is spent, e.g. on housing. Spending is more likely to reflect educational background and status, factors slower to change. In their study of Los Angeles, Shevky and Williams (1949) used, in addition to occupation and education, a third indicant — the proportion of the population paying less than a specified monthly rent (Timms, 1971), but this was omitted from the later work of Shevky and Bell on San Francisco (1955).

As measures of *urbanization,* Shevky and Bell employed three sets of data: the proportion of children under a certain age relative to the female population of child-bearing age — a measure of fertility — the proportion of adult females in the labour force, and the proportion of the housing stock consisting of detached, single-family dwellings. Use of the term 'urbanization' as well as of the measures employed to express it, are strongly suggestive of Wirth's views that urban growth is accompanied by changes in the status of the family as a social unit (Robson, 1969), relationships typical of the extended family breaking down as women go out to work. Again care must be exercised over the use of terminology and, in particular, over the distinction between 'family status', used as alternative to urbanization, and 'familism'. The latter refers to a set of value preferences and is not a description of family type (Timms, 1971), in short the individual may choose to opt out of marriage and child-rearing, preferring life styles which have been described as 'careerism' and 'consumerism' (Bell, 1958). The distinction is an important one when note is taken of stages in a family life-cycle and the relationship between these and choice of residential location.

The third construct, segregation or ethnic status, was introduced by Shevky and Bell to allow for the immigrant group which has so far failed to become assimilated with the host population of the city, the negro ghetto affording the most obvious example. It is frequently identified by data relating to birthplace but, as a separate dimension, it was ignored in early studies of a number of European cities where ethnic segregation was thought to be of little significance (Herbert, 1967).

When more than one set of data is used to indicate a particular dimension, as in the case of social rank and urbanization, it is a relatively easy matter to combine these in a composite index. Scores representing the three indices may then be plotted on a 'social space diagram' to provide a convenient summary of a city's social structure. The most common form of diagram is one in which scores relating to the individual census tracts or enumeration districts of a city are plotted against axes of social rank and urbanization. The graph is subdivided along these axes to yield 16 social area types, each of which may be further subdivided to allow for the segregation index (Fig. 11). The diagram is a useful classificatory device, its principal merit being to facilitate comparison between cities.

Alone, the social space diagram does not describe the distribution of social groups within the city, but social space can be translated into geographical (physical) space by plotting the values for individual census tracts on a map of these units, combining like values in 'social areas'. Social area studies of United States cities have been facilitated by the fact that census tract data has been available there since 1910. In the United Kingdom enumeration district data drawn from the 1951 Census was employed in studies of Oxford (Collison and Mogey, 1959) and Belfast (E. Jones, 1960), but it has been in common use only since 1961.

Although due allowance must be made for the weaknesses of social area studies noted below, the broad tendency revealed by these studies, for social rank to be distributed sectorally within the

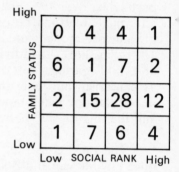

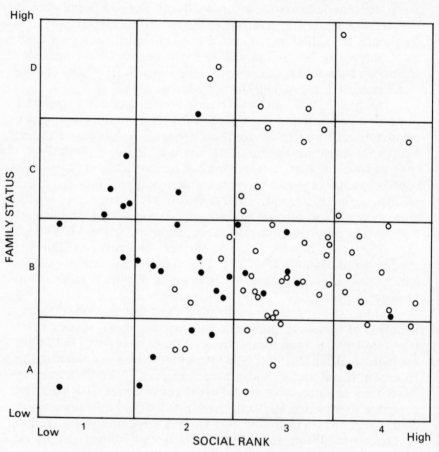

11 A social space diagram for Winnipeg, based on Herbert, 1972.
(Courtesy David and Charles)

city and for urbanization scores to be distributed concentrically should not be overlooked. As descriptions of urban residential structure, the diagrams of Burgess and Hoyt are thus seen to be complementary, a fact noted by Mann (1965, p. 96) in his composite model of the British city (Fig. 12). Where it is present, the ethnic dimension exhibits clustering, usually close to the centre, but with a tendency also to sectoral development.

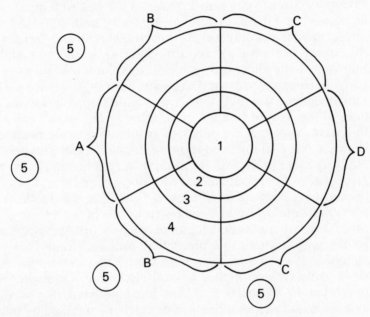

A   The middle-class sector

B   The lower middle class sector

C   The working class sector (and main municipal housing areas)

D   Industry and lowest working class areas

1   The city centre

2   Transitional zone

3   Zone of small terrace houses in sectors C and D; Larger by-law houses in sector B;
Large old houses in sector A.

4   Post-1918 residential areas, with post-1945 development mainly on the periphery

5   Commuting distance 'village'

12   The residential land use model of P. H. Mann, 1965. (Courtesy Routledge and Kegan Paul)

At the same broad level of generalization it is not difficult to suggest reasons for the distributional pattern of the three social variables. An explanation of the sectoral form assumed by social rank can be sought in the role of transport, the most formative influence on the physical growth of cities. A British example may be used to illustrate the point. Soon after the middle of the nineteenth century the Great Eastern Railway Company decided to introduce cheap workmen's fares on its routes north-east from Liverpool Street station in London. This was well in advance of legislation making such fares compulsory and the effect was to attract passengers of relatively 'low' social rank and thereby direct the social evolution of suburbs such as Edmonton and Walthamstow lying along this sectoral axis. The Great Western Company, in contrast, preferred to encourage long-distance passenger movement and was therefore slow to build stopping places along its lines to the west of London in Middlesex. The suburbanization of this sector was thus not only slower than that to the north-east of London, but also involved those of 'higher' social rank who, generally speaking, are less dependent on public transport, having greater access to private means of transport, and start work later in the morning. In spite of differences in scale and in mode of transport, the London example is mirrored in the evolution of many other cities where the development of a network of radial transport routes was a slow and piecemeal process, trams being built alongside the canal or river, long before they were able to effect suburbanization on higher ground elsewhere. Once the sectoral development of social rank has been initiated in this way, its extension and perpetuation can be further explained by reference to the operation of the housing market in which Hoyt was interested. The social reputation of a particular sector is carefully nurtured by estate agents who are able to sell their three-bedroomed 'semi' (duplex) for a higher price here than elsewhere, restricting the market to those who can, or in their quest for status seek to, afford the greater cost. A third level of explanation arises from work on mental maps which reveals a sectoral bias in the individual's knowledge of the urban area (p. 80). In so far as residential moves are influenced by what is familiar, the consequence again will be for the sectoral distribution of social rank to be maintained.

Explanation of the concentric distribution of family status rests on the assumption that the family has requirements of space and of access to certain amenities which change at successive stages in a theoretical life cycle and which involve moves towards or away

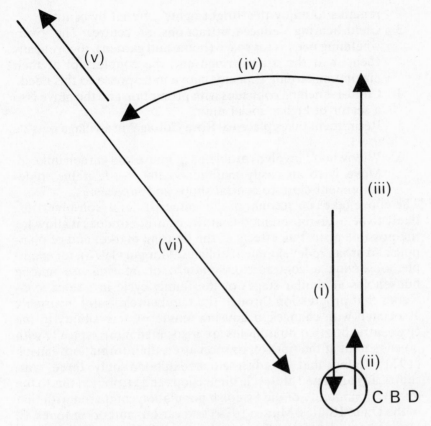

13   Theoretical sequence of residential moves within a city based on
      stages in the life-cycle and a change in social status

from the city centre. Six stages are commonly recognized once
marriage has taken place (Rossi, 1955; Abu-Lughod and Foley,
1960): Pre-child; Childbearing; Child-rearing; Child-launching;
Post-child; Widowhood.

The family may move in response to a change at any stage but
is most likely to move at the child-bearing and child-launching
phase, and least likely at the child-rearing stage when a stable
environment e.g. access to a particular school, appears most important. The succession of moves represented in Fig. 13 is intended to
serve as an example rather than a generalized model.

1   School-leaver moves to institutional residence in, or close to,
     CBD.
2   Marriage takes place and the couple seek rented accom-
     modation in sub-divided property near CBD. Leisure

remains to enjoy the 'bright lights' offered by centre.

3   Child-bearing reduces attractions of centre. The over-whelming need is for space (home and garden), theoretically cheaper at the urban fringe and the couple, not at their maximum earning capacity, move in response to this need.

4   Child-launching coincides with promotion and the move is to a sector of higher social rank.

5   Retirement takes place to 'Rose Cottage' in a village outside town.

6   Widowhood involves problems of house and garden upkeep. Move is to an easily maintained flat in 'desirable' rede-velopment close to central shops and services.

The above takes no account of the 'careerists' and 'consumerists', likely to be over-represented near the centre; nor does it allow for the possible distorting effects of the housing market and of plan-ning and urban redevelopment policies. Morgan (1976), for exam-ple, observing a contradictory pattern of housing use among households at similar stages of the family cycle in Exeter, con-cludes that progression through the family cycle is not invariably associated with changes in housing tenure or accessibility to the city centre, but that households are associated more typically with housing built at the time of, or soon after, their formation. Janson (1971) found that Swedish cities exhibited only three con-centrically arranged life-cycle dimensions and attributed this to the relative immobility of the Swedish population compared with that of the United States. Murie (1974) and various authors in Jones, E. (1975) have also noted the complexity of the factors which affect the decision to move.

The concentration of ethnically-distinct, immigrant groups close to the city centre is usually explained in terms of access to low-cost housing and certain types of employment afforded by the CBD (e.g. office cleaners) or older industrial districts (Ward, 1971). Contemporary evidence of outward commuting from the centre towards the suburbs of cities would suggest that the former is, however, the more powerful influence. Within a zone of low-cost housing the initial concentration appears to owe a good deal to the point of entry of the immigrants, clustering taking place around railway or bus termini (Busteed, 1972; Ogden and Winchester, 1975).

Criticism has been levelled at Shevky and Bell's method of identifying social areas on the grounds that the three constructs are not separate and independent dimensions of urban social struc-ture, and also that the indices used to identify them are unsatisfactory. The introduction of factor analysis has gone some way to overcoming this problem, a wide-ranging set of data being used to identify dominant factors and patterns of intercorrelation. Robson (1969), for example, employed 30 variables in his study of Sunderland, identifying four principal components which accounted for some three-quarters of the total variance. Such methods are not wholly objective, since the nature of the input data has an important bearing on the factors which emerge. Most factor analytical studies rely heavily on data obtained from the census, but this is biased by the nature of the questions asked in the first place. Other sources of data have been used—rating valuation of property, possession of a telephone or motor car, distribution of entries in Who's Who, incidence of certain diseases, and so forth—but difficulties arise over data collection, and the more exotic the data set the less easy it becomes to compare one city with another. The merits and weaknesses of factorial ecology are noted by various authors in Berry (1971).

Empirical evidence tends to confirm the importance of the three dimensions recognized by Shevky and Bell, particularly if allowance is made for the rather culture-specific nature of their own work on the west coast of the United States. But a number of discrepancies appear, the most persistent arising from the use of fertility and women in the labour force as measures of urbanization. In several cities studied by Van Arsdol, Camilleri and Schmid (1958), for example, there was seen to be a high degree of correlation between fertility and social rank. In Rome, likewise, both fertility and women in the labour force correlated highly with social rank (McElrath, 1962). Weak association between the indices used to measure urbanization, and a relationship between one or more of these and social rank, is also borne out by other studies. High fertility often appears to be associated with the extremes of social rank, whilst the proportion of females at work is related to the occupational status of the male population. Further complications arise from differences in life-style and the need to recognize the separate associational characteristics of 'careerists', etc.

The third component, segregation or ethnic status, does not always emerge as an independent dimension of urban social structure. In such circumstances there is frequently seen to be a marked negative relationship with social rank and a positive one with urbanization. In cities with more than one migrant group, subcategories are likely to appear as in the case of life-style differences.

Amongst the minor components that are fairly consistently revealed by factor analysis is one concerned with mobility. This implies the presence within an urban population of a group whose residential behaviour is largely unrelated to the other dimensions, i.e. there is a category of persons whose moves are not governed by such factors as the search for living space or social standing, or who remain in a locality after their peers have left, possibly because of their involvement in some kind of social activity in the neighbour-hood.

Another criticism that arises from the pursuit of social areas within cities is the too ready assumption that a certain set of population characteristics can be associated with a particular set of housing characteristics, i.e. that social space coincides with housing space. This may be true where first-generation, new housing is concerned, but in most cities, especially in the Old World, a large proportion of the housing stock has had a succession of occupants and the 'filtering' process may be evident in the presence of social groups of a very different kind from those for whom the houses were originally built. Housing need may be expressed in terms of stage in the life-cycle and nature of life-style, but it does not follow that there is the housing available to satisfy those needs. Supply of housing must be taken into account as well as demand (Simmons, 1968). The nature of the housing stock and the way in which the housing market operates must thus be regarded as, to some extent, an independent factor in the patterning of a city's social structure. 'The physical housing environment is the segregated backcloth against which the spatial sorting of social groups occurs' (Win-chester, 1975). The distinction, unfortunately, does not always emerge from factor analytical studies when sets of data combining population and housing information are used and composite fac-tors result. This problem is not made easier to resolve by the fact that data are usually based on enumeration districts rather than morphological regions.

Close correlations can undoubtedly be found between certain measures of the demographic and housing situation, but the nature of such correlations may differ widely from one city to another. The Victorian villa dwellings which, in a city such as Oxford, are subdivided for student occupation, are likely to be occupied by a totally different social group in a predominantly industrial city. The presence or absence of the usual household amenities (bath, W.C., etc.) is an element of the housing environment often closely correlated with population characteristics (Winchester, 1975), but whereas in one city the absence of such amenities may correlate with low social status, in another, which happens to have a high proportion of local authority housing, this will not be apparent. Instead there will be a high degree of correlation between the presence of these amenities and life-cycle characteristics, i.e., with a youthful, fertile population. High density of occupation of dwellings may coincide with student occupancy in a university town, but with newly-built council estates in the industrial city.

The degree to which publicly-owned housing distorts the 'natural' pattern of residential areas is a debateable one. Robson (1968) drew attention to the distorting effect of council housing in Sunderland, a town with 40 per cent of its housing stock owned by the local authority at the date of the study, but others have put less emphasis on this factor. C. J. Thomas (1966), for example, showed how in Nottingham there was a tendency for tenants to move between estates and for differences in social rank between one estate and another to be heightened by this sorting process. The effect of local authority housing policy on social segregation was noted in Chapter 1. Reference was also made in Chapter 1 to the effect of land-ownership on the selection of sites for municipal housing projects. Therein lies one explanation of how the location of such developments may come to distort the theoretical pattern of social areas. At the same time one must not ignore the strength of social and economic forces of the kind which built the Cutteslowe Walls and which are likely to repel housing schemes of a non-conforming social nature. Significantly, perhaps, Robson (1975) does not put any local authority housing in two sectors of his idealized British city (Fig. 14). One must be cautious over the interpretation of any such generalization, however. The distribution of private and council housing will be affected, not only by the extent to which the housing stock as a whole is publicly owned, this varying from city to city, but also by the political complexion and related policies of a particular city council. The complexity of such forces is well brought out in Pritchard's (1976) investigation of housing and the spatial structure of the city of Leicester.

The above account has drawn attention to some of the problems that arise from the application of social area and factor analytical methods to the study of urban social structure. A weakness of any such techniques may be seen in the extent to which people are treated as statistics rather than as individuals or as members of groups with behavioural traits related to those of the group concerned. To achieve a fuller understanding of urban residential structure it becomes necessary, therefore, to devote some

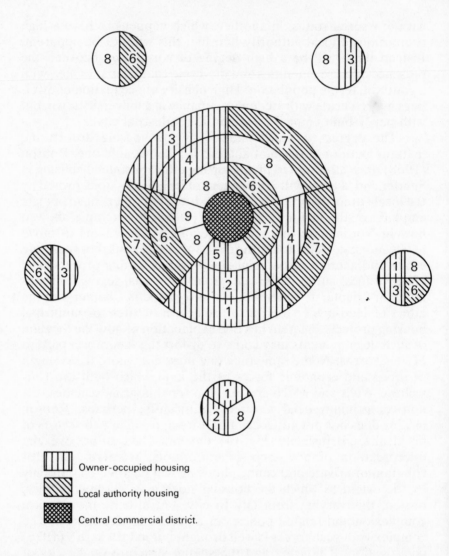

14   Robson's (1975) diagram of physical spaces in an idealized British
     city. (Courtesy Oxford University Press)

thought to the behaviour of social groups. In searching to explain
such behaviour, it may be that simple measures of segregation—
indices of dissimilarity or segregation, and location quotients—
provide some of the best clues to the reaction of one group to
another and to the preference of these groups for particular housing submarkets within the city.

Social systems

In his study of Johannesburg, R. J. Davies (1964) observed a higher degree of segregation amongst the 'lower' and 'upper' socio-economic groups than amongst the 'middle classes' and this conclusion is widely supported by empirical evidence elsewhere. The explanation is partly economic: the poor, for example, have fewer financial resources to enable them to move and are often tied to rented accommodation, whether private or public. But in part the explanation is also social, deriving from the kinds of social interaction and association that are implied by such elusive terms as *community* and *neighbourhood*. Measures of social interaction include marriage distance, friendship patterns represented by visiting and activities carried out in common, and membership of clubs and organizations. These, it is postulated, are related to common aspirations, group loyalties, a sense of territory, and other constraints. To some extent the argument is a circular one: is the pattern of social activity itself a product of geographical inertia, e.g. of inability to move from a particular area of housing, or are social areas brought about by social interaction? No doubt both influences are at work and this must be borne in mind in assessing the evidence afforded by any community-based studies.

Bethnal Green in the East End of London was the subject of a succession of sociological studies in the 1940s and 1950s and has become the type example of the 'working class' community. The area was settled by refugee Huguenots who introduced silk weaving in the late seventeenth century and out of this early manufacturing tradition have evolved a variety of industrial activities. The range is important because although in a number of industries, such as furniture making, the practice of son succeeding father is well-established, the variety of industrial employment has contributed to the residential stability of the population. The latter is marked. Young and Willmott (1957) questioned a sample of families and discovered that on average each couple had no fewer than thirteen relatives living in Bethnal Green. These kindred provided 'a bridge between the individual and the community', the ramifications of the extended family ensuring links with many other families to constitute a kind of social network. Social and economic strands are thus closely interwoven in the web of the community and the community is, in turn, identified with what Young and Willmott refer to as 'the common territory'. The sense of territory is strongest at the street level, where the pub, the shop, and perhaps the church* are regular meeting places, but residents

* As in Belfast where in half the streets, 97 per cent or more of the households are of the same religion (Poole and Boal, 1973).

also identify themselves with districts corresponding with former village nuclei. The latter constitute 'distinct ecological areas with differing styles of housing and prestige' (Frankenberg, 1966, p.176; Glass and Frenkel, 1946). Frankenberg contends that areal differentiation at these several scales, together with the associated sets of loyalties—to street, to district, to borough—contributes to the overall sense of community. Group loyalties are themselves brought about, not only by geographical association, but also by the extent to which class differences are subordinated to a common sense of status.

To what extent have communities of the Bethnal Green type survived the economic and social changes and the urban redevelopment schemes of the last twenty years? There is no simple answer to this question. Some, like St. Ebbe's in Oxford, have been swept away; others, like Oxford's 'Jericho', have survived to an age when town planners prefer rehabilitation and conservation to major surgery and transplantation. Between these extremes it is possible to find groups who have refused public housing when dispossessed by a redevelopment scheme, preferring to re-establish the community in another portion of the city (Hartman, 1963). Johnston describes them as the 'respectable working class' for whom 'public housing implies lack of privacy, high crime rates and an institutional form of existence' (Johnston, 1971). Even when redevelopment has had the effect of removing whole sections of the population to distant estates there is evidence here also which suggests that the original basis of community is not entirely destroyed (Willmott, 1963; Frankenberg, 1966). At Berinsfield, a new housing area outside Oxford, Morris and Mogey (1965) found a hierarchical arrangement of social networks strongly reminiscent of the different scales of association referred to above. Study of the older community may thus afford valuable insights into the nature of the contemporary one. Knowledge of the 'working class' community may also contribute towards an understanding of ethnic quarters and of the forces which serve to maintain them.

The persistence of 'upper class' enclaves close to the city centre has been noted by many observers, although their social structure has been subjected to less intimate scrutiny than that of the 'working class' communities. It is likely, in fact, that the wealthy, possessing greater personal mobility than the poor, maintain social networks of a far less spatially confined nature than the latter, and that the enclaves owe more to the survival of status than to the presence of a closed social system. Be that as it may, Mayfair and Belgravia in London, the *seizième arrondissement* of Paris,

Beacon Hill Boston, Nob Hill San Francisco, Chicago's Gold Coast and the Park Avenue apartment area of Manhattan in New York are well-known examples of a type that persists, often in close proximity to areas of highly contrasted social rank. High land and property values cushion them from change but they are frequently protected also by leasehold covenant and, more recently, by the designation of conservation areas. In Britain, the Civic Amenities Act of 1967 was followed by the establishment of many such Conservation Areas; they include, for example, the Victorian housing estate of North Oxford to which reference was made in Chapter One. A portion of the population of these upper class enclaves commonly resides on a permanent basis in hotels.

In Sjoberg's model of the 'pre-industrial city' (page 182) the élite live close to the centre, near to those buildings which stand for power and authority, whilst the poor and outcasts are confined to the edge of town. In the context of Sjoberg's model it is inviting to interpret those enclaves that still persist as relics of a former city structure, and studies of the once fashionable quarters of northern industrial cities in Britain lend some support to this view. In Manchester, Rodgers (1962) observed a sequence of changes in the run-down of such areas, beginning with the conversion of large Victorian villas, first into apartments of a still spacious and attractive nature, but later into smaller flats for a poor, possibly immigrant population, and in some cases into industrial use. The sequence is repeated in industrial cities such as Bradford where Manningham Lane, once known as 'Millionaires Row' is now more commonly referred to as 'the North-West Frontier' or 'the Khyber Pass'.

Environmental pollution and decay, followed by the arrival of ethnic minorities, have brought about changes in the industrial city which may be less apparent elsewhere, especially in large, administrative centres. In the United States, Schnore (1965) has distinguished between those cities which achieved the greater part of their growth before the motor car age, i.e. before 1920, and those which have largely grown since that time. Enclaves of the wealthy are more typical of the latter since competition for central sites has been less strong, other land uses being drawn to a suburban or fringe location (Guest, 1972). Bedarida (1968) views the decline of the central elite quarter as an 'Anglo-Saxon pattern' which, although evident in the United Kingdom, the United States and Canada, is not found in cities as different as Paris, Milan, Warsaw, Barcelona, Amsterdam, and Vienna, where the suburbs are 'left to the working class and seen as the worst part of the city without any facilities, with difficult transport and so on' (p.213). Persistence of high status areas may be interpreted as part economic, part behavioural. The centre affords easy access to central offices and to a wide range of social amenities; certain addresses carry status however mean the apartment may be. Even in the Anglo-Saxon world there is evidence that, far from having lost all their social status, central portions of some cities have regained it in response to changing attitudes to commuting and to the evolution of new life styles. To the professional couple with children grown up or at boarding school, the central city offers release from long journeys to work, whilst compensation for reduced access to open country is provided by ownership of a 'second home' in the country to which the family can retreat on Friday afternoon. They may be said to belong to the categories of 'careerists' or 'consumerists' to which reference has already been made in order to distinguish those who do not follow the projected course of familism. Chelsea, and more recently Islington, are parts of London which have experienced a rise in status in response to such changes. It is also possible to find localities in hitherto unfashionable districts south of the Thames, where terraces of working-class property have undergone similar 'gentrification'. The process of change is at first slow. A few middle-class pioneers purchase cheap property and restore it; the practice accelerates as others discover the convenience of living there and the locality acquires *cachet;* older residents are tempted or encouraged to sell and the process is completed. The logistic curve that represents such a sequence of changes on a graph has close parallels with that which describes the spread of the ghetto (Fig. 15).

Ethnic segregation and the ghetto

Except where it takes the form of a sudden change in house style, segregation on the basis of social rank or family status is usually less apparent to the casual observer in the city than is ethnic segregation, and it is the latter that has attracted the greatest attention from those interested in the social problems to which segregation can give rise.

At the outset it is necessary to consider what is meant by the word *ethnic*. According to Nathan Glazer (1975) it refers to 'a social group which consciously shows some aspects of a common culture and is defined primarily by descent', i.e. it combines a cultural aspect of group differentiation with an implied biological

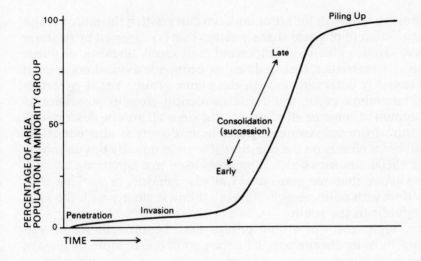

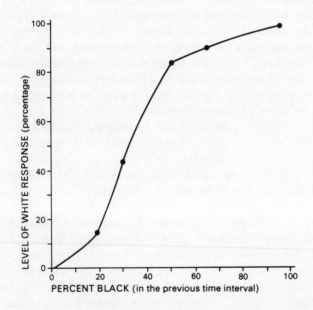

15 Sequence of changes in the population structure of an area accompanying 'gentrification' or 'ghettoization'. After Johnston (above),
1971, and Rose, 1972. (Courtesy G. Bell & Sons, and the Editor of
Economic Geography)

element, although the latter does not carry with it the more precise
association of physical characteristics that is suggested by the term
race. Groups identified in terms of their racial, linguistic or religious characteristics, their political or economic aspirations, are not
necessarily coterminous with the ethnic group. Yet it is certain
that an ethnic group will derive its identity from its possession in
common of some or all of such traits, since all may be described as
culture-forming. Awareness of ethnic identity is also important
and bears closely on the question of segregation. By this definition
the racial minority which submerges itself in a common culture is
less *ethnic* than the non-racial Catholic minority in working class
Belfast with political aspirations that link it closely with the Irish
Republic to the south.

Segregation of ethnic groups may be brought about vol-
untarily or by discrimination on the part of one or more sections of
the population against another, usually, but not invariably, a
minority. Care, however, must be taken in interpreting measures
of segregation (Peach, 1975). There are many statistical pitfalls
that arise from the nature of census data and from the nature of the
areal units for which data is available, whilst measures of segregation that seem relevant for one ethnic group may have little
relevance for the behaviour of another. Emphasis in any study
should be on the cultural cohesion of the group and on its relationship with others, i.e. on the process of segregation. A historical
dimension is also essential, both to an understanding of how segregation has been brought about, and in attaching meaning to any
particular measure of segregation.

Originally used to describe the Jewish quarter of a medieval
European city, the term *ghetto* has lost much of its precision and is
widely employed to denote a tract of segregated housing. Indeed it
may not even imply segregation when it is used, as it frequently is in
the United States at the present day, simply to refer to a run-down
quarter of the city, the kind of area to which the equally emotive
word 'slum' is sometimes attached. In such circumstances it is
scarcely surprising that there should be no simple definition even
of that best-documented example of segregation, the black American (or Negro) ghetto. 'Negroes are more segregated residentially
than are Orientals, Mexican American, Puerto Ricans, or any
nationality group. In fact, Negroes are by far the most residentially
segregated urban minority group in recent American history. This
is evident in the virtually complete exclusion of Negro residents
from most new suburban developments of the past fifty years as
well as in the block-by-block expansion of Negro residential areas

in the central portions of many large cities' (Taeuber and Taeuber, 1965).

Successors to the European migrants whose movement to the United States was checked by legislation in the early 1920s, the black Americans from the Deep South have concentrated increasingly in the inner city slums of northern and western cities. In their study of selected cities, the Taeubers recorded a segregation index* as high as 91.6 in Indianapolis and Rose (1972) has observed that only about 'ten per cent of black metropolitan populations reside outside of contiguous black residential clusters'. Although the distribution of the Negro population in the cities of the South is somewhat different, there is evidence that segregation has increased there also over the last twenty years or so.

Morrill (1965) has suggested four reasons for the black ghetto: white prejudice, characteristics of the Negro population itself, discrimination in housing and legal barriers. White prejudice is colour prejudice—'lighter-skinned members of the other groups may escape the ghetto, but black skin constitutes a qualitative difference in the minds of whites' (p.342)—but it is associational as well as racial, involving the fear of losing status if Negroes enter the neighbourhood as well as fears relating to intermarriage or simply to people who are physically different. For its part, the Negro population, like any newly-arrived minority group, derives strength and support from remaining within the group. A legacy of poverty and limited education means that status and acceptance can be achieved by many Negroes only within the Negro community. Rose (1970) sees this community as having a territorial base. 'The existence and persistence of the Negro ghetto as a spatially based social community may best be explained within the framework of the social assignment of territory. Once a slice of physical space is identified as the territorial realm of a specific social group, any attempt to alter this assignment results in group conflict, both overt and covert.' To this explanation one may now add the cultural and political awareness of the present generation of black Americans. Hannerz (1969) has examined the evolution of black culture, attributing it to the African origin of the population, to its Southern background, to subjection to racism, and to shared poverty. Political control—Black Power—comes from the growing proportion that is black of the total population of American cities with their outdated municipal boundaries. Taken together, the attitudes of whites and blacks constitute social pluralism, 'the involuntary operation of a set of forces designed to minimize social interaction and, as a consequence, promote social

*A measure of displacement, showing the percentage of the minority population who would have to move to reproduce the distribution pattern of the rest.

isolation' (Rose 1969).

Blame for discrimination in the housing market is customarily attributed to the real estate industry (Brown, 1972), although it is claimed that realtors are only responding to consumer—principally white—preference (Muth, 1969). Race restrictive covenants, written into the deeds of property in order to prevent black penetration of white residential areas, first appeared in Chicago in the early 1920s and were not outlawed by the US Supreme Court until 1948. Brown describes the race restrictive covenant as 'this most effective of all residential restrictive devices' (p.68). The response of the National Association of Real Estate Boards after 1948 was simply to rephrase the relevant article in its Code of Ethics which now reads: 'A Realtor should not be instrumental in introducing into a neighbourhood a character of property or use, which will clearly be detrimental to property values in that neighbourhood.' Protection of property values remained the cloak under which discrimination in housing was practised until Civil Rights legislation was introduced in 1968, in an attempt to eliminate it. Throughout most of this period the role of the real estate market was complemented by policy implemented by the Federal Housing Administration. This body, possibly influenced by Hoyt's report on residential neighbourhoods (Rose, 1970), carried out a policy aimed at ensuring the racial homogeneity of neighbourhoods by financing or insuring only those properties that met this requirement. Athough this practice officially ended in1949, it was, in fact, still carried on until finally banned in 1962 (Morrill, 1965).

The boundary along which one segregated area meets another is a fruitful zone in which to investigate the reaction of ethnic groups to each other and to observe the forces that underlie segregation. Morrill has described the spread of the black ghetto as a spatial diffusion process (1965), although he later preferred the term quasi-diffusionary (Morrill, 1968). In this process the Negro is the active agent, the searcher, and the white is passive, the realtor facilitating change by encouraging whites to sell ('block busting'). As block by block conversion to black occupancy takes place it can be seen that it is in the realtor's interest to maintain a dual housing market, a white market in which property values are maintained by excluding blacks (above), and a ghetto market, since the prices that the realtor can obtain from Negroes on the edge of the ghetto are higher than could be obtained from whites. Other writers have preferred to interpret the spread of the ghetto in terms of white withdrawal before a perceived threat and Rose has represented this as a series of thresholds along a continuum of change from white to black occupancy (Fig. 15). The point is not disputed by Morrill who himself observes that 'whites are willing to accept 5 per cent to 25 per cent (with a mean of 10 per cent) Negro occupancy for a long time before beginning abandonment'. According to Rose (1970), whites continue to seek housing on the edge of the ghetto until the level of black occupancy reaches about 30 per cent. Thereafter the white exodus is rapid, although the growth of the black population and the related pressure on housing space is a variable that is bound to affect the rate of white removal. Based on the idea of thresholds, Rose (1972) employs several terms to describe the ghetto: 'core neighbourhood' for those census tracts in which black occupancy has reached 75 per cent, 'ghetto fringe neighbourhood' where the population is 50 to 75 per cent black, and 'neighbourhood in transition' for those portions where the percentage black is below 50 per cent but above the critical 30 per cent. Use of such terms also points to contrasts in population and housing characteristics within the ghetto.

Typically, the ghetto extends outwards in a sectoral fashion from the inner city slums, although as in San Francisco, the pattern may be distorted by topographic variations. In southern cities, black housing areas may extend to the urban fringe but in the North, where the Negroes are a successor population—usually of the Jewish group in the first place according to Rose (1969)—the ghetto is more exclusively an inner city phenomenon. The actual pattern of ghetto development is affected by the rent-paying ability of the population, renting of property being more common than purchase. Where the ability to pay rent is low, there are likely to be several ghetto nuclei as the population seeks out low cost housing. Better-off Negroes, possibly migrants from another city, are in contrast more likely to be drawn to the transition area of the ghetto. Here, towards the fringe of the ghetto, the social rank of the black population is likely to be as high as, if not higher than, that of the retreating white population. Short-distance moves also take place within the ghetto, the middle-income Negroes moving towards its fringe, vacating property that is taken up by 'working class blacks' (Rose, 1972) who, in turn, have abandoned the 'lower class' inner core. The extent to which the anti-discrimination legislation of the 1960s will alter this pattern has yet to be seen. Rose has suggested that the effect could be a more polynucleated pattern of black residential development, but the political strength that the black population gains from segregation may militate against this.

Studies of the residential distribution of ethnic groups in the

United Kingdom have generally yielded much lower indices of segregation than corresponding studies in the USA, and there seems little justification for the use of the term *ghetto* in any comparative sense. On a ward basis the segregation index of West Indians in Birmingham in 1961 was 55.0 and of Indians and Pakistanis only 45.0 (P.N. Jones, 1967). A broadly comparable figure of 56.9 was obtained by Poole and Boal (1973) using planning units as a basis for measuring the segregation of Catholics in Belfast in 1969. This latter value rose to 79.0 when the data were analysed at street level. In a later study of Birmingham, P.N. Jones (1970) discovered a build-up of immigrant population in certain areas of the city during the early 1960s, but only in a few clusters of enumeration districts did the immigrant proportion of the total exceed 25 per cent and Jones concluded that 'ghetto-like conditions are a long way off .

Despite this, sufficient work has been carried out on residential segregation in the United Kingdom to provide additional insights into the nature of the forces which bring about such separation. Boal, for example, drawing on experience in Northern Ireland, puts forward a conflict interpretation of segregation, arguing that descriptions of urban 'sub-communities' have emphasized shared interests as the basis of community, neglecting response to outside pressures. 'The urban residential sub-community can be interpreted as a mechanism for coping with threat' (Boal, 1972). In the face of a perceived threat a group will cluster, (1) for defence, (2) for the psychological support that is provided within its own cultural area and, (3) to achieve a power base. During a phase of sectarian violence in Northern Ireland the two communities tend to withdraw into their segregated strongholds of the Falls or the Shankill which also serve as places of retreat for the terrorist or urban guerrilla. Actual conflict is most common along the boundaries where segregated areas adjoin (Poole and Boal, 1973).

With its slogans and street decorations, Belfast also illustrates well the degree to which the community can become identified with a common territory (Boal, 1969; 1970). Within its territory the cohesion of the group is maintained by separate education in Church schools, by parish-based social and sporting clubs, and by local community organizations such as the Lodges of the Orange Order. Stereotyped views of the opposite group are formulated to the extent that journeys to work, to shop and to school are planned so as to avoid the alien territory (Busteed, 1972; 1974). Alienation to this extent is not encountered elsewhere in the United Kingdom, although what Jones describes as 'the emergence of community sentiment' is apparent in immigrant localities in the form of temples, shops and cinemas catering for ethnic tastes (1967). It is strongest amongst Muslim Pakistanis (P. N. Jones, 1976).

The role of the housing market must not be overlooked, the availability of low-cost housing having an important effect on the initial concentration of immigrant groups. This has been demonstrated for cities in many parts of the world, e.g. in Rowland's (1971) study of Maori migration to Auckland. In Britain, municipal ownership of property has contributed, however indirectly, to the distribution of immigrant groups. In Birmingham, for example, coloured immigrants have avoided the innermost zones of poor housing because these are mostly owned by the municipality and scheduled for redevelopment. Instead they have been attracted to a middle ring of pre-1914 dwellings, large enough to permit subdivision and usually under leasehold tenure with short-run leases which make them unattractive to the normal purchaser but a good proposition for the speculator able to exploit a big immigrant demand. When public housing is offered to immigrant families, West Indians are found to be more willing to move than are Asians for whom privately-owned housing affords a means of capital accumulation (Jones, 1967). Jones concludes that the greater complexity of the housing market in Britain compared with the USA results in a less obvious association between zones of immigrants and the distribution of the poorest housing in the city (1970).

The urban village

The term 'urban village' was first used by Gans (1962) in his description of the West End of Boston, a low-rent neighbourhood of the city, now demolished, which had housed a succession of immigrant peoples: first Irish, then Jews, later Italians and Poles, together with small numbers of other ethnic groups including Negroes. In this respect it was no different from residential districts bordering the central business district of many other American cities which had similarly absorbed successive waves of immigrants, in time despatching most of them to the suburbs as they learnt the language and adjusted to the American way of life (Ward, 1968; 1971). 'The . . . area, typically, is one in which European immigrants—and more recently Negro and Puerto Rican ones—try to adapt their nonurban institutions and cultures to the urban milieu. Thus it may be called an *urban village*. Often it is described in ethnic terms: Little Italy, The Ghetto, or Black Belt' (Gans, p.4). Burgess had used similar terminology (Fig. 4), and the establishment of such immigrant 'colonies' has been regarded as an essential part of the initial settlement of any immigrant population in an urban area (Rex and Moore 1967, quoted by P. N. Jones, 1970).

Movement of the 'colony' to the suburbs has usually been accompanied by dispersal, although Glazer and Moynihan (1964) have found evidence of ethnicity affecting the pattern of residential development in the suburbs. The rate of dispersal is influenced by population growth within the community itself and by pressure on housing space exerted by other immigrant groups. Centralization of the working-class Catholic population in Belfast has been explained in terms of the absence of a more recent immigrant group to displace it (Poole and Boal, 1973). But the rate and the degree of dispersal is also affected by what Gans referred to as the durability of the ethnic tradition. It is the survival of such tradition, with its overtones of community and social network, which gives the urban village its unique significance. Inevitably it has much in common with both the 'working class' community and the ghetto; less exclusively class-based than the former and without the external pressures exerted on the latter, it can be said to occupy an intermediate position in any categorization of such inner city residential areas.

The strength of cultural ties varies from one ethnic group to another and is the key to the survival of the group as a territorially-based community. The Kalamazoo Dutch (Jackle and Wheeler, 1969) are a commonly quoted example of a group which underwent acculturation and dispersion, but their experience differed from that of other American immigrant communities, notably the Russians (Simirenko, 1964) and Italians. The greater part of *The Urban Villagers* was devoted to a study of the Italian community of Boston's West End and to analyzing the nature of its social system. In addition to the obvious links afforded by language, Gans stressed the importance of food because of its close connection with family and group life. 'Indeed, food patterns are retained longer than others because they hold the group together with a minimum of strain' (p.73). Additional factors emphasized included: social relationships based on kinship, ties to the church, and the role of clubs and societies. These explanations bear out the conclusions of Firey (1947) drawn from a study of the Italian community of Boston's North End. Amongst the groups retaining an ethnic outlook the Jews invite attention on account of the strength of a social network and culture deriving from religious practice. Inheriting also a tradition of working in a narrow range of occupations such as tailoring to which they were once confined, the Jews have often exhibited a high degree of segregation. This was particularly notable in cities of Western Europe and North America, following the migration of East European Jews in the late nineteenth century. The resulting Jewish quarters well deserved the epithet of urban village (Connell, 1973).

In their study of 'New Commonwealth' immigrants in Sparkbrook, Birmingham, Rex and Moore describe the 'tight-knit' community in which the newcomer lives but they also refer to the area as one in which the newcomer is 'launched into a larger society in which he has new rights and obligations as a citizen and in which, in time, he will be able to make his own way' (Rex and Moore, 1967). It is inviting to apply the term urban village to such an area despite the less concentrated nature of the immigrant community. Comparisons, however, must take into account the effect of modern transport and communications on the maintenance of social networks. Webber (1964), for example, uses the phrase 'community without propinquity', suggesting that communities can survive without being tied to a single locality. The constraints of distance will, nevertheless, continue to affect some groups more strongly than others and also certain age groups more than others, so that one must be cautious of generalization. Still greater care must be taken in seeking to make comparisons between the social systems, territorially-based or otherwise, of cities in the Western World and those which may be observed in the rapidly growing cities of the Third World (Chapter 9).

The 'zone in transition'

Socially or ethnically defined communities of the type described above are most commonly associated with that part of the city to which Burgess gave the name *zone in transition*. In an age more sceptical of the ecological concepts underlying such a definition, the phrase *inner city* is likely to be preferred (Brooks et al., 1975). 'Surrounding the CBD are areas of residential deterioration caused by the encroaching of business and industry from Zone 1. This may therefore be called a Zone in Transition, with a factory district for its inner belt and an outer ring of retrogressing neighbourhoods, of first-settlement immigrant colonies, of rooming-house districts, of homeless-men areas, of resorts of gambling, bootlegging, sexual vice, and of breeding-places of crime. In this area of physical deterioration and social disorganization our studies show the greatest concentration of cases of poverty, bad housing, juvenile delinquency, family disintegration, physical and mental disease. As families and individuals prosper, they escape from this area into Zone III beyond, leaving behind as marooned a residuum of the defeated' (Burgess, 1929).

Omitting the overtones of Al Capone, Gans (1968) defines the inner city as 'the transient residential areas, the Gold Coasts and the slums that generally surround the central business district, although in some communities they may continue for miles beyond that district.' He distinguishes five categories of resident who live within this inner city:

1 *The 'Cosmopolites'* They live close to the centre of the city in order to take advantage of its cultural facilities and the category includes students, artists and 'professionals'. The latter, if they are wealthy, maintain a second residence in the suburbs or out of town.

2 *The unmarried or childless* Gans subdivides this category to distinguish the young adults and the newly-marrieds who will move to the suburbs when they have children, from those who remain permanently unmarried or childless. Like the 'cosmopolites' this type of resident lives in the inner city by choice. The phrases 'consumerists' and 'careerists', used earlier, would apply to many of the representatives of these two categories.

3 *The 'ethnic villagers'* They had already been described in *The Urban Villagers* and the category includes all the immigrant communities (except Negroes) with their emphasis on kinship and the primary group. Their presence in the inner city is partly a matter of necessity, partly one of tradition.

4 *The 'deprived'* They include the black Americans of the ghetto, together with other sub-categories experiencing hardship such as the very poor, broken families, and some who are physically or mentally handicapped. Having no other choice of place of residence, and living under bad housing conditions, they have much in common with,

5 *The 'trapped' and downward mobile* Many of these are old people, staying behind as others move away, either because of poverty or because socially, they have come down in the world. In the more picturesque phrases of Burgess, they may be said to make up the 'residuum of the defeated'.

The Gans typology is derived from observation of the North

American city and in relation to European cities it may be thought that he has omitted the category of the 'respectable working class'. The omission is partly explained by the emphasis which he placed on the transient nature of much of the population living in the inner city. In fact he distinguished this zone, not only from the suburbs, but also from an intermediate *outer city* of stable residential areas which housed the working and middle-class tenant and owner (p. 98).

An inner city of mixed land use and transient population would seem to defy the search for spatial order. But it has already been suggested that the change and instability which characterised the Chicago of the 1920s is a less obvious feature of the contemporary North American city (page 36) and Bourne (1968) has gone so far as to state that the area which Burgess distinguished as the 'zone in transition' is now 'essentially non-transitional'. Failure of the CBD to continue to grow outwards is accompanied by reduced investment in property resulting in gradual deterioration rather than renewal or replacement. The residential portions of the inner city are occupied by 'stable' communities so that transition is less typical of this zone than of residential neighbourhoods in any other part of the city. Whilst not accepting that transition is necessarily slowest in the inner city, Griffin and Preston (1966; 1969) contend that land use change has slowed or largely ceased in *portions* (their italics) of the inner city. Outward growth from the CBD still takes place but it is uneven and interrupted. Griffin and Preston represent this in the form of a sectoral model (Fig. 16). Within the three sectors which they distinguish are to be found residential areas of either high or low status, together with clusterings ('multiple nuclei') of other types of land use: wholesaling, car sales and parking, government establishments, miscellaneous retail establishments, and certain kinds of industry, both heavy and light.

On the basis of a study of twelve United States' cities, Davis (1965) noted an increasing compartmentalization of the inner city into areas of either high or low value housing. 'Middle class' housing had been displaced because the difference in value between 'upper' and 'middle' class housing served to prevent the latter filtering down to the former. Areas of high value housing were able to guard themselves from invasion by low income groups, hence the observed polarization of housing types. In the Griffin and Preston model the area of high value housing corresponds with the *Sector of Active Assimilation*. As the name suggests, they see this as the most fluid portion of the inner city

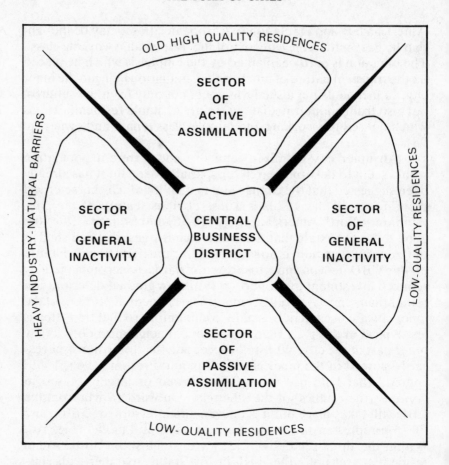

16   Griffin and Preston's transition zone model. (Reproduced by permission from the *Annals of the Association of American Geographers,* vol. 56, 1966)

environment but although change takes place, 'the basic theme (remains) . . . the existence of higher-quality land uses' (p.346). The high status of the locality serves to attract land uses from the central business district and the former mansions of the wealthy are gradually taken over as doctors' consulting rooms, lawyers' offices or the headquarters of professional organizations. But the wealthy population is by no means wholly displaced, and elsewhere the old villas are replaced by luxury apartments. Typical of the shopping parade serving this residential neighbourhood are small restaurants, high-quality clothing shops, book and antique shops.

    Similar changes to those which Griffin and Preston describe can be observed in many British 'county towns' which escaped nineteenth century industrialization. Victorian villas lining the Banbury Road which bisects the fashionable enclave of North Oxford have almost all been converted to language schools, surgeries or offices. Away from the main road the area retains its residential character, although the completeness of the former Victorian townscape has been eroded by modern flats and the occasional college annex as owners have obtained permission to build in their gardens or even to replace the more decayed buildings which lie outside the designated Conservation Area. With its family businesses, including restaurant, antique shop, and florist, North Parade continues to serve the commercial interests of the neighbourhood.

Areas of low quality housing are associated with the *Sectors of General Inactivity*. They are not absent from the *Sector of Passive Assimilation* but in the Griffin and Preston model this latter zone is given over most typically to light industry, the railway, wholesaling and low-grade retail land uses. Change takes place within the Sectors of General Inactivity but in comparison with the other parts of the inner city these are zones of 'general quiescence'. Stability is partly related to the survival of heavy industry which affords a source of local employment, but it is a product also of social forces: ethnic concentration, the survival of older immigrant neighbourhoods, and the presence of residents 'in their advanced years' ('the trapped' according to Gans). Rapid changes may be brought about by urban redevelopment schemes in any part of the zone, but until such measures are applied there is a degree of stagnation about the area which renders inappropriate the use of such terms as 'invasion and succession' or 'transition'.

Perception of the residential environment

To the economist's interpretation of the city as a kind of battleground on which locational advantages are 'traded off' one against another, the sociologist has contributed the idea of 'community', suggesting that like-minded people cluster together in order to enjoy certain social benefits. Geographical studies of the city have been influenced still more recently by the psychologist's concept of the 'city of the mind', the idea that the individual's spatial behaviour within the city is related to his perception of urban space.

The individual's knowledge of the city in which he lives is incomplete and biased by the fact that he spends most of his time in just one or two small parts of it. The phrase 'action space' may be used to describe the collection of all urban locations about which the individual has some information, whilst 'activity space' corresponds with the smaller subset of urban locations with which the individual is brought into contact as a result of his normal daily activities: journeys to work, visits to friends, etc. (Horton and Reynolds, 1971). From these activities he builds up a mental picture, or map, of the city which is far from being a 'precise, miniaturized model of reality, reduced in scale and consistently abstracted'. Rather is it 'made by reducing, eliminating, or even adding elements to reality, by fusion and distortion, by relating and structuring the parts . . . It was as if the map were drawn on an infinitely flexible rubber sheet; directions were twisted, distances stretched or compressed, large forms so changed from their accurate scale projections as to be at first unrecognizable. But the sequence was usually correct, the map was rarely torn and sewn back together in another order. This continuity is necessary if the image is to be of any value.' (Lynch, 1960, p.87).

According to Lynch, the individual's mental map of the city is made up of five principal elements, paths, edges, districts, nodes and landmarks, and it is by reference to these elements that the cityscape becomes 'legible' to its inhabitants. *Paths* are the routes which the individual customarily takes in the course of moving about the city, either on foot or in a vehicle, and for most people they constitute the strongest element of the map since impressions of the city are recorded during these journeys. The planner can respond to this fact by introducing legibility to a city's path networks. A new housing estate can be made more legible to children who have to learn their way home from school if the roads are not all of the same width or angle and if they have different kinds of houses, fences or trees bordering them. *Edges* constitute the boundaries of the map, or of portions of it, and help the individual to see the city in terms of discrete areas. Railways and trunk roads may be seen as virtual barriers. In an early study of Bethnal Green, Self (1945) observed that 'the main streets are very real social barriers and to some residents the Cambridge Heath Road resembles the Grand Canyon'. The American phrase 'wrong side of the (railway) tracks' is expressive of social distance and illustrates the barrier-effect, both physical and mental, of the railway. In some of the British New Towns, such as Stevenage (Fig. 17), the network of main distributor roads was designed so as to help newcomers identify themselves with particular neighbourhoods by providing well-marked 'edges' to these portions of the town.

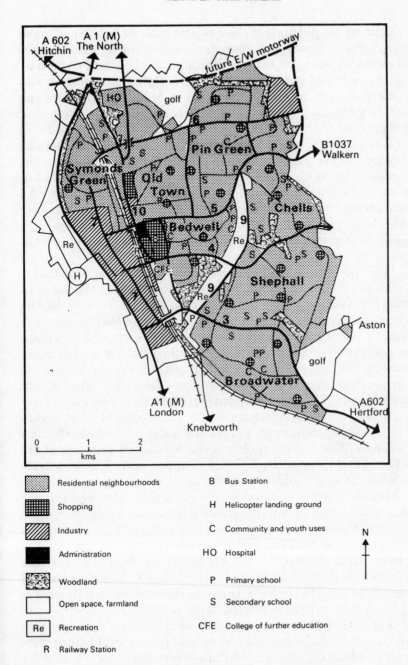

17 Master Plan of the new town of Stevenage. Names refer to the neighbourhoods. (Courtesy Stevenage Development Corporation)

Districts are portions of the city which, to the individual, have some common, identifying character. Such character may be physical in the sense that it is derived from, say, the street pattern or the architecture of the houses, or it may relate to the people who live there. Lynch quotes the example of Minneapolis where the observer's mental image 'typically breaks down each time the street gridiron changes its orientation' (Peterson, 1916). *Nodes* as the name suggests, are focal points and take the form of junctions or squares where paths converge. *Landmarks* take many forms. The most obvious examples are the church spire or skyscraper but the landmark may be external to the city and take the form of a mountain peak which serves as a point of reference to the traveller within the city. Alternatively it may be quite small, the post box, signpost or tree that adds legibility to the path network referred to above.

In his own work on Boston, Jersey City and Los Angeles (in *The Image of the City)*, Lynch clearly demonstrates the value of mental maps in identifying the residential districts of a city. But he has been criticized on the grounds that individuals also have images of the city that cannot readily be mapped. These may be described as visual rather than spatial although they have a spatial component and represent what people find attractive or unattractive in an urban landscape. It is not easy to isolate such images, and Lowenthal (1972) has drawn attention to the problems involved in interpreting verbal preferences, but a knowledge of what makes for personal attachment to a particular locality must clearly contribute to a fuller understanding of the residential structure of the city (Ford and Fitzsimons, 1974). Even the ghetto may be attractive in so far as it projects a strong sense of place.

Studies of residential mobility suggest that most migrants are conservative when they move house within the city, preferring to avoid unfamiliar places or groups of people, and for this reason often selecting a dwelling that is satisfactory rather than optimal for their needs (Rossi, 1955). For many of them the search is confined to that part of the city of which they have a clear mental image. This may be quite a small portion of the whole and is frequently sector specific, related to the individual's activity space. Journeys into and out of the town centre make an important contribution to the learning process, and the sectoral bias in residential preference and intra-urban migration is confirmed by studies such as those of Johnston (1972a) in selected cities of Australia and New Zealand and of Adams (1969) in the United States.

So far reference has been made only to individuals but, in fact, mental images are shared by groups. Underlying such group perception are differences based on, for example, age, sex, education or ethnicity. 'People who see themselves as working class, accordingly, also see themselves as being suitable for those areas and homes thought appropriate to the working class' (Duncan, 1976). Shared images are built up through interpersonal communication within the group, other groups being excluded by what Horton and Reynolds describe as a 'communications barrier'. Lynch also recognizes the fact that images are held jointly: 'The landscape plays a social role as well. The named environment, familiar to all, furnishes material for common memories and symbols which bind the group together and allow them to communicate with one another' (p.126). The individual, of course, may belong to more than one group, a point stressed by Wirth, and mental maps will therefore overlap, but this is not inconsistent with observations already made concerning attachment to territory at several different scales.

In so far as environmental perception is affected by group membership, it becomes necessary to ask whether the study of mental maps and images can contribute anything to the analysis of urban residential structure that is not already available from examining the behaviour of urban 'communities'. Tuan (1974) has little doubt when he states that 'the perceived extent of neighbourhood does not necessarily correspond with the web of intense neighbourly contacts'. The slum dweller of the inner city may have little awareness that he occupies a definable area in spite of his kinship and other ties with those around him. Conversely the middle-class suburbanite, with a web of social contacts that extend throughout the city, will defend his territory with brick walls in order to keep out undesirable outsiders. In such circumstances there would seem to be every reason to explore the city of the mind, and we may even sympathize with Carr's (1970) view that 'in a very real sense the city is what people think it is'.

4

The Commercial Structure of the City

The centre of the city in the ancient world was the hub of political and religious activity. Imposing buildings dominated the centre, symbolizing power both spiritual and temporal. Indeed such powers were frequently combined in the one priest-king. Commerce was tolerated for the profit which it brought to the ruling class but its status was generally low, and if the market place happened to be located near to palace or temple it was placed there under licence and to take advantage of the prestige and pedestrian traffic, and therefore potential custom, which proximity to the palace afforded. Such a city was very different from downtown New York, and at the outset of an analysis of the commercial structure, even of the western industrial city, it is worth reminding oneself that the urban core has not always resembled the popular image projected by the view of Manhattan from the Staten Island ferry.

The Central Business District

A Central Business District (CBD) is common to all three models of urban form: Burgess, Hoyt and Harris and Ullman. Two definitions suggest why the CBD should be such an important element in the make-up of the western city:

1   'An area of very high land valuation, an area characterised by a high concentration of retail businesses, offices, theatres, hotels and "service" businesses, and an area of high traffic flow.' (United States Bureau of the Census)

2   'That part of a metropolitan area which comprises the locus of high-order service activities, the characteristics of each being their unique accessibility or convenience to the greatest number of people.' (J. H. Dunning)

Several reasons may be put forward to explain the concentration of service activities at the heart of the city, one of them being suggested by Dunning's phrase 'unique accessibility'. Traditionally the CBD has been the most accessible point, not only to the city's own population, but also to the population of villages and smaller towns within the city region who have therefore looked to it for the provision of higher order goods and services. According to central place theory, the greater the population and the more extensive the transport network, the higher is likely to be the order of services available. An indication of the importance of accessibility is to be found in the fact that, in large cities, the CBD is typically enclosed within a ring of main line rail terminals. Chicago's famous Loop is defined by the elevated railway system, and office complexes have been built above railway stations—for example the Pan American building above Grand Central Station, New York—just as out-of-town airports are now beginning to attract not only hotels, but also conference and high order shopping facilities (Gottmann, 1966). Within the CBD, accessibility is provided by various forms of transport including the taxi, the movements of which have been used to express the pattern and nature of linkages within city centres (below). Several major world cities have either built new or have extended their underground railway systems in recent years. At a different scale, the personal messenger service is a commonly used form of communication within certain parts of the CBD.

Accessibility may also be interpreted in terms of access to a labour force for the CBD employs not only the businessman, who frequently commutes long distances to work, but also the office cleaner, waiter and newspaper vendor. This supporting labour force is more commonly drawn from close at hand, from the residential quarters of the inner city described in the previous chapter.

A second explanation is economic, concerned with the advantages to be derived from clustering. There is the advantage first to the customers whose movements are minimized when shops, banks and other services are close together. Clustering also permits comparison of prices and quality, and the phrase 'comparison goods' is frequently used of the range of retail goods which exhibit concentration for this reason. Medieval cities had their Butchers' Row or Fish Street; the modern city likewise displays various degrees of clustering amongst, for example, shoe shops, lawyers' offices, furniture stores and car showrooms.

Clustering of activities within the CBD also offers benefits to those who provide the services. Despite their apparent variety, most of the functions of the CBD are complementary and interdependent. They make use of each others' products, not in the sense of manufacturing firms exchanging their goods for further processing, but in the more abstract sense of dealing in the title to goods (Dunning, 1969). The transaction is no less real for the fact that it is made on paper rather than by lorry or van, and meetings or conferences may be regarded as the 'markets' for such abstract dealings (Gottmann, 1970). The CBD also enables firms to achieve external economies by having access to what is, in effect, a common pool of services. These can range from photo-copying to consultancy and warehousing. The wide variety of such services means that a particular firm is able to obtain a 'package' of services which may involve, for example, licensing, insurance and shipment. High buildings characterise the CBD and Gottmann accounts for this phenomenon, not only as a response to high land values, but in terms of the ease of communication which a single tower structure, served by a lift (elevator), affords to closely related service activities. One such tower may house a million square feet of office space which, if distributed horizontally, would involve considerable loss of time on the part of, for example, messengers or secretaries, who move between departments or related firms.

There is a third, less tangible, reason for the concentration of activities within the CBD which may be described as behavioural. Prestige attaches to a city centre address and the foreign businessman is more likely to be impressed by a visit to an office in the CBD than to an obscure location in the suburbs. In addition a central position permits easy access to places of entertainment, specialized stores and sophisticated restaurants, as well as to sites of historical and tourist interest. Concentration also facilitates personal contact, whether it be in the office and the conference room or in the less formal atmosphere of clubs and coffee houses. The introduction of ever-more-sophisticated communications equipment would appear to have reduced the need for such contact except for purely social reasons, and in some activities this has been the case, but there are others for which face-to-face contact remains valuable, even essential (Meier, 1962). Dunning draws attention to the fact that many financial transactions take place on the basis of trust and confidence and for such deals the personal visit is still preferred to the telephone call or letter. And the benefits of personal contact are not limited to the financial world: the newspaper reporter has his sources of information, and one does not have to search far for parallel examples in the fields of politics, the law, and even of entertainment.

For convenience, a distinction has been made between the

three reasons put forward for the concentration of service activities in the city centre, but in practice no clear-cut division exists. Personal contact, though based partly on tradition and custom, is economic in the sense that understanding and confidence bring gain. Linkages, whether personal or transactional, also involve accessibility, to each other if not to the customer who travels into the centre from the suburbs or beyond. Since the advantages are so interwoven it becomes necessary to employ a single measure of a city centre's attractiveness, or pulling-power, and that may be described as its *centrality*.

Delimiting the CBD.

A variety of methods have been employed to delimit the CBD, although most practitioners agree that there is rarely a clear-cut boundary. Land uses are frequently mixed towards the fringe whilst non-central uses, for example residences, appear on the upper floors of buildings which at street level are still given over to shops or other services.

The use of *building height* acknowledges the functional importance of high buildings in the CBD but fails to distinguish land uses. Thus tall apartment blocks will be included as well as office towers; some cities also have building height regulations. The intensity of *traffic* or *pedestrian movement* provides a crude indication of the general magnetism of the CBD, but allowance must be made for the introduction of traffic control measures in most modern cities in assessing vehicular movements. The *pattern* of vehicular flow based on, for example, the monitoring of taxi movements, reveals far more about the CBD as a functional system, than do flow diagrams derived from simple observation of the number of vehicles. Pedestrian counts give an idea of the bustle that is characteristic of the CBD in daytime and are of interest to companies seeking to discover the most profitable sites for new stores, but tell one nothing about the nature of pedestrian trip movement. To establish linkages it is again necessary to search out patterns of movement: the calls made by the messenger boy, or the visits of the company director to office, conference room, restaurant, sauna and so forth. Delimitation of the CBD has in some cases been carried out on the basis of the difference, commonly found, between a small resident population and a large daytime working population. Data collection is required to be on a very detailed basis and allowance has to be made for the presence of such buildings as churches, but the method can be supported by information relating to commuter flow. Detailed information regarding the distribution and movement of population was used in the early 1960s to delimit the central area of Zurich (Zwingli, 1967).

The use of *land values* to delimit the CBD is based on the land rent theory which supposes that land uses compete for the most desirable central location (page 37). In an early study of Stockholm, William-Olsson (1940) employed a shop rent index—rent divided by length of frontage—to distinguish the central shopping area of that city, and others have made use of a similar trade index based on the usually more elusive data relating to retail turnover. Valuation of property for taxation purposes provides a more general source of data and rateable values, usually expressed in terms of front-foot values, have been widely employed in British studies. Where there is standardization of valuation procedure it becomes possible to employ the technique for comparative purposes. Actual land values have been more commonly used in studies in the United States. Where these are not available it may be possible to piece together a map from information relating to sales.

By far the most common approach to delimitation is one which takes account of *land use* within the CBD and methods range from the simple transect study based on observation of ground floor street frontages to the more elaborate indices taking account of floor space and height of buildings which were pioneered by Murphy and Vance in the early 1950s (Murphy and Vance, 1954 a, b; Murphy, 1971). Their method involved recording land use on the basis of building blocks and floors, this data being presented in the form of maps relating to three storeys, land use for the upper storeys having first been generalized. Delimitation of the CBD was achieved on the basis of two indices derived from the maps, a Central Business Height Index (space given over to central business uses ÷ ground floor area), and a Central Business Intensity Index (space given over to central business uses ÷ total floor space, expressed as a percentage). Applying the method to nine medium-sized United States cities they were able to produce a generalized model of the shape of the CBD in the form of a quadrate cross (Fig. 18). Such a generalization assumes a chequerboard pattern of streets, and even in North American cities the precise form of the CBD will be affected by barriers such as parks and railway lines. Nevertheless, the diagram is useful in illustrating the tendency for central business land uses and related land values to extend out furthest along the main roads which

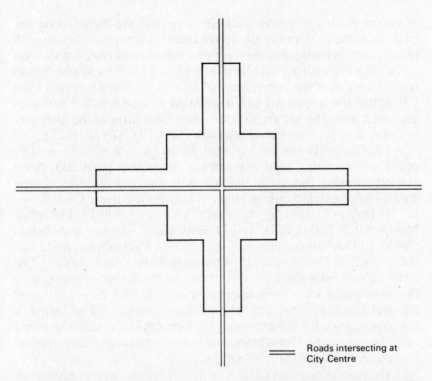

Roads intersecting at
City Centre

18 Quadrate cross, representing the idealized outline of the CBD
    according to Murphy and Vance, 1954. (Courtesy the Editor of
    Economic Geography)

converge on the centre — the Peak Land Value Intersection
(PLVI) in North American studies — and to occupy the minor
streets, which constitute the interstices, to a lesser depth from the
PLVI. Alternative shapes of CBD which might arise under different conditions have been suggested by Hartman (1950).

Interest attaches to the criteria which Murphy and Vance used
to distinguish central business land uses from other categories of
land occupance. The presence, or absence, of what they described
as 'the normal profit motive' was the principle applied in selecting
land uses, thus retailing and various financial and office functions
are included, whilst the following are excluded: permanent residences; government and public property including parks, schools
and administrative headquarters; churches and colleges; industrial
establishments with the exception of newspaper publishing which
involves advertising and the sale locally of its product; wholesaling
with stocks, and commercial storage, railway tracks and yards; and
vacant sites. The problem of distinguishing between different types

of office use is recognized and all categories are included on the basis that 'they undoubtedly derive benefits from association with places such as banks, lawyers' offices, hotels, and restaurants, that do belong in the district' (Murphy, 1971). There is a suggestion in this statement of the importance of linkages in the structure of the CBD, but the argument is not pursued in any depth. Land uses excluded from the list are said to 'contribute little to the interplay of retail activities that characterizes the CBD' (1971, p.27).

Publication of the work of Murphy and Vance was followed by other studies using land use indices to delimit the CBD. Scott (1959) applied the technique to Australian cities and similar studies were carried out on cities in Southern Africa: Cape Town D. H. Davies, 1959), Port Elizabeth (Young, 1961), Lourenço Marques (de Blij, 1962), and Durban (R. J. Davies, and Rajah, 1965). In Durban the effect of segregation has been to create two quite distinct CBDs, one European and the other Indian. The latter differs from the former, notably in the higher proportion of the area given over to residential land use and to schools and cultural organizations. This the authors account for in terms of cultural factors, the immaturity of Indian CBD services compared with those provided for whites, and the effect of legislative controls on residential land for non-whites.

Delimitation of the CBD has, as one would expect, proved an easier task in the more geometrically laid-out cities of the New World than in those of the Old with their historic cores and legacy of former land uses. Carter and Rowley's (1966) attempt to identify the CBD of Cardiff illustrates the problems that arise in the European city. They employed four criteria: land use, a measure of intensity of development, gross rateable values and land values, on the basis that no one of these alone was able to yield a satisfactory definition. They concluded that 'under British conditions, it is most difficult to derive objective CBD boundaries without accepting a gross simplification or generalization which defeats its own end' (pp.125-6) and warned that 'in areas such as Europe, where every central area is the product of a long evolutionary process, there is always danger in lifting out of context arbitrarily defined parts of cities' (p.134). This observation is borne out by work on Amsterdam by van Hulten (1967) who came to the conclusion that 'the urban core of Amsterdam is not an area, but rather a "web" of streets' and within the meshes of the web are 'streets and building blocks which lag behind'. In a study of the CBD of Glasgow, Diamond (1962) found similarities with the central areas of cities in the United States, Australia and South Africa, but also noted a number of differences. One of these arises from the concentration of wholesaling within the central area of Glasgow. This activity includes 'credit warehousing' which involves personal customer visits as well as mail order business. Diamond accounts for the contrast with the United States situation in terms of the different history of transport development. Other points noted were the presence of tall buildings, especially those serving a local government function, the location of which owed more to history than to competition for space, and a tendency for land and property values to reflect past rather than present economic conditions.

Spatial organization of the CBD

The intensity of central business land use is not uniform throughout the CBD and many writers have distinguished a 'hard core' with the highest land values, tallest buildings etc., from a fringe possessing a lower concentration of central land uses. D.H. Davies (1960), for example, used the central business index method to distinguish such a hard core in Cape Town. Adopting a wider concept of the central area, Horwood and Boyce (1959) have put forward a core-frame model of the CBD (Fig. 19). The *core* is characterized by retailing, offices, banks, hotels and theatres; it is an area of tall buildings and concentrated daytime population. Government offices are included as well as those of business, these and other functions sometimes emerging as distinct nuclei within the core. Smaller nuclei also appear towards the edge of the core, and court houses, libraries and telephone exchange buildings are quoted as examples. Functional nodes are even more characteristic of the *frame* and these include wholesaling, warehouses, transport terminals, car sales and servicing, light industry, multi-family dwellings and certain institutional land uses, for example hospitals and consulting rooms. Core and frame together make up the CBD although it is clear that the frame extends well beyond the CBD as defined by Murphy and Vance and indeed has much in common with the 'zone in transition'. Horwood and Boyce did not establish any method of delimiting their core and frame but the concept has some value in suggesting that it may be possible to distinguish, at least in large cities, a *central area* that is more extensive than the CBD as defined according to the rather strict *business* criteria employed by Murphy and Vance.

Notwithstanding their more limited idea of the CBD, Murphy and Vance noted that land use within it was far from homogeneous

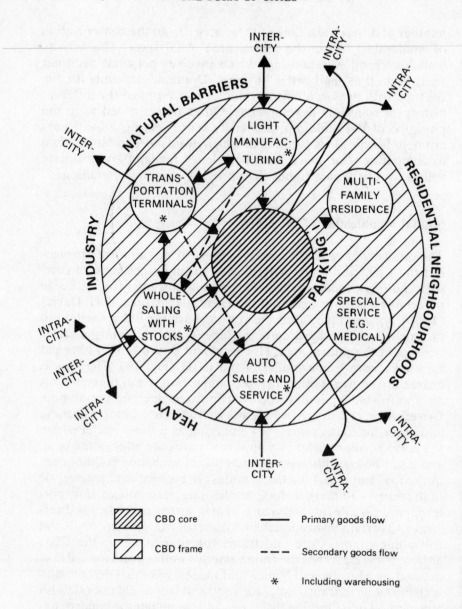

19 The central area core-frame model of Horwood and Boyce, 1959.
    (Courtesy University of Washington Press)

(Murphy, Vance and Epstein, 1955). Changes take place with
increasing distance from the centre. Around the peak land value
intersection are clustered department and clothing stores, restaurants, drugstores and specialized services which cater for the large

daytime population. The tallest buildings are to be found a short distance from this central point with shops and financial institutions on the ground floor and offices above. Banks are most common, together with hotels, some 200-300 yards from the centre. Furniture and automobile accessory stores appear towards the edge of the CBD, with petrol filling stations and supermarkets in an 'automobile-orientated' area beyond. Finally, zones of 'assimilation' and 'discard' are recognized on the fringe of the CBD. Car showrooms, speciality shops, headquarter offices and drive-in banks are typical of the growing edge of the CBD whilst credit stores and pawn shops, cheap cinemas and bars are likely to be found where other central business land uses are withdrawing. Within this broadly concentric pattern of land use the authors note the tendency for establishments that are mutually dependent to cluster together: smaller shops close to the department stores, lawyers' and estate agents' offices adjacent to law courts, men's clothing shops near the main offices and banks. Vertical clustering is also observed, 'office buildings contain a number of individual units, and frequently these units do a considerable amount of business with one another' (Murphy, 1971, p.61), but the nature of the dependence is not explored further. It has been the task of subsequent studies of urban centrality to demonstrate the form and extent of such linkages.

Case studies of other cities enable the conclusions of Murphy, Vance and Epstein to be viewed in a rather wider context. In his attempt to isolate the 'hard core' of Cape Town's CBD, D. H. Davies (1960), for example, found that certain activities, requiring less than average centrality, were more commonly found near the edge than the centre. These included newspaper publishing and printing, hotels, cinemas and headquarter offices. In the case of department stores, a contrast is noticeable between those near the PLVI which offer high quality goods to a wide range of customers, and those towards the edge of the CBD which resemble suburban stores serving a low-income population. Scott (1959) also distinguished between inner and outer retail zones in his study of Australia's state capitals. The inner zone is compact and made up principally of department, variety, and women's clothing stores, together with other shops and service outlets catering for women. Shops in the outer zone are more concerned with household goods. Scott also recognized a third, office zone, distinct from the two retail districts. Historical influences are stressed in the British studies of Glasgow and Cardiff. Glasgow has two shopping nuclei, the location of which is related to that of the city's bus stations.

Fashion and exclusive shops, together with entertainment facilities are, however, found between the two primary nodes. Offices occupy a compact area in the centre and between the two main railway stations. Wholesaling and certain types of light industry are also central, but peripheral to the shopping and office quarters. In Cardiff there is a sharp contrast between the medieval core which has retained small family shops and most of the banks, and a newer extension of the CBD with the much larger chain stores, furniture stores and cinemas. The emergence of separate office quarters was initiated by the conversion of large houses in the higher-status residential area near the centre.

In seeking to explain the internal structure of the CBD, account must be taken of urban redevelopment schemes as well as of historical factors. Giggs (1972) observed that planned redevelopment in Nottingham gave rise to a marked zonation of new buildings. Additions to the retailing sector took place mainly within the core of the CBD whilst new building for other uses was in the 'frame' beyond this inner zone. This conclusion is confirmed by R. L. Davies (1972b) who found the core-frame concept to be consistent with the planned redevelopment of Coventry. Here the pedestrianised shopping precinct constitutes a core, with department and variety stores at the centre and supermarkets, small shops and a retail market towards the edge and close to the car parks. In the 'frame', beyond this precinct, sites have been given over to other uses: the new cathedral, local government offices, higher education, swimming pools.

Retail area models

Attempts have been made by Garner (1966) and R. L. Davies (1972a) to devise models of retail distribution on the basis of the observed clustering of particular types of retail activity within the CBD. Getis (1968), however, in a comparative study of thirteen United States cities, was unable to discover sufficient association between shops of similar type to permit any such general conclusions to be drawn.

The central area models of both Garner and Davies are, in fact, microcosms of the retail structure of the city as a whole. Garner stresses the relationship between land values and the distribution of different kinds of retail outlet (Fig. 20). Shops with the steepest bid rent curves are thus located at the heart of the CBD; these also have high threshold values and typically serve a popu-

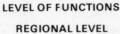

LEVEL OF FUNCTIONS

REGIONAL LEVEL

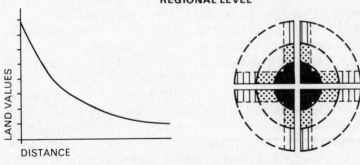

COMMUNITY LEVEL

NEIGHBOURHOOD LEVEL

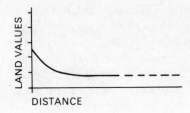

Regional

Community

Neighbourhood

20   The internal structure of different orders of city centre according to
     Garner, 1966. The diagram illustrates the relationship between land
     values and the distribution of different kinds of retailing. (Courtesy
     Northwestern University)

lation that looks to the city as its regional centre. Shops selling convenience goods, similar to those in small suburban centres, are to be found on the fringe of the CBD, whilst retail outlets of intermediate threshold values, comparable with those in neighbourhood centres, occupy the middle ground.

Davies takes as his starting point the retail area model of Berry (1963) and distinguishes three categories of retail cluster within the CBD displaying, respectively, nucleated characteristics, ribbon characteristics and special area characteristics (Fig. 21). The first of these types exhibits zonal variation, corresponding closely with that noted by Garner, and is considered similarily to be a response to land values and to threshold values. Thus clothing stores are found at the centre whilst food shops are more typical of the fringe of the CBD. Car-orientated ribbon developments appear towards the outer edge of the CBD where they extend into the 'frame' and Davies describes them as representing in embryonic form the outlying commercial ribbons. Banks, cafes and garages are regarded as typical of these inner city ribbons which, however, are a less pronounced feature of British than of North American cities. Other types of retail outlet cluster in particular locations, usually related to factors of accessibility. Streets of 'quality' shops are most often found near the centre because they cater for high income customers drawn from a wide area. But stores selling furniture or domestic appliances are located further out where they can satisfy their requirements for space and access to good road facilities. Specialized functional areas overlap the edge of the CBD into the 'frame' within a zone which Davies represents on his 'complex model' by the pecked boundary line.

Davies found evidence to support both his own and Garner's model in Coventry (1972b). Within the central area (defined by the inner ringroad), clothing shops, especially those dealing in women's wear and shoes, occupied key positions within the precinct; shops selling household goods occupied less centralized positions and exhibited a lower degree of clustering; food shops were largely absent from the precinct, occupying dispersed sites towards the periphery. Clustering of outlets with 'special area characteristics' was confirmed, particularily with regard to furniture stores and high quality shops, and ribbon development was noted, the most common elements in the ribbons being cafes and public houses, banks, building societies and allied services. Davies drew attention to the 'obviously strong locational linkages' exhibited by both banking and building societies, a pointer to the importance of office linkages in the CBD.

NUCLEATED CHARACTERISTICS

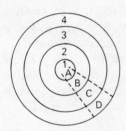

SHOP TYPES	EXAMPLE CLUSTERS
1 Central area	A Apparel shops
2 Regional centres	B Variety shops
3 Community centres	C Gift shops
4 Neighbourhood centres	D Food shops

RIBBON CHARACTERISTICS

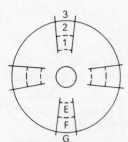

SHOP TYPES	EXAMPLE CLUSTERS
1 Traditional street	E Banking
2 Arterial ribbon	F Cafes
3 Suburban ribbon	G Garages

SPECIAL AREA CHARACTERISTICS

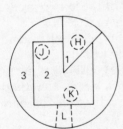

SHOP TYPES	EXAMPLE CLUSTERS
1 High quality	H Entertainments
2 Medium quality	J Market
3 Low quality	K Furniture
	L Appliances

THE COMPLEX MODEL

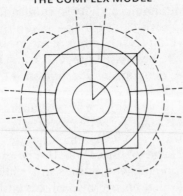

21 R. L. Davies's (1972) model of the internal retail structure of the city centre. (Reproduced by permission from the *Transactions of the Institute of British Geographers*, no. 57, 1972)

The degree to which other cities 'fit' the retail area models must depend upon several factors of which size is probably the most significant. In a study of cities of widely varying population total, R. W. Thomas (1972) observed a much lower degree of segregation of retail functions in the smaller than the larger cities and put forward the tentative conclusion that this was related to the distance which customers were prepared to walk on any given shopping trip.

Office location

London has been the subject of a number of studies that have sought to establish the nature of office linkages and to map functional sub-regions on the basis of observed patterns of linkage. In an early paper, Morgan (1961a) drew attention to the presence of two main office districts in Central London and suggested ways by which one kind of office establishment becomes functionally involved with another (1961b). Selecting one of those two areas, the City, Goddard (1968) carried out a multivariate analysis of local authority data relating to eighty different types of office and was able to identify thirteen office regions within which there was a high degree of internal linkage. Dunning (1969), also working in the City, drew up a map of ten regions using a simpler method involving the calculation of coefficients of localization for particular activities (Fig. 22).

Goddard suggests that the linkages which exist between office firms constitute a definable activity system and that within the system corresponding with the City as a whole (the CBD, let us say), it is possible to identify a number of interrelated sub-systems. Linkages, in fact, are to be found both within and between the main branches of the City economy: 'The pattern of inter-correlation might be summarized as sets of inter-locking activities — within group bonds — with certain elements common to several sets' or between-group bonds.' All activities exhibit strong internal linkages with the exception of wholesaling and manufacturing which are located on the edge of the City. Inter-branch linkages are marked between shipping, commodities and insurance — the trading group; close connections are also observed between banking and insurance — the financial 'core', and between banking and 'other finance' — the financial 'ring' (Figs. 23 and 24). Dunning noted that wholesaling and newspaper publishing had the weakest links with other groups and concluded that these were the activities

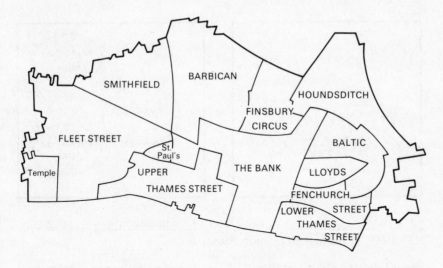

22   Districts of the City of London according to Dunning, 1969.
(Courtesy the Editor of *Town Planning Review*)

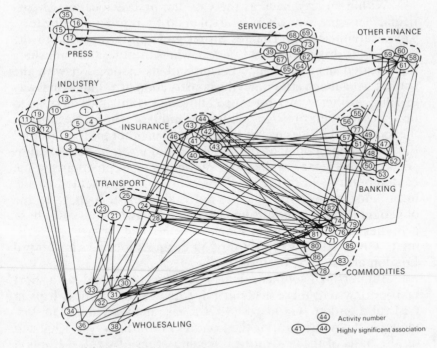

23   Spatial linkages between different types of office activity in the City
of London according to Goddard, 1968. (Courtesy Pergamon Press)

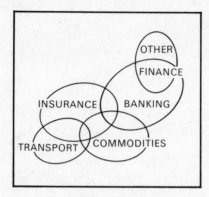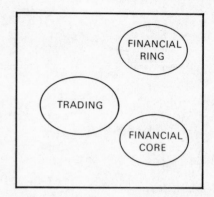

24   'Office activity sets' in the City of London according to Goddard, 1968. (Courtesy Pergamon Press)

most likely to abandon their City location in the future. The nature of internal linkages is further explored by Daniels (1975) who utilizes 'indices of contact' in order to measure their importance.

Within an area such as the City the precise location of particular activities can often be explained by reference to history. Thus warehousing in Thames Street grew up in response to the needs of the original port of London, whilst printing and publishing was located near St. Paul's because of its association with the church. At a much later date, the construction of a road, Kingsway in 1902, attracted life insurance and other companies anxious to find sites for their prestige buildings (Goddard, 1967). Negatively, the location of offices has been restrained in other parts of Central London by the policy of the big leasehold estates. Yet superimposed on this legacy of the past are the distance constraints of the contemporary world, the need for contact as represented by the intra- and inter-activity linkages noted above. The highest degree of geographical concentration is likely to be associated with those activities involving a high proportion of personal contacts. According to Goddard (1975) a third of all business journeys in Central London are, in fact, on foot.

But personal contact can also be achieved by making a short taxi journey and these account for a quarter of business trips in Central London. Goddard (1970) has analysed data on taxi movement obtained during the London Traffic Survey of 1962 and on the basis of these identifies five sub-areas of Central London which exhibit a high degree of internal circulation. The compactness of these areas, he suggests, may be due to the relatively high cost of taxi journeys. One of the regions corresponds to the eastern (financial) part of the City, described above. The others are in the West End with its high-class shopping facilities and related activities, such as garment making; Westminster, the government quarter which also has a concentration of civil engineering businesses; Soho, Covent Garden and Fleet Street where entertainment and publishing activities are concentrated; and Bloomsbury which is the University district but also has trade union offices which favour a site close to main line rail terminals.

The five sub-systems, or districts, revealed by taxi flow data are set within a matrix of more varied and less intensive land use, confirming one of the observations made by Horwood and Boyce in their core-frame model. Any attempt to interpret the overall land use in as diverse an area as Central London must also take account of functional linkages which do not encourage a high degree of spatial association. For some business activities the telephone is a perfectly adequate means of maintaining contact and those office sectors which rely on the telephone rather than on personal visits are less likely to exhibit as intensely clustered a pattern as, say, banking or government. Goddard (1973) conducted a sample survey of the telephone calls made by a wide range of businesses in Central London. A complex pattern was revealed. Close intra-group linkages were noted in the case of some activites, for example civil engineering, where it was necessary to maintain contacts between architects, engineers and the manufacturers of construction materials. Complicated inter-group linkages also emerge and the example is quoted of a firm wishing to place an advertisement which approaches the newspaper publisher via an advertising agency. Such findings as these have considerable relevance so far as office decentralization is concerned. Use of the telephone may not necessitate close spatial association in an area the size of Central London but the firm with a large number of contacts there is unlikely to welcome the much greater cost involved in maintaining these from beyond London.

Evolution of the CBD

The CBD is a dynamic region of the city, not only in the sense that its activities constitute definable systems, but also because the relative importance and spatial extent of these activities change with time. Technological progress and developments in transportation are amongst the factors which lead to the appearance of new functions and to the decline, or decentralization from the

CBD, of others. What is now the CBD was once the city itself, and change studied over a sufficiently long period of time thus involves displacement of the residential population as well as the emergence of specialized functional areas in the place of a typically mixed form of land use with sites serving many purposes. In some form the sequence can be observed in any European city. Buissink and de Widt (1967) have described how, in Utrecht for example, there was a more or less fixed ratio between 'central' land use, other non-residential land use, and residential land use until about 1850 when the balance was upset by the onset of the Industrial Revolution in the Netherlands. Then followed a 'process of centre formation' as the number and range of central land uses grew rapidly. In a much larger city, London, there was already movement of business functions from the City to the 'West End' by the end of the sixteenth century . By the early nineteenth century the principal shopping district was clearly detached from the rest of the central district (Kellett, 1969).

In the course of an early attempt to explain the nature of inner city linkages, Rannells (1956) showed how, in Philadelphia, the pattern of these activities was constantly changing and with it the pressure on space. The character of these changes as they affected the historic American city was subsequently described by Ward (1966) for Boston. His study, which is concerned primarily with the period from 1840 to 1920, traces the emergence of 'modern' functional areas from three small specialized nuclei. The financial quarter emerged from a high status residential district in which the buildings served both as places of residence and as counting houses for wealthy merchants. Warehouses, which had originally housed workshop manufacturing, gradually shed this latter function, which subsequently moved out of the CBD altogether, and a wholesaling district developed, with retailing becoming concentrated along the streets first served by electrified streetcars. Appearance of this specialised shopping area was further encouraged by the division of food marketing into wholesale and retail sectors. Expansion of government activities led to the establishment of a separate administrative area by expansion, again into a former residential area, from a nucleus around the seat of state government. The changes are summarized in 'model' form in Fig. 25.

During the period with which Ward was concerned the CBD was not only evolving internally but also expanding physically. Yet even then the pattern of growth was irregular and fluctuating, and by the late nineteenth century there were residential districts adj-

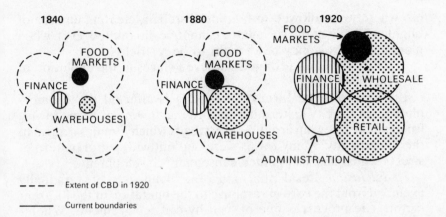

Extent of CBD in 1920

Current boundaries

25   Stages in the evolution of the American CBD according to Ward, 1968. (Reproduced by permission from the *Annals of the Association of American Geographers,* vol. 58, 1968)

acent to the CBD which were not experiencing pressure from commercial interests and which were, therefore, left free to house immigrants (Ward 1968). Expansion of the CBD was also affected by barriers, both natural and man-made, and the effect of such barriers on the growth of the CBD has been investigated in the case of Harrisburg by Mattingly (1964). Three ways by which additions were made to the CBD were recognized by Bowden (1971) in a study of the evolution of San Francisco's CBD: by small-scale accretion, as certain functions expand during a period of general quiescence; by 'bursting' in all directions but especially in linear fashion, during brief phases of economic prosperity; and by separation into at least two discrete parts, a characteristic of rapid growth in the largest cities when a process which Bowden describes as 'leapfrogging' took place. The movement of retailing from the City of London to Oxford Street exemplifies this process.

Behavioural, as well as economic, factors have also influenced the growth of the CBD. They are well illustrated in the 'skyscraper infatuation' which swept through American cities after 1920 (L. R. Ford, 1973). Tall buildings were erected, not only to economize on site costs and to permit easier personal contact, but as monuments to the entrepreneur and as landmarks for the city. Ford cites as examples the two Mid-Western cities of Cleveland and Columbus where prestigious tower buildings were erected in the 1920s, the effect of which was to shift the direction of growth of the CBD. Formerly run-down areas were suddenly made attractive to commercial development by the new buildings, whilst older properties elsewhere were allowed to fall into disrepair, creating an area of blight. The role of the speculator cannot be discounted, even when planning controls may be thought to be restrictive.

Vance (1971a) distinguishes seven stages in the evolution of the American CBD:

1   *Inception* The form of the CBD is affected by the morphology of the city's site and by its original functions. Some towns, for example, grew up around a crossroads which remains central to the modern city. Many towns were laid out with a grid pattern of streets which has also guided subsequent development.

2   *Exclusion* Residential and other land uses are gradually excluded from the core in response to the operation of the bid-rent factor. The process is one of 'cell-by-cell replacement'. Wholesaling and manufacturing industry are pushed to the edge of the zone.

3   *Segregation* Spatial sorting into sub-areas takes place in response to the need to maintain close linkages between activities of a similar nature. 'The salvation of the downtown is the ability it has to segregate functions into coherent subdistricts which are manageable in size and shape.' Self-contained units move out of the CBD to save rent. High-class shopping may be able to survive outside the CBD.

4   *Extension* Ribbon-like expansion takes place after 1918 along arterial roads, especially in the direction of those parts of the city where 'style (is) higher than rent'. Car sales and establishments dealing in business equipment and services are typical of such linear extensions.

5   *Replication and Readjustment* Certain functions move out of the CBD and relocate in outlying shopping centres. The process is not confined to shopping and may involve the movement of headquarters offices, theatres etc. Within the CBD adjustment takes the form of growth in other, principally office, activities but where several towns are close together in a metropolitan situation, the CBD may never fully adapt itself to these changes. In others there is increasing specialization on a narrow range of central functions, i.e. segregation of activities between cities takes place.

6   *Redevelopment* Planned redevelopment schemes are carried out in an attempt both to reinvigorate the commercial life of the centre and to replace the slums. Vance does not make the point, but renewal is more likely in some parts than others because of the pattern of property ownership.

7   *A City of Realms* 'There is "central business" all over the city' and the suburban centres undergo the processes outlined

above. Downtown, however, retains its symbolic status and remains a focus of highly specialized activities. These include financial, government and cultural activities, and both specialized and mass shopping 'but only for that population for whom the downtown is the most convenient place to shop'.

Future of the CBD

There is abundant evidence that activities move out of the CBD but no universal agreement that the CBD is in decline, even in the United States. Some have pointed to the loss of certain forms of retailing and office work to the suburbs and interpreted this in terms of decay and absolute loss at the centre. A CBD function has been defined as 'a function that has not yet left The Central Business District' (Allpass et al., 1967, p.103). But others have taken a more optimistic view, seeing change in the CBD as continuation of the process of evolution noted above.

Most controversy has arisen in connection with retailing. Investigations carried out between 1920 and 1948 by a firm of consultants in the United States revealed that the proportion of retail sales that took place in the CBD fell sharply with city size, from over 80 per cent in cities with a population of under 25 000, to between 15 and 35 per cent in cities over 750 000 (L. Smith, 1971). Such figures, however, fail to reveal whether the expansion of retailing in the suburbs is at the expense of the CBD or only in proportion to population growth. A study of Madison, Wisconsin (Ratcliff, 1953) suggests stability in the CBD, outlets for convenience and speciality goods being taken over by those for comparison goods. Common sense suggests that experience will vary from city to city depending on such variables as rate of population growth, the nature of property ownership, parking provision and accessibility, the quality of public transport, private enterprise and municipal planning.

The same factors influence the dispersal of offices, though not necessarily in the same way. In some cases offices may move from the centre, despite a desire for close contacts, because there is a lack of space for expansion or because old buildings are no longer suitable for the firm's purposes. More usually, moves take place when there is no longer any need for close spatial association (Daniels, 1975). Such moves may involve whole sections of business as with the well-documented removal of book publishing from Central London to the Home Counties. But movement also affects branches of a single activity; those forms of routine office work not requiring close contacts with other firms moving to the suburbs, e.g. accountancy or research, whilst the decision-makers remain in their central location. For offices not caught up in the web of inner-city linkages, a suburban situation offers the advantages of cheaper sites and better access to those sections of the workforce, for example married women who, because of the demands of their children, are unwilling to travel long distances to work. In Britain the Government has been successful in dispersing a number of relatively self-contained branches of its own administration from London to the Development Areas, e.g. pensions to Newcastle and car licensing to Swansea. The Location of Offices Bureau, set up in 1964, has assisted decentralization by providing advice to firms and amongst the moves from London which it has helped to promote are those of several insurance organizations. Moves of this kind may also be thought of as part of an evolutionary process. Goddard (1967) has referred to the Soho-Covent Garden district of London, one of very mixed land use, as 'a birth zone for newly formed office-based firms; those firms that flourish and grow soon move out to more desirable locations', and there is reason to think that the same sequence is followed in other parts of the central area.

Modern telecommunications have facilitated the removal of routine office functions from the CBD but even video equipment is not a perfect substitute for face-to-face contact or for the informal group meeting. It is also expensive to install. Paradoxically, progress in telecommunications may in fact encourage centralization as well as permitting decentralization. Directors and other top officials, freed from the necessity of maintaining close physical contact with their factory, data-handling unit, or typing pool, are able to take advantage of a location which permits easy and frequent personal contact with other executives (Thorngren, 1967). Office employment thus continues to increase in the CBD by growth in what have been defined as 'quaternary' activities (Gottmann, 1970). The building of rapid transit facilities to serve an increasing number of world cities must be seen as another factor that will maintain the CBD as a focus of high level office activities.

Vance (1962) has put forward the suggestion that the urban core may be 'falling apart'. The needs of the shopper are less well served by rapid transit and similar peak hour transport facilities than are those of the office commuter and the preferred location for retailing is likely to be one where there is car-parking nearby. He concludes that 'if this trend continues, the single focus which has in the past characterized the core will be lost and we may find ourselves a generation from now restricting the term central business district to the office area and coining a new name, perhaps metropolitan speciality district, for what we still by tradition consider the downtown business district.'

Ranking service centres

Burgess (1929) drew attention in Chicago to what he called 'satellite loops', suburban centres catering for the needs of the wealthier, residential population: 'This typical constellation of business and recreation areas includes a bank, one or more United Cigar stores, a drug store, a high class restaurant, an automobile display row, and a so-called 'wonder' motion picture theatre.' Carrying out a government-sponsored survey of retail trade in Baltimore, Rolph (1929) went much further and identified for the first time a hierarchy of such centres. Five types of business area were recognized, each with its typical range of activities:CBD, retail sub-centre, string street, neighbourhood facility group, and non-concentrated business.

Rolph's five-rank hierarchy was confirmed by Proudfoot (1937) in a comparative study of nine United States cities. His terminology has been widely adopted in subsequent classifications:

1   CBD
2   Outlying business centre
    a CBD in miniature, developing at focal points within the city; shops sell comparison goods, e.g. clothing and furniture.
3   Principal business thoroughfare
    derives its customers principally from through traffic; stores are often widely spaced.
4   Neighbourhood business street
    depends primarily on the neighbourhood, i.e. is within walking distance for shoppers; convenience goods, e.g. grocery, are most typically sold; storeys above the shops are often used as residences.
5   Isolated store cluster
    most commonly found in the sparsely settled fringes of the urban area; includes stores of the corner shop type.

In another American Government publication, Canoyer (1946) introduced a distinction between what he described as cluster types of commercial area and strings (or ribbon develop-

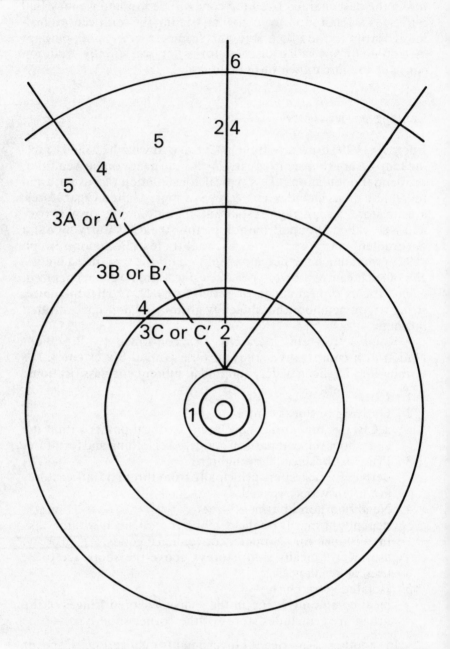

26 Schematic representation of the retail structure of a large American city according to Kelley, 1955. (Courtesy Methuen Publications)

ments). The former comprised CBD, community shopping district, and neighbourhood centre. Kelley (1955) added further dimensions to the classification in the form of the 'controlled' (i.e. planned) sub-centre, and the regional shopping centre built near the edge of the city to serve the car-borne population of the whole, or part, of the city region. Unlike the 'unplanned sub-districts', usually located on main roads radiating from the town centre, the 'controlled sub-centres' incorporated off-street parking facilities and were planned as an integrated unit by a single agency. Three levels of such centres were distinguished on the basis of location, number of people served and types of shop represented (Fig. 26).

1 CBD
2 Main business thoroughfares (string streets) — car dealers and furniture stores are typical.
3 Secondary commercial sub-districts (unplanned)
  A Suburban or outer—serve 30 000-100 000 people
  B Community or district—serve 15 000-30 000 people
  C Neighbourhood—serve 3000-15 000 people
3a Controlled secondary commercial sub-centres (planned equivalent of 3)
  A^1 Suburban or outer
  B^1 Community or district
  C^1 Neighbourhood
4 Neighbourhood business streets — convenience level shops along busy streets
5 Small store clusters and scattered individual stores — shops complementary rather than competitive.
6 Controlled regional shopping centres — decentralized substitutes for downtown-parking space may occupy 3 to 9 times the floor space devoted to the sale of goods.

The search for a hierarchy

Empirical studies of intra-urban service centres have frequently sought to verify the occurrence of a hierarchy of such centres. Methods of classification have ranged from simple, single-parameter approaches based on the number of businesses present of a particular type, to rankings based on multivariate procedures or indices of centrality (Beavon, 1974). Collins (1965) set out a four-fold classification of service centres in south London based on number of shops alone, without reference to their use. It has been more common, however, to take account of the nature and variety of such outlets, although this has sometimes been reduced to the search for a 'trait-complex'. Typical of this latter method is the classification of 292 centres in Greater London carried out by Hartley and Smailes (1961). Three categories of centre are noted, the trait-complex of the middle-ranked 'suburban centre' being a combination of a Marks and Spencer store, Dunn the hatter, a representative of a jewellery chain, and at least four chain shoe stores. Weekley's (1956) detailed breakdown of suburban centres in Greater Nottingham exemplifies the same approach. In this the selection of particular indices such as a Woolworths store or a cinema is justified by reference to the threshold population required to support outlets of a particular kind. But problems of comparison arise, certain firms having more stores in one part of the country than another (the Nottingham study significantly chose to make use of Boots the Chemist), whilst the threshold value changes with time. The minimum population needed to support a cinema is much larger now than it was in the mid-fifties. McEvoy (1967) ranked shopping centres in the Manchester conurbation by four alternative methods and found that key indices were useful only at the higher level of the hierarchy. Problems arose when using the method in a study of centres of greatly differing size.

For such reasons later classifications have usually been based on a wider range of variables, Berry (1963), for example, employed the following kinds of information in his study of commercial centres in Chicago: number of business types and of establishments; total front footage and floor area; retail sales, payroll and employment*; size and population of largest trade area; trade area's total income.

Factor analysis of the data revealed four levels of centre below that of the CBD (page 112).

Use has also been made of land and property values on the basis that these reflect competition amongst commercial interests for access to nodes of secondary accessibility within the city. Bus services, e.g. the average number of buses per hour on weekdays reaching a centre between 9.30 a.m. and 4.00 p.m. (outside commuter hours), have likewise been employed as a measure of attraction. In another study of Greater London, Carruthers (1962) employed a combination of rateable values, bus services and type of service provision to achieve a four-fold classification below the level of CBD. Carol (1960) used pedestrian counts as well as detailed information relating to shopping facilities in his search for a hierarchy of centres in Zurich. His four levels included the CBD.

---

*For Britain, Jay and Hirsch (1960) found a close correlation between numbers employed and sales by establishment, a useful observation in view of the difficulty that may be encountered in obtaining the latter data.

Relevance of Central Place Theory

Carol claimed that when his survey of Zurich was begun in 1952 it was 'the first attempt to use the central place concept for analyzing the pattern of central functions within the city'. It is inviting to interpret an empirically-derived hierarchy in central place terms and indeed Berry and Garrison (1958) have claimed that, since central place theory also serves as a theory of tertiary activity, it does serve to explain the observed hierarchy. They argue that if central place theory is formulated in terms of the simple concepts of threshold and range it is thereby freed from 'complicating assumptions about the shape and homogenous character of city trade areas' and becomes applicable at the intra-urban as well as the inter-urban level. Furthermore, 'whatever the distribution of purchasing power a hierarchial spatial structure of central places supplying central goods will emerge'. Their ideas were tested in a detailed analysis, involving the calculation of a correlation matrix, of 285 business centres in the city of Spokane (Garrison et al., 1959). Comparison with other American studies (Berry, 1962; 1963) supported the conclusion that the intra-urban commercial structure exhibits four levels of centre:

1 Major regional centre
1a Other shopping goods centre*
2 Community business centre
3 Neighbourhood business centre
4 Isolated convenience stores and street corner developments

Additional confirmation came from the work of Simmons .(1964; 1966) and Garner (1966). The latter's contribution goes further in attempting to explain the structure of individual service centres in terms of bid-rent curves (Fig. 20, page 93), and in its exploration of the spacing of such centres. He discovered a broad resemblance to the $k=4$ (transport-orientated) pattern of Christaller and concluded tentatively that 'some underlying and fundamental spatial relationship exists in the spacing of different order centres in a hierarchy'. Few others have attempted to investigate the spatial arrangement of centres, following Garrison and Berry in relaxing assumptions concerning the shape of trade areas. Yet central place theory cannot be divorced from the principle that an individual will travel only so far to buy a low order good, a little further to buy goods of higher order, still further for goods of even higher order and so on. Collins (1965) is one of the few who have tried to relate hierarchy to accessibility, his 20 minute isochrone

*The sub-category allows for the fact that centres at the upper end of the hierarchy, whilst displaying similar features, nevertheless differ in importance. Berry (following Kelley) also distinguishes between planned and unplanned centres.

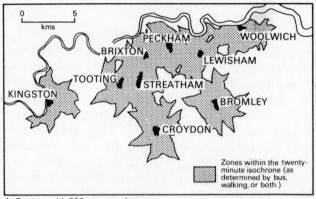

A. Centres with 300 or more shops

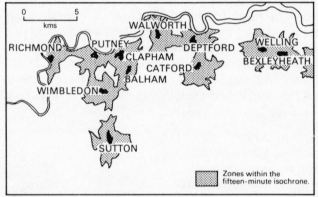

B. Centres with 200 to 300 shops

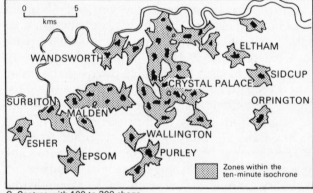

C. Centres with 100 to 200 shops

27   Service centres in south London and associated travel times according to Collins, 1965. (Courtesy Methuen, *Frontiers in Geographical
Teaching*)

corresponding with centres offering at least 300 outlets, 15 minutes with 200-300 outlets, and 10 minutes with 100-200, whilst centres with under 100 shops serve only the most local needs (Fig. 27). Burns (1959) has also produced a diagram to illustrate nesting of centres within a theoretical British town, but the underlying concepts are not worked out in depth (Fig. 28).

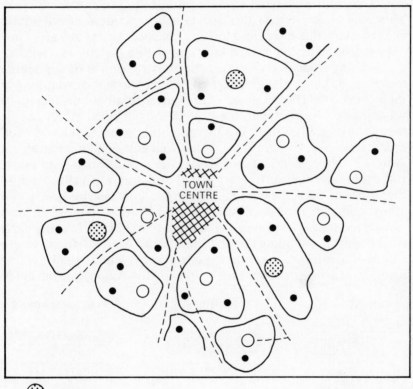

District centre
Neighbourhood centre
Sub-centre

28 Distribution of a four-tier system of intra-urban service centres according to Burns, 1959. (Courtesy Edward Arnold)

According to Berry (1963) the hierarchy of service centres is just one of three components which make up the commercial system of the city as a whole. Following the lead of Canoyer and others, he recognized both ribbon developments and 'specialized areas' as distinctive elements (Fig. 29). The former include what he

calls 'highway orientated commercial ribbons' which are characterised by petrol stations, restaurants, ice-cream parlours, fruit and
vegetables stands, and motels and, secondly, 'urban arterial commercial developments' with car repair facilities, furniture stores,
suppliers of building materials, and office equipment stores. There
is no functional association between these types of commercial
outlet, customers making a single-purpose trip to patronize them.
This is in contrast with the 'specialized functional areas' within
each of which there are close linkages and economies of scale. They
appear to occupy haphazard locations within the city as a whole.

Arising from Berry's classification is a problem of the degree
to which the three elements are complementary or overlapping in
their functions. The presence of low-order retail outlets in a highway ribbon ('beads') will, for example, have some effect on the
hierarchy of such centres. For this and other reasons, it has proved
much less easy to adopt the three-fold division outside North
America, whilst Berry's typology has been questioned even there.
From observations in Calgary, Boal and Johnson (1965) found
that ribbons served both passing traffic and nearby residential
areas, and that the specialized functional areas likewise drew a
certain amount of patronage from these two sources. In some parts
of the world, including New Zealand and South Africa, where
suburban centres frequently exhibit a linear rather than nuclear
form, it has been shown that no valid distinction can be made

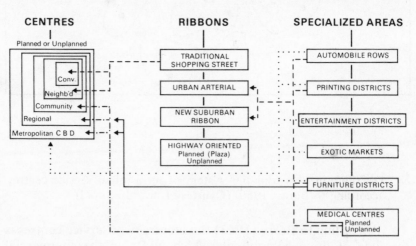

29   B. J. L. Berry's (1963) classification of intra-urban service centres.
     (Courtesy University of Chicago)

between the clustered (i.e. hierarchical) and ribbon types. W.K.D. Davies (1966) questions the definition of 'centre' in many British studies, especially those which select key criteria to identify the centres. 'If, as so often happens, the key criteria cluster in certain places within a linear continuum of functions, then the fact that only a few functions are investigated means that distinctive nodes will appear when these are mapped. Thus it is possible to observe both a linear pattern and a series of nodes in the same area, simply because of this method of classifying functions.' He quotes the example of Whitechapel-Mile End Road which Carruthers treats as one unit, Hartley and Smailes as three.

R. L. Davies (1972b) questions the value of looking for hierarchical relationships in British cities where the central business district has retained a more important role as shopping and service centre compared with American cities and where, in consequence, any rank sequence of small centres is bound to be less well developed. The British system of commercial centres is compared with the primate pattern of size relationships observed in the urban 'hierarchy' of certain whole countries whereas American experience conforms more to the log-normal, i.e. rank-size (Zipf, 1941), form. Intermediate stages may be recognized (Fig. 30), American cities usually exhibiting a pattern approximating to stage 3 although he suggests that some of them may be approaching stage 4. Certain European cities, where planning is a less powerful restraint on decentralization than in Britain, have patterns resembling stages 2 or 3.

Allowance must also be made for the historical dimension in accounting for the distribution of suburban service centres since, in Europe at least, this has frequently been fixed by the presence of some older village nucleus. In his study of a part of Leeds, Leeming (1959) contrasts the scatter of shopping and other service facilities amongst the pre-1914 back-to-back terraces with the more regularly spaced 'parades', about half a mile apart, which were built to serve the later, lower-density, council or private housing estates. There is greater duplication of retail outlets in the older areas and some which 'represent a pattern of social and economic life antecedent to the present'. History cannot be ignored, even in the New World, as Cohen and Lewis (1967) have demonstrated in relation to Greater Boston. Factors which may be seen to have influenced the siting and growth of retail centres in Boston, include the evolution of the highway network and of public transport services; the plan of the city with a general absence of the type of intersections associated with a grid pattern; and the multiplicity of local government units encouraging the proliferation of shopping centres.

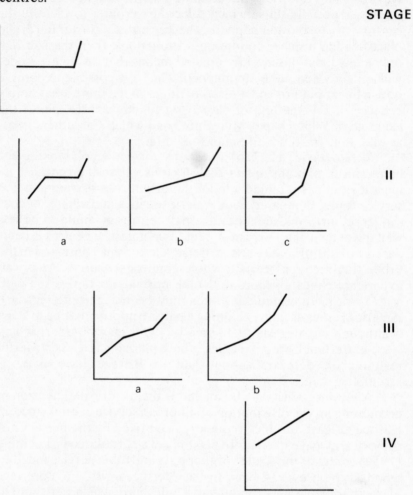

30 Berry's (1961) diagram of city-size relationships used to illustrate the evolution of an intra-urban system. (Courtesy University of Chicago Press)

Internal structure of service centres

Reference has been made to Garner's use of bid-rent curves to explain the internal arrangement of shopping centres. The point is taken up by Scott (1970) whose diagram suggests that every kind of retail establishment has its own rent gradient, the angle of which 'will depend upon the sensitivity of the retailer's output and costs to changes in accessibility' (Fig. 31). Such an explanation is of a traditional profit-maximization kind, of course, and does not make allowance for economic ignorance, sub-optimal 'satisficer' decisions, or the trading policies of particular companies. The value of corner sites, with their greater window space, is illustrated for certain forms of retailing in the higher bids which they are prepared to make for these positions. Scott quotes the example of Oxford Street in London where, in November 1968, there were more corner sites occupied by shoe shops than by any other kind of store. Retailers of men's clothing also show a preference for corner sites as the position of Burton the Tailor often demonstrates. Banks bid for corner sites, not for the window display, but for status and to be near points of maximum pedestrian movement. In contrast, the shop selling a specialist item such as postage stamps or saddlery is more likely to select a cheaper site at the back of the shopping parade because customers are more likely to make a special trip to patronize it.

Like the CBD, but on a different scale, local centres also exhibit clustering of similar or complementary outlets. The most common form of association is of shops in the same or closely

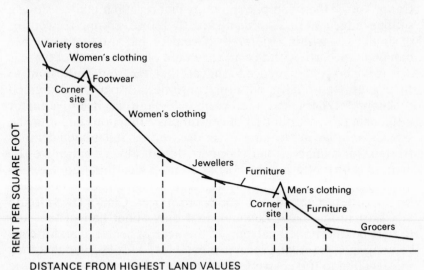

31 The relationship between land values and the distribution of different forms of retailing in an unplanned shopping centre according to Scott, 1970. (Courtesy Hutchinson, *Geography and Retailing*)

related trades in order to achieve external economies from access to a greater number of potential customers. The degree of clustering clearly varies from trade to trade and Scott quotes the retail affinity of antique dealers as an extreme example. The association of clothing and shoe shops is often noted. Somewhat different is the clustering of satellite outlets around some 'leader'. In an early study of store affinity, Ratcliff (1939) noted the tendency in American shopping centres for 'variety stores' to locate close to department and clothing stores because the goods they sold were small and cheap and did not themselves act as 'shopping trip generators'. Petrol stations similarly attract confectionery and ice cream stalls. More specialized are the forms of complementarity which involve proximity to markets or sources of supply. The former category is illustrated by the sale of law books and of specialist clothing — wigs and gowns — in close proximity to the law courts; the latter by the sale of remnants or damaged goods from outlets, perhaps a market stall, near to the factory manufacturing these' items.

A behavioural approach

Central place theory implies not only that certain functions share a similar range and threshold and are, therefore, grouped in centres of similar size within a hierarchy of centres, but also that consumer behaviour accords with this arrangement of functions. Yet there is a growing body of evidence to suggest that, far from conforming to such a gravitationalist pattern, consumers display well-defined space preferences and that such behaviour is, itself, a factor influencing the distribution of central place functions and thus the size and relative importance of service centres. It has been demonstrated, for example, that shoppers do not always patronize the nearest centre offering the sort of goods which they require, frequently travelling longer distances than would appear to be necessary in order to obtain such goods or services. Clark (1968) found in Christchurch, New Zealand, that only about half of the customers he questioned patronized the nearest centre even for convenience goods (meat, grocery, vegetables). He observed that they were willing to travel significantly greater distances to shop in the CBD or at other larger centres; it follows that the range of a good is enlarged as the size of centre increases. Ambrose (1968) investigated shopping behaviour in a number of coastal towns in Sussex and found that more than a third of all purchases were made at points beyond the nearest outlet. The degree to which shoppers were prepared to travel 'excess distances' varied according to the nature of the goods to be purchased as one may have expected, longer journeys being undertaken for certain types of clothing than for foodstuffs. The description, 'spatially flexible goods', has been applied to those items for which people customarily 'shop around', or which have travel characteristics corresponding to those normally regarded as higher order items (Golledge, Rushton and Clark, 1966). Curry (1962) adds a further explanation when he quotes the shop consultants' maxim that customers are drawn more strongly to a shopping centre that is in the direction of the CBD than to one towards the edge of the city.

Ambrose suggests that irregularities in the pattern of consumer behaviour arise from the variety of reasons for which shopping journeys are undertaken. He cites the desire for fresh air, or for an antidote to boredom, and the need to take the baby out. Some of these are likely to be of most benefit to the local centre. The most common reason for travelling further than necessary to purchase a good is the multi-purpose shopping trip. Low order goods and services may be obtained in the course of a trip to obtain ones of a higher order, a fact confirmed by Garrison's work on Cedar Rapids, Iowa, which showed that distances travelled to a particular centre were similar whether for high or low order goods (Garrison et al., 1959). The larger centre frequently offers the added attraction of lower prices on certain goods. Stores there are able to reduce prices, both because of the possibility which is open to them of thereby attracting greater custom, and also because of the scale economies that arise from a greater emphasis on supermarket-type trading. In actual fact the financial advantage to the customer of bulk-purchasing may be wholly offset by the cost of transport and parking, but the perceived advantages would seem to be greater than the actual ones so that the shopper is not easily deterred (Rowley, 1972). Account must also be taken of shopping that takes place in close proximity to place of work. Nader (1968), for example, found that the workplace of employed wives had a very strong influence on the shopping habits of residents on a new housing estate which he studied near Sunderland.

It was noted in the previous chapter that mental images of the residential environment can be related to group perception. It can similarly be shown that there is a group element in consumer space preferences. Huff (1960) found that the most powerful influences at work were related to differences in age, sex, education, occupation, income and, what he called, 'mental synthesizing abilities'.

In a more general paper, Thompson (1966) referred also to race and length of residence and concluded that 'the fundamental factor affecting the geographic distribution of retail trade is the manner in which customers organize their perceptions of the external environment with which they are faced.' There is an interesting degree of correspondence between the factors noted by Huff and Thompson and the measures used to differentiate social areas by Shevky and Bell.

The significance of differences on age structure are noted by Scott (1970). The elderly and mothers with young children depend heavily on the local shops as one may expect. At a broader level of generalization, and based on evidence from the United States, the older age groups retain more loyalty for a city centre than do younger ones.

Rather fuller investigation has taken place of the significance for the spatial arrangement of service centres of differences in socio-economic status. In a study of Melbourne, Johnston (1966) observed that the uneven distribution of purchasing power was reflected in that of shopping centres, and Nader (1969), in an investigation of consumer behaviour in the Tyneside industrial region, noted the tendency for households of higher economic status to obtain a greater proportion of both convenience and shopping goods in the larger centres than was the case amongst households of lower economic status. R. L. Davies (1968) compared two outlying residential areas of dissimilar social rank in Leeds, one (Middleton) an estate of predominantly council housing and the other (Street Lane) of largely private development, and his conclusions are of considerable relevance to the idea of a hierarchy of service centres. The total number of business outlets is smaller in Middleton than in Street Lane, yet the variety of goods and services offered in the former is much greater than in the latter, stores being less specialized in any particular trade. Davies concludes from this that, in hierarchical terms, the shopping centre in Middleton extends both above and below the functional role that might be suggested by number of establishments alone. It offers certain goods and services of a higher rank than one might expect; at the same time certain low order convenience goods are overrepresented. Such conclusions bear out the work of Schell (1964) in Boston who found low order centres exhibiting high functional complexity notwithstanding their small market areas. From a parallel enquiry into consumer movement, Davies (1969) draws certain related conclusions. Shoppers in Middleton use their local centre, both for convenience and shopping goods, to a greater extent than

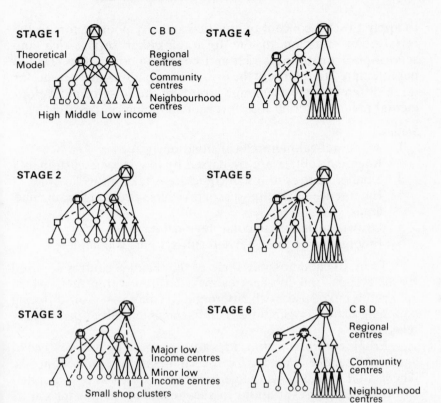

32   R. L. Davies's (1972) model of the development of a hierarchy of
     intra-urban service centres. (Reproduced by permission from the
     Transactions of the Institute of British Geographers, no. 57, 1972)

do those of Street Lane. The latter patronize other retail centres
elsewhere in the city to a proportionately greater extent, whilst
movements to the CBD are more nearly similar, though with a
slightly higher movement from the lower status area except
amongst the oldest age groups. In short, the 'higher socio-
economic classes tend to use a hierarchy more widely and
variously, when lower socio-economic groups limit themselves to
local facilities or the larger centres easily accessible along major
bus routes' (Davies, 1972b).

It follows from the work of Davies and others that, far from
exhibiting an overall hierarchical arrangement of service centres, a
city must be expected to develop distinctive sub-systems which
reflect the spatial distribution of socio-economic groups. Furthermore, Beavon (1974) has suggested that since the distribution of
socio-economic groups is typically sectoral, it may be appropriate

to apply Lösch's concept of city-rich and city-poor sectors to the intra-urban situation in the form of either service-rich and service-poor or business-rich and business-poor sectors. Davies has attempted to represent the evolution of contrasting systems for three different socio-economic groups in the form of a developmental model covering four levels of shopping centre (Fig. 32):

Stages
1   A theoretical hierarchical situation
2   Regional centres are by-passed by low-income customers
3   Smaller centres in low-income areas take on wider roles
4   Emergence of an almost separate sub-system in low-income areas
5   Growth of middle-income regional centres
6   Emergence of three related sub-systems is complete

The CBD and possibly some of the regional centres are used by all groups, and sub-centres may develop within them which reflect this mixed use. Such differentiation may arise from differing shopping habits, possibly from embarrassment felt at patronizing 'class' shops.

Ethnic contrasts within cities are evidenced by the presence of shops and services catering for special dietary and cultural needs. The spatial implications of such differences are likely to parallel those arising from variations in socio-economic status insofar as immigrant groups are frequently of low status. In their studies of service centres in Chicago, both Berry and Garner allowed modifications to their hierarchical systems to take account of predominantly negro and other low-income areas.

The significance of intra-urban migration has been investigated in Tyneside by Thorpe and Nader (1967) who found that suburban housewives who had previously lived close to a large regional centre tended to return there for shopping, even for the purchase of food. Nader's (1968) study of the Penshaw estate near Sunderland yielded similar results, people who had moved from Sunderland continuing to obtain a high proportion of their purchases there. Scott (1970) also quotes evidence to support the view that newcomers to an area are more likely to assess stores in terms of their prices, quality of service etc., than are old-established residents, whilst the latter group includes more who feel under an obligation to patronize a certain store or who are anxious to minimize the effort which shopping requires. Such differences further complicate the geography of service centres.

Consideration of consumer behaviour cannot be divorced

from that of the retailers on the other side of the counter, and allowance must be made for company policies in any realistic analysis of the nature of service centres. In their work on Tyneside, Thorpe and Rhodes (1966) discovered that a different location pattern was exhibited by each of the seven main organizations involved in the grocery trade there. In part the contrasts could be explained by reference to the history of mergers and take-overs by which a particular company had come into being. Some companies are quick to eliminate their unprofitable outlets following such amalgamations, whilst others retain stores even in areas from which many of the former customers have now moved. Companies receive different kinds of locational advice depending on which estate agent or marketing organization they consult. They also pursue different policies both with regard to location and to the nature of trading. Some prefer to maintain a widespread presence; others concentrate their activites on a few profitable sites. They also differ in the extent to which they go in for self-service or retain a greater degree of personal contact with the consumer. Cohen and Lewis (1967) similarly emphasize the importance of store policies in the United States. They note the practice which some companies have of associating geographically in a shopping parade with certain other kinds of firm with which they are not in competition. They complement each other and, by association in this way, attract more customers to both.

Alternative patterns

Attention has been drawn to the possibility of several recognizable sub-systems of service centre coexisting within the same city. But as the use of the motor car for shopping trips becomes more and more common, the likelihood grows of cities displaying complementary rather than hierarchical arrangements of centres. Within such a system, individual centres are likely to offer a similar variety of convenience goods to the neighbourhood population, but will specialize in the provision of certain high order goods and services to a population that may be drawn from the whole, or a large part of, the city. The nature of this specialization will depend on various factors, some historical, some related to the policies or simply the success of particular companies. The intra-urban pattern suggested is similar to that which may be found amongst a group of closely related cities and which Burton (1963) described as 'the dispersed city'. The provision of 'parcels' of goods and

services from a non-hierarchical system of centres does not preclude competition, and change will also take place in response to
such influences as population migration, new road construction
and planning policies.

5

Industry in the City

It is far from easy to discern order in the distribution of manufacturing industry within the city. Certain influences on location are not difficult to recognize — transport arteries, localized markets such as the CBD, zoning regulations, etc. — but the variety of manufacturing activity is so great, and the restricting effect of the past so strong, that few geographers have achieved a classification of intra-urban industrial location that goes beyond generalized description. The well-known theories of urban structure are of little help, failing to view industry on a more disaggregated basis than that represented by the dubious distinction between heavy and light manufacturing. Burgess confines industry to a zone immediately beyond the central business district, and Hoyt to a single sector in a way which does no more than emphasize the localizing role of transport. The multiple nuclei model goes somewhat further, implying that industries cluster for economies of scale, making use of particularly favourable sites, and that some of them are located away from residential areas and beyond the edge of the city where land values are lower, but the diagram is of little value as a classificatory device.

Of the many problems that arise in the search for spatial order in manufacturing, the greatest are likely to result from geographical inertia. 'Because of the large investments involved and the greater inflexibility of manufacturing establishments, industrial inertia is more characteristic than is the inertia of commercial and residential districts. Succession and replacement are not as often encountered in manufacturing districts' (Northam, 1975). Many firms choose to remain in locations that have become sub-optimal because of the high disinvestment costs that would be incurred in moving. The cost of a move is likely to involve the purchase of land and erection of new buildings, the transfer of machinery and other equipment from the old site to the new one, loss of interest on capital until the old site and buildings are sold and, depending on the distance involved, possibly even a contribution to workers' removal expenses. Uncertain as to whether these costs will be outweighed by the advantages occurring from a more efficient factory layout in a better location, manufacturers often prefer to reorganize their operations in situ rather than risk a move. Another strategy that frequently commends itself as an alternative to a complete move, especially when expansion is contemplated, is the establishment of a branch plant. 'Complete relocation is, therefore, less common than other forms of adjustment and usually occurs only where a firm is forced to move, as in a redevelopment scheme. Wherever possible managements prefer to augment existing capacity than relocate, especially where the latter decision involves a large capital expenditure' (Goodall, 1972). It follows from such a statement that any attempt to discover regularity or pattern in the distribution of industry in cities must incorporate a study of change over time, i.e. an evolutionary element.

An evolutionary viewpoint

The need for an historical perspective is stressed by Pred (1964) who prefaces his own definition of intra-urban locations with an examination of the stages by which the present pattern was achieved. Five phases are distinguished. In the first of these — before the 'Industrial Revolution'—manufacturing took place in or close to the home, except for a number of industries processing raw materials which, in the case of the American colonies, were largely confined to the water front. Water-power sites attracted industry during the early years of the Industrial Revolution, leading to the creation of new settlement nuclei that were later to be absorbed by the expanding city (cf. the reference to Marshall's 'industrial colonies' in Chapter 1). The early iron industry was also drawn to riverside sites because of the need for power. Expansion of the railway network from the middle of the nineteenth century led to the growth of manufacturing districts in close proximity to central railway stations and yards, often in association with wholesaling. At the same time, by permitting manufacturing to take place on a much larger scale, the railway also created a demand for space. This was satisfied, in the fourth stage, by the creation of the first industrial suburbs, some of these planned by philanthropic entrepreneurs such as George Pullman in Chicago or Titus Salt in Bradford. These incorporated housing for the workers but, by the end of the century, tram and street railways were making it possible to commute several miles to work in the largest cities.

During the present century the motor vehicle and a manufacturing technology that favours horizontal rather than vertical layout of factories have encouraged the decentralization of industry to sites in the suburbs or on the edge of the city. Yet, adds Pred, 'not all industries have decentralized to non-central and peripheral areas of the metropolis; nor have all of those industries decentralized identically. The forces of inertia and precedent have left a deep imprint on the industrial landscape of the modern metropolis.' Two questions are posed. What kinds of industries remain in or near the core of the metropolis? What patterns, if any, are to be distinguished among the decentralized industries?

Berry and Horton (1970) also point out that the location of industry in cities can often only be understood by reference to historical events, and most of the section of their book which examines this subject is devoted to a study of the evolution of industry in Chicago. Groves (1971) adds another evolutionary stage to the five recognized by Pred. In a study of industry in the San Francisco Bay Area he suggests that the decentralizing effect of the motor vehicle was largely over by mid-twentieth century and that subsequently a variety of forces have combined to bring about renewed concentration. The electronics industry of Palo Alto is cited as an example of a modern industry which displays a highly clustered pattern of location. This results from the need to keep abreast of the latest innovations in an industry that is evolving rapidly and from a desire to be on hand when new contracts are being placed. Siting is also affected by the industry's use of air freight and of piggy-back forms of transport. Airports and terminals with piggy-back facilities both involve high capital investment and, once built, tend to remain, attracting industry to them. 'The history of manufacturing growth in the San Francisco Bay Area is largely that of the growth of subsidiary centres of industrial concentration at the expense of the dominance of the original "core" cities of San Francisco and Oakland.'

In his study of the American City, Murphy (1966) includes a schematic diagram of a typical manufacturing town and five types of location are represented (Fig. 33). Three of these are described as 'older developments' and, for the most part, they and their sub-categories accord with the evolutionary stages noted by Pred, though with rather more emphasis in Murphy's scheme on redevelopment and planning. It is interesting, however, to observe that Murphy also includes a category which he describes as 'scattered factories in residential areas'. Bakeries and ice-cream plants are quoted as examples of such industries which he also refers to as

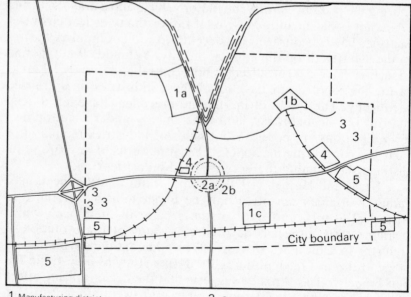

1 Manufacturing district
  a on waterfront
  b at waterfall
  c on railway
2 Central business district
  a light manufacturing serving the
    central business district
  b loft-type factories in outer portion

3 Scattered factories in residential areas

4 Industrial district resulting from clearance
  and redevelopment, may or may not be
  organised or planned

5 Outlying industrial area, may or may not be
  organised or planned

33 R. E. Murphy's (1966) schematic diagram of the distribution of manufacturing in a middle-sized American city. (From *The American City*, with permission of McGraw-Hill Book Company)

community or service industries. Yet industries can also be found scattered throughout the built-up area of the city which do not serve local markets. The textile towns of Yorkshire and Lancashire or of the Lille-Roubaix conurbation in France illustrate this pattern well. Processes in the textile industry that did not require large quantities of water or great amounts of power were relatively free from river- or railway-side locations, even in the nineteenth century, and manufacturers built their plants where there was space for the workers' houses. As the textile industry has contracted during the present century the weaving sheds and other premises have been taken over by a miscellaneous array of enterprises, adding still further to the problem of sorting out location patterns which represent the manufacturing conditions of the contemporary world from those which are inherited from the past.

Economic considerations

In his *Theory of the Location of Industry,* Weber (1929) suggested that the location of industry within cities would be affected by the same factors as he had observed at the inter-urban level. Such a view has been challenged by, for example, Logan (1966 a) who argues that not only does traditional theory largely ignore such influences as site rent and changes that occur with scale, both of great significance for industry in cities, but that it makes no allowance for non-economic behaviour, the personal factor in location. The need for a behaviouralist approach to the study of industrial location has also been stressed by many other authors, e.g. Pred (1967) and D.M. Smith (1971).

Yet, despite the importance that attaches to 'imperfect knowledge' and the pursuit of 'satisficers', the significance to the manufacturer of the traditional factors such as transport costs must not be overlooked. The significance of these costs varies greatly, according to whether the market for a firm's products is within the city or is at a regional, even national, scale. Another consideration is the degree to which the firm incurs all, or only a part of, the costs involved in assembling materials and delivering products. A firm may profit from a special arrangement that delivers raw materials cheaply; products may be delivered at a fixed rate or bear the full cost involved; on the other hand the customer may pay. The value, weight and perishability of the product must also be taken into account. The degree to which many of these other factors bear on location depends, however, on the nature of the market, and in fact often comes back to the question of whether the market is in or outside the city. This distinction appears in the early attempt by De Meirlier (1950) to group industries according to the more important influences on their location:

1 Local market industries with locally-obtained basic raw materials.
2 Local market industries with nationally-obtained basic raw materials.
3 National market industries with locally-obtained basic raw materials.
4 National market industries with nationally-obtained basic raw materials.

Later studies have continued to lay stress on market location whilst paying less attention to the source of raw materials (but cf. Pred, below). Historical considerations can be seen to support emphasis on the market. It has been pointed out that in the United States, for example, the motor lorry became the principal means of intra-city freight movement well before it took over from the railway as the dominant form of inter-city movement (Moses and Williamson, 1967). Its effect was to lower the cost of moving goods, thereby giving manufacturers greater freedom to select sites offering other advantages such as cheap land, but industries serving distant markets were at first denied these advantages, and remained tied to sites adjoining the rail freight depots. Change came with the growth of inter-city trucking after World War II and at this stage the regionally- or nationally-orientated industries were encouraged to leap-frog the city-serving ones to seek sites on the edge of the built-up area. There is thus a time/technology element to the explanation of industrial segregation.

The value attached to market access is supported by empirical evidence. In a sample study of firms in Sydney, Logan (1966) found that closeness to market was the main reason for site selection in the case of more than a third of the firms questioned. The next most important explanation of location, stated as the main reason by a fifth of the firms, was the availability of land at a suitable price. Site rent would thus appear to be a major determinant of location at the intra-urban level. Goodall (1972) puts this plainly when he states that, 'Although differences in land costs between urban areas may not be as significant as other inter-urban factor cost differentials, variation in land costs between parts of an urban area may be highly significant in determining intra-urban manufacturing location because of the relative ability of manufacturing to compete for urban land. This is especially the case when scale of plant is related to the total amount of land needed. Scale of operation thus becomes a significant factor determining actual location within an urban area.' Since land rents usually decline from the centre of the city towards the periphery, firms for whom the centre is no longer an attractive location, e.g. in terms of access to market, are likely to respond to the burden of high rents by moving out to the suburbs or the urban fringe.

Space for re-organization or expansion is a major consideration behind the decision to move as Goodall implies. A survey of firms who had moved from London to the 'expanding towns' of Swindon and Aylesbury found this to be the principal reason for moving in more than two-thirds of the cases (Scargill, 1968), and the conclusion is confirmed by other studies, e.g. by Lever (1972). Historical evidence points to the long-established tendency for moves to take place in response to change in the nature of manufacturing and to the acquisition of new markets. Thus, for example, the establishment in 1862 of a new factory at Small Heath, Birmingham, for the manufacture of military arms marked the beginning of a process of specialization and contraction in the gun quarter of the inner city (Wise, 1949). Many are the instances of firms 'born' in backyard premises of the central area which, having succeeded in winning a market for their products, have moved to new sites further out. William Morris, who began to assemble cars in stables behind an Oxford college, moved to a disused barracks on the edge of the city in 1912. Herein lies further reason for viewing industrial location in evolutionary terms.

Firms frequently cluster in particular quarters of the city or on industrial estates in order to gain external economies of scale. For some of them, sub-contractors and others who are involved in the intermediate stages of manufacture, clustering can be interpreted in terms of access to market. But as Keeble (1969) has pointed out, industrial linkages take many forms, and the advantages that derive from agglomeration must therefore be treated as a separate influence on location. They were recognized as such, for example, by Chinitz (1960) who grouped industry in the city into three broad categories: those serving local markets; those serving national markets; and those which were 'communications-orientated'. The location of this final group is dictated by the need for close communication with suppliers, sub-contractors, customers etc., i.e. by external economies. In his study of the industrial areas of north-west London, Keeble found that, although in general linkages were weaker than in the inner quarters of the city, they were nevertheless strong in particular industries, especially engineering. He noted the presence of many firms engaged in sub-contract engineering, some of which later 'graduated' to the manufacture of finished products, and of firms providing engineering 'services' such as tool or pattern making, metal-finishing and electro-plating. Many of these ancillary trades were to be found, not on the industrial estates, but in converted premises such as disused laundries in the adjacent residential areas where rents were cheaper. Within this middle industrial belt of London the convergence of transport routes affords particular advantages with regard to linkages (Fig. 34). When firms move out, or establish branch plants, migration tends to be in a radial direction in order that links may be more easily maintained.

The benefits of clustering are not easy to isolate or to quantify, depending as they do on the nature of the industry, the size and

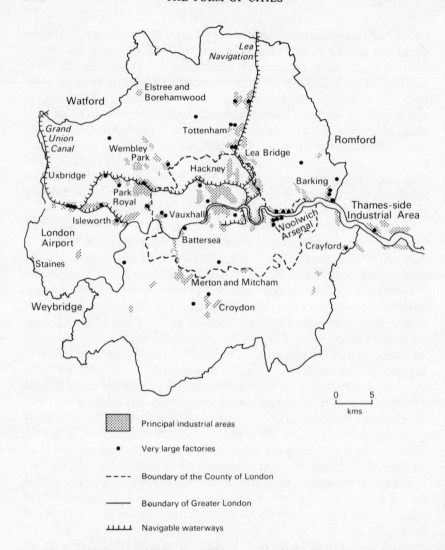

34 The principal industrial areas of Greater London. After Martin,
    1964. (Courtesy Geo. Philip)

organization of the firm, and other variables. Trends in the structure of modern industry would suggest, however, that the significance of linkages is growing and experience in the electronics
industry of San Francisco, referred to above, supports such a view.
    Amongst the advantages of north-west London to engineer-
ing industries noted by Keeble is the pool of skilled labour that has
been built up there, an example of cumulative causation, and

representative of a special form of linkage. Firms may be drawn to such an area by the possibility of poaching skilled labour from other enterprises. On the other hand the central city offers the advantage of access to a wide variety of labour, especially if the city has a good radial system of public transport. 'Labour pool economies are maximised at the city centre. This is particularly important for firms with specialist skilled labour demands' (Richardson, 1971). As commuting becomes more time-consuming and expensive, firms requiring highly skilled labour may be tempted to relocate in the suburbs. Conversely, as Goodall points out, firms which rely on relatively low-paid, unskilled labour are more likely to remain in an inner city location close to those areas where unskilled new arrivals can find a place in the housing market. Generalizations must be treated with caution, however, especially in view of the relatively low priority given to access to work in the decision over where to live (Chapter 3), and to the option which is open, at least to some firms, of reducing the wage bill by substituting other costs. Substitution is, of course, least likely where firms have specialist labour requirements. Some employ mainly married women, perhaps on a part-time basis, and for such firms a location in a residential area offers the best opportunity of staff recruitment. The scatter of small manufacturing enterprises in textile towns owes much to the need for ready access to this kind of labour.

Many other considerations enter into the locational decision which cannot easily be built into a typology of manufacturing locations because of the extent to which they vary in nature and importance from city to city. Amongst these are what Logan (1966 b) describes as 'institutional forces', the zoning or planning regulations imposed by the municipality, and the level of service provision. In his description of manufacturing in the state capitals of Australia, Logan observes that industrial estates on the periphery of the cities tend to be so inadequately provided with essential services such as roads, electricity, sewerage and the telephone, that they are 'virtually useless to industry'. Within a metropolitan area shared between several local government authorities there may be differences not only in the quality of public services, but also in local taxation policies, and such differences have frequently played a major part in influencing the locational decision.

In pursuit of a typology

Reference has already been made to the generalized schemes of urban industrial structure put forward by De Meirlier, Chinitz and Murphy, schemes which lay stress to varying degrees on the locational influences noted above. In a further search for order, Loewenstein (1963) drew land use maps of a selection of American cities and superimposed upon these the five concentric rings of E.W. Burgess. From his maps he deduced that certain industries, such as printing and newspaper publishing, which he described as labour or market-orientated, tend to be attracted to the central city. Location there offers access to the largest possible labour market, and industries can afford to pay high rents because they produce goods which are 'highly competitive in price'. By contrast industries that are 'essentially component assemblers and distributors', e.g. the motor vehicle industry, are aligned along railways and roads where rents are lower and they are able to reserve land for future expansion. Loewenstein also refers to two other categories of industry: basic processing industries such as petroleum refining and steel manufacture which use bulky raw materials, demand large amounts of land, and avoid residential areas because of the noise or smell which they generate; and a group which he designates simply as one involving large plants outside the city. The manufacture of paper goods is cited as an example, but the distinction between these latter two locations is far from obvious.

Hamilton (1967) employs a similar method of analysis, and achieves almost identical results, basing his synthesis on Martin's (1964) map of industrial areas in Greater London (Fig. 35). His central city category (A) is of industries which benefit from having access to skilled labour drawn from the entire city (e.g. instrument manufacture), or which seek to supply markets in the central business district (office machinery) or the entire city (newspapers). Such industries characteristically 'swarm' in clearly-defined industrial quarters where there are external economies to be gained by clustering. In contrast with the latter are those industries which seek cheaper sites, employ unskilled or semi-skilled and female suburban labour, and are attracted to sites alongside radial or 'ring' transport arteries to facilitate assembly of materials and the despatch of products. A sub-category of port industries is distinguished from the others which are said to include 'food manufactures, electrical engineering and light industries', but the distinction between locations B and C is not apparent from the map.

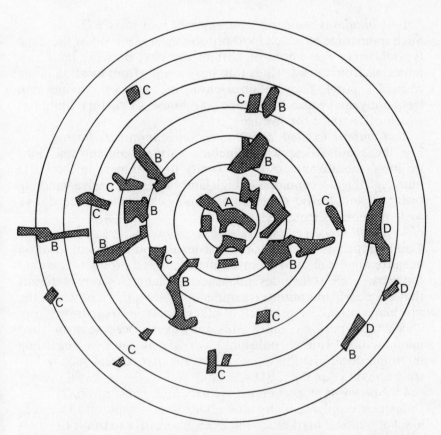

35   Hamilton's (1967) model of the industrial structure of a large city
      based on Martin's map (Fig. 34). (Courtesy Methuen, *Models in
      Geography*)

The final group of industries (D) seek large sites on the outskirts of
the city for assembly-line production and to permit storage and
waste disposal; they include industries handling dangerous or
obnoxious materials. Hamilton quotes as examples the vehicle,
heavy engineering, oil-refining and heavy chemicals, metallurgical
and paper industries.

     The most widely quoted typology is that of Pred (1964) who
based his generalizations on observation of 'the logical patterning
of locational trends' within the ten largest metropolitan areas of
the United States. Drawing also on previous work, notably that of
Chinitz, he grouped industries into seven 'flexible types'. In his
scheme he also recognized what he described as the fortuitous
element in location by allowing randomness in the distribution of
particular industries.

1   *Ubiquitous industries concentrated near the CBD*
Such industries, of which food processing is regarded as the most
typical, serve the whole or part of the city, drawing their raw
materials from outside (they thus have a waterfront location in the
case of a port). They retain a close link with wholesaling and
frequently make use of former warehouse or factory buildings
which offer space for storage.

2   *Centrally located 'communication-economy' industries*
For these industries, which include garment-making and job-
printing, the advantages of proximity to customers in the CBD
outweigh the diseconomies of high land values, expensive handling
facilities and traffic congestion. Small-scale enterprises derive
scale economies from clustering.

3   *Local market industries with local raw material sources*
Common to this category of industries is randomness of location
because almost all movement of materials and products is within
the urban area. It includes industries which employ raw materials
that are nearly ubiquitous (manufactured ice); those of which the
raw materials are by-products of other industries (e.g. drawn from
a local meat-packing plant); and ones which process semi-finished
manufactures (metal polishing). 'Vestigial notions regarding
minimum local distribution costs' means that several such industries remain near the CBD.

4   *Non-local market industries with high-value products*
Industries supplying high value goods (e.g. computers) to a regional or national market are relatively insensitive to transport costs
and also exhibit a random distribution within the city. The convenience afforded by freight-forwarding services may, however,
encourage location near the CBD.

5   *Non-centrally located 'communication-economy' industries*
These industries have much in common with those in category 4,
but they show a strong tendency to cluster in order to have access to
the latest ideas and technologies relating to the industry and to win
contracts. They are often highly technical and scientific, and Pred
quotes the examples of the electronics and space-age industries of
Boston which concentrate along Route 128, and those of the San
Francisco Bay Area.

6   *Non-local market industries on the waterfront*
Most typical of the waterfront industries are shipbuilding and
repair and industries which process imported raw materials, e.g.
petroleum or sugar refining. Amongst the riverside industries are
many which no longer employ the river for their transport but are
'anchored by inertia'.

7   *Industries orientated towards national markets*
In order to overcome the high cost of transporting bulky products
over long distances, these industries show a marked tendency to
locate towards the edge of the city on the side facing their most
important regional or national market. In addition to American
examples, Pred notes the attraction of north and north-west London to metal and engineering industries supplying markets in the
Midlands.

Pred's scheme has been criticized on the basis of overlap
between the categories and for placing too much emphasis on
'communication-economies' as a factor affecting the location of
industry outside the CBD (Wood, 1974). But a degree of overlap is
inevitable, and the second criticism appears harsh in view of the
importance of linkages in non-central locations noted by other
observers such as Keeble and Logan. Pred's typology is successful
in combining a variety of factors, the significance of which is
supported by other studies, and in its attempt to allow both for
inertia and for chance. If there are weaknesses in the scheme the
most striking would seem to arise from the neglect of considerations to do with labour.

The balance is restored by Carter (1972) who, in a classification which draws on the ideas of Loewenstein, Hamilton and
Pred, includes a sub-group of centrally-located industries which
are there principally because of labour requirements:

1   *Centrally located industries*
    a   labour-orientated.
    b   market-orientated (includes Pred's categories 1 and 3).
    c   CBD-orientated (includes Pred's category 2).
2   *Non-local market high value industries*
    These tend to have random locations (cf. Pred's category 4).
3   *Large basic processing industries*
    They include Pred's category 7 but Carter makes the point
    that many chemical and metallurgical industries remain in
    the older industrial districts of the inner city because of heavy
    investment there. Such inertia, it is suggested, is under-
    estimated in the other three typologies.
4   *Waterfront or port industries.*
5   *Integrated industries along communication lines*
    (include Pred's category 5).
6   *Suburban industries*
    These are so-located as a result of decentralization.

By including this final group, Carter makes some allowance for the effect of planning controls on location. Recognizing also the force of inertia, the scheme is one which demonstrates 'that industry can be found in every zone and sector of the city from CBD to outer suburb'.

The most elaborate scheme so far proposed—13 categories— is that of Groves (1971). Based on his research in the San Francisco Bay area, the classification emphasizes the market area served. But in the sub-divisions he stresses the role of other factors, noticeably the mode of transport used (on the grounds that some forms, e.g. railways, are more locationally constraining than others, e.g. road transport—cf. Carter's category 5), the space needs of the industry (which may be just a room in a disused dwelling), the nature of the product or raw material including its perishability (allows for the importance of market gardening in the San Francisco Bay Area), and the need to take advantage of external economies:

1 *Local Market Serving Industries*
   a *CBD concentrated, communication orientated* e.g. printing.
   b *Dispersed location, large plants urban core orientated, general consumer market* e.g. newspapers.
   c *Bulky product, linked to local manufacturer* e.g. glass containers.
2 *Local/Regional Market Industries*
   d *Urban core orientated, rail transport* e.g. paint and varnish manufacture.
   e *Urban core orientated, road transport* e.g. bread-making.
3 *Regional Market Industries*
   f *Strong urban core orientation* e.g. distilling.
   g *Located outside urban core areas* e.g. motor vehicle assembly.
4 *Regional/National Market Industries*
   h *Concentrated 'communication-orientated' industries, located outside urban clusters* e.g. electronic products.
   i *Random location within urban clusters* e.g. defence equipment.
5 *National Market Industries*
   j *Concentrated outside urban core locations, based on local/regional raw materials which are perishable* e.g. fruit and vegetable canning.
6 *Waterfront Industries*
   k *Urban core locations* e.g. shipbuilding.

    l   *Non-urban core locations* e.g. oil refining.
7   *Additions from the Literature*
    m   *Local market industries with local raw material sources*
    e.g. manufactured ice.

The West Coast bias is quite evident in Groves' scheme. This, and the large number of subdivisions, make it less valuable as a generalization than some of the simpler classifications outlined above. But it remains important as a reminder of the range and complexity of factors which help to bring about the distribution of industry within cities.

Linkages in the inner city

A recurrent element in all the classifications of intra-urban industrial location is the presence of a group of industries, close to the city centre, which rely on 'communication economies'. They appear as the 'factory zone' with which Burgess encircled his CBD, and as 'light industry . . . found in upper storey lofts' in Griffin and Preston's transition zone. Characteristic of most of these industries is their tendency to cluster in separate 'quarters', classic accounts of which appear in Wise's (1949) description of the jewellery and gun quarters of Birmingham, in the work of Hall (1962) and Martin (1964; 1966) on the industries of Greater London, and in Kenyon's (1964) account of the New York garment industry. Individual manufacturing units are usually very small, involving skilled and often highly specialized work, but requiring little in the way of raw materials or power. They commonly make use of converted dwelling houses ('lofts' in the American literature) which have been left unprotected by the absence of restrictive covenants. Urban redevelopment may see these replaced by 'flatted factories' which offer similar advantages of proximity to other, closely associated, branches of the trade, but at higher rents. Many of the older industries trace their origin to crafts practised in what is now the CBD, having evolved from these by a process of 'industrial transmutation', i.e. the transference of skills in response to changing tastes and fashion. The Birmingham jewellery industry evolved in this way from buckle-making and toy manufacture. Immigrant skills have, in some cases, contributed to the growth of the industry. The clothing industry in both London and New York expanded rapidly with the arrival of Jewish refugees from Eastern Europe in the late nineteenth century. Shops and offices, hotels and hospitals in the CBD continue to provide a market for the products of such industries as clothing and printing, certain food trades, and the manufacture of specialized equipment. An intricate web of linkages unite the individual manufacturing units in a particular trade, permitting frequent changes of product (within a narrow range) in response to changing demand, but requiring coordination on the part of merchants or 'jobbers'. The latter often maintain showrooms along a 'trade street' and organize the putting out of work to contractors and possibly to outworkers in their homes. In this way the quarter becomes functionally structured around the trade street: Vyse Street in the Birmingham jewellery district, Curtain Street in the furniture quarter of Shoreditch and Bethnal Green, and Broadway between 34th and 40th Streets in the case of the New York clothing industry.

No quarter is permanent, although some show a high degree of persistence. Decline of a particular industry may be brought about for many reasons—changing space requirements, the search for cheaper labour, shifts of fashion—yet unless it is cleared away by redevelopment, the district is likely to remain one in which new firms 'incubate'. The centre of the city may well remain an important market even when movement takes place, and this is likely to be betrayed in both the distance and direction of the moves. Thus industries from the East End of London have largely moved towards the north and east, clothing firms to Hackney and Stoke Newington, and the furniture industry to Tottenham and Edmonton. A degree of clustering and of market orientation is maintained even when firms have moved as far out as the New Towns. The furniture trade, for example, has favoured Harlow to the north of London, whilst the clothing industry has been drawn eastwards to Basildon.

Integrated industries of the urban periphery

Evidence of industrial linkage is by no means confined to the inner city (Keeble, 1969) and the classificatory schemes refer to 'integrated' or 'communication-orientated' industries which cluster, often on industrial estates, in the suburbs or on the fringe of the city. Most typical are the technologically advanced engineering and electronics industries.

The industrial estate takes many forms and Bale (1974) has found it necessary to propose a definition in order to avoid confusion over the use of the term. He writes 'An industrial estate is a

grouping of industrial establishments provided with certain common services and utilities laid down in advance of demand, and
established as a result of enterprise and planning by an independent organization.' The organization concerned may be public
or private, or indeed a combination of both, and its responsibility
may or may not extend to the actual erection of factory buildings.
Manchester's Trafford Park estate, begun in 1896 following the
completion of the Ship Canal, was the forerunner of many later
estates in the north of England as the Slough estate, started in
1920, was in London. Military depots and airfields used in the two
World Wars have provided many of the sites of later industrial
developments. Designation by the Government of Special Areas in
1934 and of Development Areas in 1945 has led to the establishment of numerous estates as part of a policy of attracting new
forms of employment to the depressed areas; in some cases the
enterprise has come from a local authority as in the case of the
estates built by the City of Liverpool at Speke and Kirkby.

Factories are large by comparison with those of the inner city
'quarters' and frequently appear much larger because of the
amount of space reserved for car parking, storage and for future
expansion. But there are small units, too, especially amongst the
satellite subcontractors and suppliers of services, and indeed some
estates, such as London's Park Royal, have a large number of such
factories which Hall (1962) interprets as a continuation of the
city's workshop tradition. Favoured sites are alongside main roads
and, more particularly in the United States, near to an airport for
the convenience of executive travel and the movement of air
freight. Noise and danger reduce the value of the land beneath the
flight path for housing which may therefore be reserved for industrial use. Linkages take many different forms, involving the movement of goods between firms, provision of services of all kinds from
paint spraying to banking, marketing, and the communication of
information (Wood, 1969). A 'campus-like atmosphere' is claimed
for some American estates where scientifically-based industries
profit from exposure to a flow of new ideas.

H.M. Mayer's (1964) description of the Centex estate in
Chicago provides a useful illustration of what linkage involves.
Established by a Dallas company in 1956, adjacent to an ex-
pressway and international airport and with associated residential
development, the estate had acquired 149 industrial units (7500
employees) by 1963 when the study was carried out (Fig. 36). Of
these firms, 83 were engaged in manufacturing or processing, and
no fewer than 66 in services, storage or distribution. Amongst the

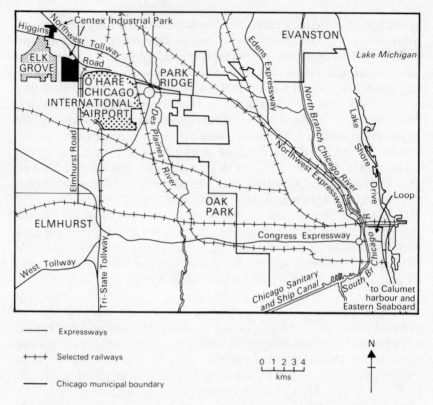

------- Expressways

+++ Selected railways

------- Chicago municipal boundary

0 1 2 3 4
kms

N

36   The Centex Industrial Park, Chicago. After Mayer, 1964. (From *Focus on Geographic Activity,* with permission of McGraw-Hill Book Company)

latter group were 7 firms engaged solely in packaging, one of them serving a quarter of all the other firms on the estate.

It would be wrong to suppose that industrial estates are occupied only by firms which have moved out of crowded or obsolescent premises in the city centre. Wood (1974) refers to this as 'the decentralization myth', contending that much growth takes place *in situ.* 'In these circumstances it is no longer sensible to regard outer metropolitan areas merely as industrial satellites of the central city. In fact they have been the key regions for modern industrial growth during most of the twentieth century.' In order to appreciate this point of view it is necessary to take account of the complex organization and control of modern industry. There is much 'spin-off' from existing firms. Branch plants are set up by major companies in order to carry out a new process or to man-ufacture some product as a sideline; alternatively, such work is put out to smaller firms the expansion of which is financed by the larger organization. Under different circumstances, trained staff may be tempted to leave the big firm in order to establish a small manufacturing unit of their own. In these and other ways, new firms are created, and growth takes place without necessarily involving migration from elsewhere. A historical element is clearly as important to the understanding of linkage patterns amongst modern industries as it is to an investigation of the more traditional ones of the inner city.

6

The Planned Town

The planned town is not a new phenomenon. The history of urbanization is punctuated by phases of town planting, and names such as
Newton, Neustadt, Villanuova or Novgorod point to the widespread popularity of the 'new town' idea in the past.

Towns have been founded for a variety of reasons. Many have
originated in the course of movements to colonize and settle new
lands; some have been built to assist in the defence of a vulnerable
frontier, others to house workers engaged in the exploitation of
mineral deposits or employed in a major new industrial project.
Social motives have featured more prominently in the twentieth
century with schemes to rehouse populations from overcrowded
conurbations.

Certain types of layout have been favoured by those who have
established towns *de novo*. Of these by far the most popular has
been some variation on the gridiron. What more natural when
laying out a settlement on a green-field site than to be orderly and
draw up a rectangular or chequerboard framework of streets? Such
a plan makes it easy to allocate building plots within the regularly-
shaped pieces of land created by the grid and is helpful to the
surveyor. As the population of the town grows, additions can be
made to the original layout without destroying the basic symmetry
of the plan. But despite the convenience it affords, the grid has not
always been the most favoured design. The dictates of religious
observance coupled with the needs for ceremonial have, in some
parts of the world, played an important part in the orientation of
town streets and in the arrangement of its principal buildings. Even
more exotic designs have resulted from the search for the ideal city,
or the city-beautiful, a recurrent theme in the history of town
building. The nature of the ideals pursued have, of course, varied,
but in general some version of the radial-concentric plan has been
favoured in preference to the grid where aesthetic considerations
have been to the fore. Linear designs have had little popularity
despite their convenience for the movement of vehicles. Sig-

nificantly, however, linear elements have been built into some of the most recent new towns in connection with traffic control schemes.

Cities of the Ancient World

A distinction must be made at the outset between order and planning. Order is apparent in many of the features of Mesopotamian cities, such as that of Ur which flourished around 2500 BC. Two-storey brick houses were arranged around a courtyard for privacy and shade; there was a temple precinct and a number of broad streets that probably had a processional function, whilst the overall layout of the town suggests the presence, even at this period, of segregation on a social or tribal basis. Collectively these characteristics are sufficient for Hiorns (1956) to describe Ur as a planned city, but Morris (1972) rejects this view, pointing to the narrow winding lanes, similar to those in the older parts of Middle Eastern cities at the present day, which to him are indicative of 'organic' growth. The Egyptian civilization of the Nile valley has left much less evidence of urban forms than that of Sumeria but has contributed undoubted examples of formal, planned layout in the workman's settlement of Kahun and in the 'model village' of Tel-el-Amarna, built to house construction workers in the 14th century BC. Parallel streets and regularly-shaped housing plots characterize both settlements, but as short-lived colonies erected for a specific purpose, it would be unwise to regard them as indicative of a town planning tradition. Instead, Morris prefers to regard the Harappan cities of the Indus valley (2500-1500 BC) as representing the earliest examples of conscious town planning. Both Mohenjo-dara and Harappa have what are described as a 'modified gridiron' pattern of streets and, on the basis of evidence here, Morris suggests that the title of 'father of town planning', traditionally given to the Greek, Hippodamus, is earned by some 'anonymous Harappan priest',

Whatever its origin, the practice of building to something approaching a formal plan was carried around the eastern Mediterranean by colonists and traders. It is apparent in the Minoan palace cities such as Knossos and in smaller towns, of which Gournia (c. 2000 BC) is the best known example. But the systematization of the plan was the achievement of Hellenic culture and it attained its most formal expression in the colonial settlements established under the Roman Empire.

Miletus, on a peninsula of the Ionian coast, was rebuilt in the 5th century BC after destruction of an earlier town by Persians, and is probably the earliest town to exhibit overall, chequerboard planning. It was also the home of Hippodamus, described by Aristotle as 'discoverer of the method of dividing cities'. Born in Miletus c. 480 BC he was responsible for designing towns with wide streets intersecting at right angles, the main crossing determining the site of the public open space — the *agora*. Towns for which he was responsible included Piraeus, the port of Athens, built for Pericles about 450 BC, but his ideas were disseminated widely as a result of the Greek practice of founding daughter settlements of established towns. Miletus alone is said to have spawned sixty such townships which were created to facilitate trade and the supply of food. Priene, another town of the Ionian coast, rebuilt in the 4th century, illustrates the arrangement of a typical Hellenic city: parallel streets and rectangular building plots, central agora surrounded by public buildings, facilities for leisure which here included a theatre and sports complex, and the *acropolis* — the early defensive site which in many cities became the religious centre (Fig. 37). Greek housing, though incorporating courtyards, and sometimes having more than one storey, lacked the comforts and amenities that were so much a part of the Roman tradition, and the rather mean conditions of the residential portion of the city contrasted with the thought that was put into the arrangement and architectural style of the noble buildings and colonnades which looked out on the agora.

Dispersal of settlement arose partly from the idea that Greek towns should, ideally, not exceed a predetermined size. Aristotle considered that town growth should not be permitted to go beyond the point at which a sense of community is lost. The citizens should know each other so that they might know for whom to vote when choosing magistrates and other officials. They should be able to maintain easy social contact, lead a 'good life', and not be so numerous that they could not gather to hear the public speaker in the agora. No figure was specified, but Plato suggested as optimum a total of around 5000 free citizens. Double this number was preferred by Hippodamus. In summary, Hellenistic planning involved control over the design of the whole city and layout in the form of a regular grid; aesthetic considerations are apparent in the attempt to create an attractive communal centre but do not extend to the residential area; and there is evidence that town building was affected by notions of community and the relationship between this and town size.

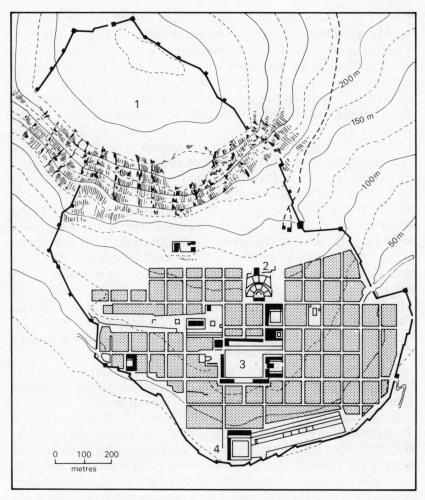

1	Acropolis	3	Agora
2	Theatre	4	Gymnasium and Stadium

37 Plan of Priene, rebuilt about 300 B.C. After Hiorns, 1958. (Courtesy Geo. Harrap)

Continuity between Greek and Roman planning is, as may be expected, most evident where the latter took place on previously occupied sites. Such was the case at Pompeii and at Leptis Magna in North Africa. Roman construction is evident in the use of more advanced engineering skills, in road-making, drainage and water supply, and in the perfection of architectural techniques, notably the arch and the vault. With these methods they were less inhibited

by site constraints than their predecessors had been. Plans tended
to be very formal, even stereotyped, a chequerboard grid of streets
being built up from the intersection of two broad axes running
north/south and east/west (*cardo* and *decumanus*). Morris suggests
that the simplicity of this plan was related to the rules which
governed the building of the legionary camp (*castra,* hence cas-
trametation). Within this grid of right angle streets, building plots
(*insulae*) would be square, and the *forum* was usually centrally
situated in an angle formed by the main crossroads. Like its Greek
equivalent, the agora, this public open space was flanked by imposing buildings, colonnades and statuary. Here, or close to it, would
be found assembly rooms (*basilicae*), law courts and municipal
offices, public baths, theatre, temple and, possibly, shops. Of the
major public buildings, only the amphitheatre was consigned a
position on the edge of the town, this for much the same reasons as
govern the siting of a modern circus or football stadium. The best
examples of Roman planning are to be found, not in Rome itself,
which, like Athens, experienced more of organic than planned
growth, but in colonial towns like that of Timgad in North Africa,
with its eleven parallel streets running in each direction. In Britain
chequerboard layout is well illustrated in the plans of Colchester
(Camulodonum) and Caerwent (Venta Silurum).

The importance of symbolism in town design can be observed
in the plan of early cities in east and south Asia, the religious
significance that attaches to such design having been described for
Chinese cities by Wheatley (1971) and Tuan (1968). In the Hwang
Ho basin of northern China, cities of the Shang dynasty (1776-
1122 BC) were laid out to a geometrical design which symbolized
order in the cosmos. 'The traditional form and layout of the Chinese city is an image of the Chinese cosmos, an ordered and con-
secrated world set sharply apart by a massive earthen girdle from
the disorderly and profane world beyond' (Tuan, 1968). The walls,
which cut out this profane world, were entered by twelve gates,
three to each wall, which represented the months of the year. The
city was square in shape and within it the pattern of north/south
and east/west streets was arranged around a main axis representing
the celestial meridian. At its northern end, in the position of the
polar star, was sited the royal residence. Sacred buildings were
built alongside the main street and around it the four quarters of
the city represented the four quadrants in the heavenly vault.
According to Tuan, the design of Chinese cities retained this
cosmic symbolism until as late as the 10th or 11th century AD.

Symbolic meaning can be found elsewhere, in the design of

Etruscan cities, and in the royal capitals of India built 'after the mythical model of the celestial city' (Rowe, 1973). Laws relating to the cosmos are enshrined in the various designs of the *mandala*, plans which govern the arrangement of buildings and streets. But order in the Indian city, according to Rowe, extends beyond the siting of temple and palace to include also the apportionment of space to the different social groups within the population. Caste, kinship and association are the bases on which places of residence are allocated in cities which provide a 'symbolic representation of the social order'. When tradition is so deeply rooted in religious belief it is not difficult to understand why segregation on the basis of caste etc. is so slow to break down in the modern city.

Proof of town planning is less easy to sustain in the case of the ancient cities of Meso-America, either because of modifications which followed occupation of these sites by the Spaniards (cities of the Aztec and Inca), or because the urban civilization was already in decline before Europeans arrived (Mayan). The Aztec city of Tenochtitlan, forerunner of Mexico City, provides some evidence of gridiron layout, however, and Morris refers to the 'rectilinear base' of the Peruvian (Inca) city of Cuzco (1972).

The Medieval tradition

Following the decline of Rome and the 'Dark Ages' that followed, town building revived in Western Europe under the stimulus of trade and manufacturing in the eleventh and succeeding centuries. New towns were founded; others grew from village nuclei following the grant of market charters and acquisition of such privileges as burgage tenure. With the exception of the *bastides* and other planted towns one may say that the medieval town was characterised by greater informality of plan than those of the classical period. Layouts were more adaptive, the conventions that had regulated Greek or Roman town design being rejected in favour of a freer interpretation of what the functions of the town required and the possibilities offered by its site. This more flexible approach produced towns some of which were circular, oval or polygonal in broad outline and within which the arrangement of streets was radial-concentric rather than gridiron. Such outlines and curving street lines were especially common in the Low Countries where, as in Amsterdam, there were practical advantages to be gained from relating the street pattern to the curvature of the canals. In many smaller towns the streets were irregular in direction and of varying width. Certain constraints operated on urban form, however, one being the need for defence. The wall played some part in the arrangement of internal space, its gate fixing the direction of certain town streets for example. Other constraints arose from the requirements of the market and from the demand for space outside the church where the people could gather and plays could be performed. In unplanned towns the market place was often as irregular in outline as the town itself and in some cases evolved by widening of the village street. But at the opposite end of the spectrum there was the *grand' place* of such cities as Brussels and Bruges which, flanked by town hall, court and other distinguished buildings, could be said to carry on the civic tradition of the agora and forum. The medieval town may not have been 'planned' but it displayed a good deal of logic in its layout and, in the case of the larger cities at least, managed to combine aesthetic awareness with a sense of what was practical.

Many new towns were founded in the Middle Ages, especially during the thirteenth and first half of the fourteenth centuries. Some were laid out to a predetermined plan. This was true of the bastides, towns established in Gascony by French or English kings and their vassals, and those built in England and Wales by Edward I. Other towns were planned and closely resemble the bastides, but it would be wrong to suppose that all planted towns were so laid out.

Military control and the settlement of newly-won or developing country were the main reasons for town foundation in the Middle Ages. Defensive burgs had been founded in tenth-century England during the wars between Saxons and Danes. Oxford and Wallingford were both built to control crossings of the Thames and had gridiron plans. But the most remarkable examples of fortified defensive settlements in the United Kingdom are the bastides established by Edward I in the late thirteenth century to control the Welsh. Ten were built, all with castles and a street layout within the walls that was broadly gridiron. Edward's other foundations were the ports of New Winchelsea, which failed to live up to the expectations of the 1280s since many of the chequerboard insulae were never built upon, and Kingston-upon-Hull.

Military considerations played a part in the foundation of bastides in Gascony since this was a frontier over which French and English fought for control. But there was economic incentive also, particularly that provided by the expanding wine trade (Beresford, 1967). Settlers were attracted to the newly-planted towns by the promise of various privileges whilst tolls and taxes were collected from them by the king's agent who, often in partnership with some local landowner, had been responsible for the layout of the initial settlement. Hill-top or river-crossing sites were favoured for their strategic value, none being more spectacular than that of Domme which sits on a limestone crag rising several hundred feet above the River Dordogne. It was not always possible to impose a strict gridiron pattern of streets on such difficult sites and there is a good deal of variation in the plan of the bastides although rectilinear forms predominate. Monpazier is the town which exhibits the most geometrical plan (Fig. 38). Within a rectangle that was once walled, three long and four short streets intersect at right angles and there is a centrally located market square or *place*. The position of the church is also typical, occupying a site to one corner of the square. Churches are strongly built and were usually fortified as a place to which the population could retreat if the walls failed to resist attacks. It was common to give up the whole of one building plot (*ilôt* or chequer) to the market place and another, or half of one, to the church. House plots were allocated within the *ilôts* and are typically long and narrow in shape, separated by narrow passageways. As at Winchelsea some towns failed and plots were never built upon.

Monpazier possesses another feature that was found in many of the bastides although subsequent rebuilding has often resulted in their destruction elsewhere. These are *cornières,* arches that support the projecting upper storeys of houses and shops around

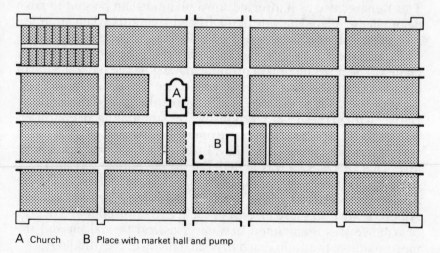

A Church   B Place with market hall and pump

38 Sketch plan of the bastide town of Monpazier

the *place* and form a kind of cloister, although the atmosphere, especially on market day, is far from cloistered.

Medieval planned towns are to be found in other parts of France, notable examples being the crusading port of Aigues-Mortes and the *ville-basse* of Carcassonne which was built to house population removed from the older, hill-top *cité* across the river. Salisbury in England has a history which in some respects parallels that of Carcassonne. In this case the earlier settlement of Old Sarum was wholly abandoned in favour of the new planned town laid out adjacent to the site of his new cathedral by the bishop about 1220. Elsewhere in England, planted towns were usually of more modest proportions, sometimes consisting of no more than a linear extension to some already existing settlement. Such was the case at Thame in Oxfordshire where house plots were allocated on either side of a wide market street following a thirteenth-century diversion of the road from Oxford to Aylesbury.

Similar market-based towns were founded in other parts of Europe, the most impressive of those in which form was dictated by the 'market-street' being the towns such as Berne which were founded in the upper Rhine basin by the Dukes of Zähringen in the late twelfth and early thirteenth centuries.

The Renaissance

The Renaissance as it affected town planning can be said to have begun in the second decade of the fifteenth century when attention was drawn to the manuscript of a Roman architect, Vitruvius, which had survived with other ancient texts in the monastery of St. Gallen. The introduction of printing made possible the diffusion of his ideas and the first of what was to be a succession of commentaries on Vitruvius appeared towards the end of the century. Between them these were responsible for stimulating an enormous interest in all aspects of Graeco-Roman life, including the layout of towns, but the legacy of medieval town-building was not wholly lost. That this was so was largely due to the appearance in 1485, some years after his death, of Leon Battista Alberti's *De Re Aedificatoria*. Whilst it did much to publicize Vitruvius's ideas, Alberti's work was also critical of them and ensured that a degree of balance was maintained between classical formalism and the more adaptive tradition that had been built up in the Middle Ages.

Strangely, since no Roman towns had actually been built in this way, Vitruvius favoured a city that was based on a circular outline with a radial-concentric network of internal roads. The radials were to converge on a central open space, the forum area. Vitruvius's preference for a radial-concentric plan guaranteed its subsequent popularity although some writers, aware of the forms which classical cities had actually taken, could not wholly abandon the gridiron, and rectilinear street patterns were incorporated rather uncomfortably in the plans of cities having a circular or, perhaps octagonal, outline. Such was the case with the designs of Pietro Cataneo (1554) and Danieli Barbaro (1567). In his work Alberti drew attention to the merits of the medieval curved street — the natural line of the walker on foot — which helped to protect the core of the city and presented ever-changing views to the pedestrian. For such reasons as these he wished the city to retain a concentric street pattern but the radials which, in the medieval town, had often been little more than lanes approaching the centre by devious paths, were now opened up into straight, wide streets which created vistas looking both inwards to the city centre and outwards beyond it. In this way Alberti sought to incorporate the new (classical revival) and the best of the older (medieval) tradition.

Although Alberti's writing was unaccompanied by a plan, that of many other commentators was. Emphasis was laid during the Renaissance on the importance of establishing the overall layout of a town and they produced many designs of what was thought to be 'the ideal city'. Numerous schemes appeared from the late fifteenth century, including those of Antonio Filarete, Francesco di Giorgio Martini, and Vincenzo Scamozzi who, like Cataneo and Barbaro referred to above, produced an ideal city plan which was based on a grid pattern (Fig. 39). These, and others, are described and illustrated by Morris and by Burke (1971). Some of the designs were wholly impracticable and few complete towns were built to a 'Vitruvian' plan. Principles derived from the designs were, however, incorporated in rebuilding or town extension schemes and before referring to particular examples of these it is necessary to establish what such principles were.

Fortification of the city was a major preoccupation of Renaissance city designers, so great in fact that Morris is able to point to city defences as the main determinant of urban form in continental Europe. It was the use of cannon from the middle of the fifteenth century that revolutionized urban defences, adding to city walls, unable alone to withstand the new weapon, elaborate systems of bastions, earthen ramparts, gun emplacements and wide moats.

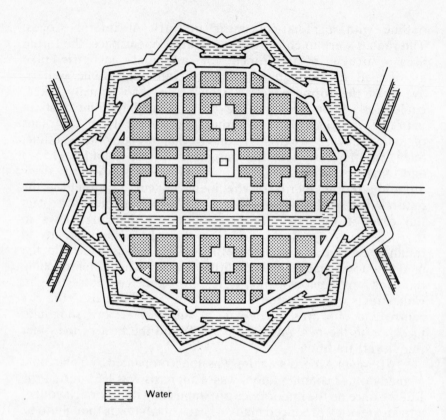

Water

39   Scamozzi's 'ideal city'

One of the principal objects was to increase the distance between enemy cannon and the city. A consequence of this was that the outward growth of the built-up area was checked and housing densities rose. In some cases the fortifications have continued to influence the spatial structure of the city to the present day.

The sixteenth century witnessed increased use of horse-drawn carriages and town streets were widened and straightened to accommodate the new traffic. This, as we have seen, applied most typically to the radials linking the town gates to the centre. It, too, had military significance, permitting cannon to be fired from within the city as a final line of defence, if the gates could not be held. In addition these processional ways had great aesthetic appeal, creating vistas, and it became common practice to add to their visual impact by adding sculptures and other architectural devices at road crossings or to round off the view at the end of the street.

A third feature of the Renaissance city distinguishing it from its medieval predecessor lay in its use of open spaces including the ornamental garden. At first these were modest and restrained. Town villas set in their own gardens were to be found in the cities of sixteenth century Italy. Small *piazzas* and squares were built, sometimes but not always symmetrically arranged within the new town or urban extension. In time the use of open space became more elaborate and formal. Private parks, tree-lined avenues, statuary and fountains were all incorporated into the design of the city, being most typical of seventeenth-century Paris and other French cities. By the following century the popularity of such embellishments had grown to the extent that in a number of towns the arrangement of open spaces and vistas can be said to have taken over the plan of the town as a whole. This was true of Versailles and of Karlsruhe where the grandiose design triumphs completely over the needs of the ordinary population who had to live there. Similar strictures apply to L'Enfant's plan (1789) for the new American capital of Washington. The Renaissance brought back systematization to town planning. Reasoned principles were applied to design and where possible the town was treated as a single unit. This gave coherence and much that was attractive and satisfying. But the plans for towns such as Karlsruhe show how easy it is for guiding principles to become formalized and rigid, as indeed was the case with later classical design from which the inspiration of the Renaissance was drawn.

Although the influence of the Renaissance lay more in the restructuring of existing towns there were, nevertheless, new foundations which reflect in their overall plan the principles outlined above. Since many were created, either to add to the defence of a vulnerable political frontier, or in connection with the building of some palace, it is hardly surprising that they should do so. An example of the former category is Palma Nova, a Venetian frontier town begun in 1593, its design usually attributed to Scamozzi. It is radial-concentric in plan with small piazzas and complete encircling fortifications, in many ways the epitome of the 'ideal city'. Similar fortress towns were built in the frontier zone between French and Dutch influence in what is now Belgium. Here both Mariembourg and Philippeville date from the mid-sixteenth century. A gridiron layout of streets was preferred in some planned towns although these, too, incorporated open spaces and were protected by elaborate defences. Vitry-le-François, Francis I's new town on the Marne, founded in 1545, is a very restrained and formal example, almost Roman in its grid plan. But at Charleville, built alongside the Meuse between 1608 and 1620, there is more imaginative use of *places* and of formal gardens, the beginning of that process of 'naturalization' referred to above.

The example of Charleville was influential in the redesign of many French cities, including Paris. Opportunity also arose from the capture of Flanders in 1667 and the appointment by Louis XIV of Sebastian de Vauban to undertake the defensive reorganization of towns. He is credited with having fortified some 300 of them and of having built about 30 new towns. Of these the Rhine garrison town of Neuf Brisach, begun in 1698, is probably the best known. It was built to a regular gridiron plan and incorporated a large central parade ground. This particular tradition of militaristic planning survived and is seen in the rebuilding of the Vendéan town of La-Roche-sur-Yon under Napoleon in 1804. The desire to create an appropriate setting for some noble building is the other main thread running through Renaissance rebuilding and many cities acquired their *place royale* or similarly named space during the seventeenth and eighteenth centuries. In a few instances a new town was built at the palace gates. Examples include both the restrained and orderly little town of Richelieu, begun in 1631, and the far more artificial Versailles which, between them, represent the range of opportunity that was afforded to the Renaissance planner when the necessity of defence was removed.

In other European countries the influence of the Renaissance was felt in urban redesign especially of the capital cities. Of the relatively small number of 'new towns', Mannheim, rebuilt and refortified more than once in the seventeenth century, is interesting as a further example of the survival of strict gridiron planning of a kind associated more with the colonial tradition. The town planting movement that began in Ulster in 1609 was also responsible for the creation of gridiron settlements, Londonderry and Coleraine providing good examples, but the circumstances here were clearly ones of colonization. In Britain, Renaissance ideas were popularized through the work of Inigo Jones who began the Queen's House, Greenwich, the first important building in the classical style, in 1619 and created the first London square, Covent Garden, in the early 1630s. The building of squares, palladian terraces and crescents followed in other cities. The addition of Craig's New Town to Edinburgh after 1765 is, however, on a scale more commonly associated with continental than with British cities. Elsewhere the nearest approximation to planned town development is to be seen in the Georgian and Regency spa towns, Bath being the outstanding example of what the classical revival could offer.

Nineteenth-century idealism

Whilst it is generally true to say that the Industrial Revolution led to the expansion of existing towns rather than the creation of new ones, and that urban growth was at first largely uncontrolled, it is inevitable that there should be exceptions to such generalizations. Some towns were established *de novo* and the initial layout was usually planned, albeit rarely going beyond a simple gridiron. Whitehaven, Middlesbrough and, later, Barrow-in-Furness are well-known examples, but there are numerous other small settlements in North-East Scotland, North Wales and elsewhere which were founded in connection with expanding linen, fishing, slate and other industries in the eighteenth and nineteenth centuries. The building of canals and subsequently railways gave rise to what were virtually company towns (Porteous, 1970). Goole in Yorkshire was the creation of the Aire and Calder Navigation Company in 1826 and had several categories of housing, those for company officials presenting an imposing facade when the town was approached by water. Examples of railway towns are more numerous and include New Swindon built in the 1840s, its parallel rows of cottages with small front gardens representing a higher standard in 'working class' housing than was common at the time.

But townships like New Swindon were exceptional and urban development in early nineteenth-century Britain was more often mean, unplanned and squalid of the kind described by Friedrich Engels in his *Condition of the Working Class in England* (1845). Reaction to this took many forms. Some, like the Chartists, advocated a return to the land. Others, more realistically, sought to improve the urban environment from within by attention to factory conditions, public health and other matters. Out of the mainstream of this concern for the city as a place in which to live came a movement which, tracing its origins from the experiments carried out at New Lanark by Robert Owen at the beginning of the nineteenth century, culminated in the Garden City Movement and the founding of Letchworth in the early years of the twentieth century. It was a movement that embraced a variety of ideals: the Aristotelian principle aimed at limiting urban growth to a certain size; the socialist idea of the commune; Renaissance preoccupation with city-plan; and romanticism with its interest in nature and a belief that town and country could be brought together to create a new and more satisfying urban environment. Much was utopian; some schemes never left the drawing board, and experiments were tried which failed. But from it all came a range of ideas which in the present century have had great influence in urban planning, not least on the design of new towns built since 1946.

The industrial township of New Lanark, with its four cotton mills and rows of workers' cottages, was built by a Scottish banker, David Dale in partnership with Richard Arkwright. Owen took over its administration in 1799 after marrying into the Dale family and proceeded to enlarge the houses in order to relieve over-crowding, to abolish child labour, and to establish a school, cooperative shop and an 'Institute for the Formation of Character'. More influential, however, than his alterations to the fabric of New Lanark were his publications which drew attention to the need for social considerations in planning. He advocated communal 'vil-lages of unity and mutual cooperation', but attempts to set up these model communities all failed including Owen's American exper-iments which included New Harmony in Indiana.

More ambitious than Owen's villages was J. S. Buckingham's plan for a town which he called Victoria and which appeared in *National Evils and Practical Remedies* published in 1849. It was a symmetrical design made up of eight concentric squares inter-sected by eight radial avenues to which he gave the improving names of Faith, Hope, Charity, Fortitude, Concord, Peace, Unity and Justice (Fig. 40). It was intended that each of the squares would accommodate a different land use or category of society, ranging from 'members of the government and the more important capitalists' whose mansions would surround the innermost square to 'the lowest orders' on the periphery. Three of the squares were reserved for light industry, shops and public open space; the others for intermediate social classes which included 'superintendents of labour' and professional persons. Buckingham intended his town to have a total population of no more than 10 000. If it grew beyond this, 'home colonies' would be founded as had happened in Hellenistic Greece.

Buckingham's plan seems rigid in design and naive in its treatment of social classes. Yet in its incorporation of open space, in the separation of industry from housing, and in the provision it made for sanitation, is offered living conditions that were far superior to those which prevailed in many industrial towns and it points the way to the garden city. There were other plans, just as utopian. In *The Happy Colony* (1854), Robert Pemberton pro-duced a design for Queen Victoria Town which was to be built on an island in the Pacific. Apart from being circular, rather than square in outline, it had much in common with Buckingham's Victoria. A later scheme, reflecting the concern that was felt for public health in the 1870s, was Benjamin Ward Richardson's plan

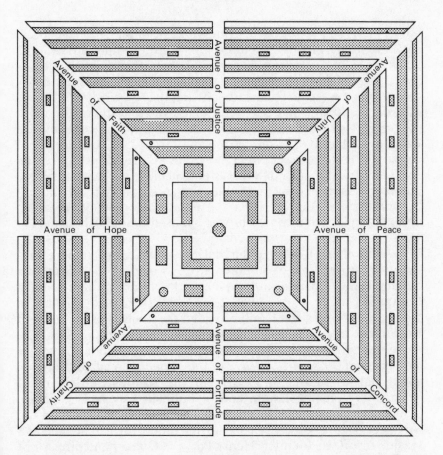

Avenue of Justice

Avenue of Faith

Avenue of Unity

Avenue of Hope

Avenue of Peace

Avenue of Charity

Avenue of Fortitude

Avenue of Concord

40 J. S. Buckingham's plan for the model town of Victoria

for a city of 100 000 people which he called Hygea, the city of
health.

It is one thing to draw plans, another to build cities, as experience in sixteenth-century Italy had shown. The nineteenth century
did not lack industrialists who, from philanthropic or other
motives, were prepared to build housing for their workers, but
their efforts were largely confined to the establishment of planned
'industrial colonies' (Chapter 1) and few were interested in the
creation of whole new towns. Copley and Akroydon in Halifax
belong to the former category (Scargill, 1963) but Saltaire, four
miles outside Bradford and with 850 houses in its 22 streets, may
be considered a planned new town. It is unremarkable in its layout
of dwellings, parallel rows having no open spaces between them,
but provision was made for the social needs of the population that
was well in advance of its time. There were almshouses, a hospital,

public baths and washhouse, schools and a Congregational church, park, and an institute building for cultural and educational activities. The houses too, in spite of their rather sombre appearance, were of far better quality than those being built in nearby towns. There were no back-to-backs and the rows included houses of differing height and size. This made them aesthetically more pleasing; it also ensured a degree of social mixing since houses were available for different income groups or categories of employee. Saltaire was built in the 1850s and 1860s and it may be considered that social mix was easier to achieve in the years before public transport became available. But such comment should not be permitted to detract from the importance of Saltaire as an attempt to plan for a community as opposed to simply housing the workers.

A number of other industrial townships were being established about the time of Saltaire. Bromborough in the Wirral was built by J. and G. Wilson around the works of Price's Patent Candle Company, which had moved from Battersea. Near Newry in Northern Ireland a linen mill provided the nucleus of the town of Bessbrook, begun by J. G. Richardson, a Quaker, in 1846. The movement was not confined to the United Kingdom. Examples may be cited of the *cité ouvrière* of the Menier chocolate company at Noisiel-sur-Marne in France, of the Krupps' settlement of Kronenberg outside Essen, and of Pullman City near Chicago. Unusual circumstances surrounded the origin of Saltburn on the North Yorkshire coast, perhaps the first model town to be built as a seaside resort. Its founder, Henry Pease, a Quaker and director of the Stockton and Darlington railway company, claimed to have had a vision of the 'celestial city' as he sat on a nearby cliff. He persuaded the company to extend its line to the coast, built the magnificent Zetland hotel, and adjacent to it the town. White brick was used to accord with the vision and the streets were given the names of jewels: Emerald, Pearl, Ruby etc.

Pease, like other new town builders in the nineteenth century, was a man of deeply-held religious beliefs with a desire to better the lot of his fellow men, as had the Cadburys. As a young man George Cadbury had studied the progress of Bessbrook and in 1893 he began to lay out an estate around the chocolate-making factory that had been moved from central Birmingham some years before. Bournville deservedly became famous, not only for the quality and design of its housing, but also for the use made of open space including gardens, recreation grounds, parks and tree-lined roads. A similar informal layout with low density housing and abundant open space was used by W. H. Lever, the soap manufacturer, at Port Sunlight begun in 1888.

The creation of Port Sunlight and Bournville owed much to the lead of Salt and others in establishing model townships — a 'Society for Promoting Industrial Villages' had even been formed in 1883 — but it was also a product of nineteenth-century romanticism, the age of Ruskin, William Morris and W. R. Lethaby. Influential so far as the planning of towns was concerned was the publication in 1889 of *The Art of Building Cities* by the Viennese architect, Camillo Sitte. He had studied the use made of open space in European cities of the Middle Ages and Renaissance and wrote of the need to restore art and beauty to those of the nineteenth century. In the United States his and other writing gave rise to what became known as the 'City Beautiful' movement. In Britain this attitude to beauty in towns is to be found in the work of the architect Raymond Unwin, whose *Town Planning in Practice: An Introduction to the Art of Designing Cities and Suburbs* was published at the turn of the century. In 1901 he and his partner, Barry Parker, began work for the Rowntree family on the building of New Earswick outside York and two years later he was invited by Ebenezer Howard to produce a plan for the first garden city at Letchworth.

Born in London in 1850, Ebenezer Howard spent most of his life as a shorthand writer. It was an unlikely background for a new town visionary but he had two qualities which, combined, were to make him the most influential British planner of the last hundred years. The first was his inventiveness — he spent much time trying to perfect a shorthand writing machine — and the second was a desire for social reform that sprang from his religious convictions. Like Titus Salt, he was a Congregationalist and it was with his socially-concious nonconformist friends that he looked into the housing problems of cities and the relationship between these and such factors as land values and ownership. As a young man he spent some time in Chicago, known up to the fire of 1871 as the Garden City, and he may have been impressed by the opportunities that existed in the Mid-West at that time for new town design. He was aware of Buckingham's plan for Victoria and was influenced also by the work of the American Edward Bellamy who, in 1888, had published *Looking Backward,* a utopian account of a city in which men were equal and most labour was performed by machine. Such writings led Howard to picture the ideal town as a socialist community in which all work was carried on collectively. These views became modified as he sought to design a town that was workable.

Howard's garden city diagram appeared in his book *Tomorrow: A Peaceful Path to Real Reform* which was published in 1898 but revised in 1902 under the title of *Garden Cities of Tomorrow* (Fig. 41). The city was to have a population of no more than 30 000, be self-supporting in terms of manufacturing employment, and around it there was to be a green belt of agricultural land, a part of the town estate that would support an additional 'rural' population of around 2000. The outline of the proposed garden city was circular to minimize distances for pedestrians and six radial boulevards divided it into six sectors or wards. At the centre was to be a garden overlooked by the principal public buildings of the town. Surrounding this would be parkland

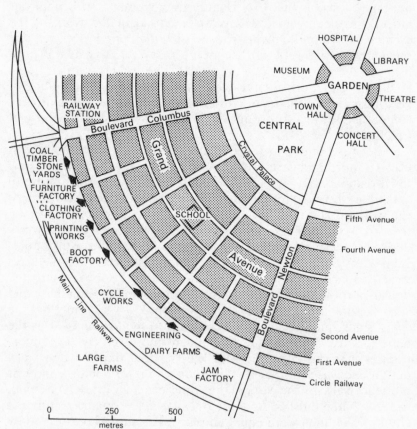

41   A portion of Ebenezer Howard's proposed garden city. (Courtesy Faber and Faber)

with, further out, successive rings of shops, housing grouped around village green nuclei, more open space as a setting for churches and schools and, on the perimeter, a factory belt served by railway. To ensure that development was controlled, ownership of the town estate was to be held in trust by a company which would receive ground rents and, after payment of interest on money raised to build the town, would pay the balance to the town council.

Howard went beyond the design of a single garden city. As population grew this would be channelled into other such towns until a 'social city' had been built up consisting of six satellites around a central core city of some 60 000 population. The satellites were to be linked by road and rail both to this central city and to each other. The total population of a quarter of a million would enable the social city to support services of a higher order than a single garden city could have done, without the problems that arise when these are concentrated in one place. This part of Howard's plan received little attention at the time but it has acquired considerable relevance in an age of metropolitan and sub-regional planning (Fig. 42).

It was never intended by Howard that his 'diagram' would be reproduced in precise detail when a garden city came to be built. It established guidelines for the architects — Unwin and Parker at Letchworth, Louis de Soissons at Welwyn — who were free to relate the detail of the plan to local circumstances. Work on Letchworth, 35 miles north of London, began in 1903 a few years after the formation by Howard and others of the Garden City Association in 1899. The plan anticipated a population of 30 000 but only one grand boulevard was incorporated in the design for the town. Other roads, however, were of generous width (40-100 feet) and had tree-lined grass verges. Houses, of varied design, all had front and rear gardens and the overall density ranged from 6 to 12 houses per acre. Land was set aside for industry next to the railway, and also for what proved to be a rather conventional shopping centre.

The Letchworth experiment was not followed by the rash of garden cities for which Howard had hoped, yet it had great influence, particularly on the layout of housing estates in existing towns. 'Garden Suburbs' were also built. Hampstead Garden Suburb was begun in 1905, to the design of Unwin and Parker, and the example was followed in other cities. Not all were middle class. Woodlands, a colliery township near Doncaster was established in association with a new coal mine sunk in 1906. Well-built houses with gardens

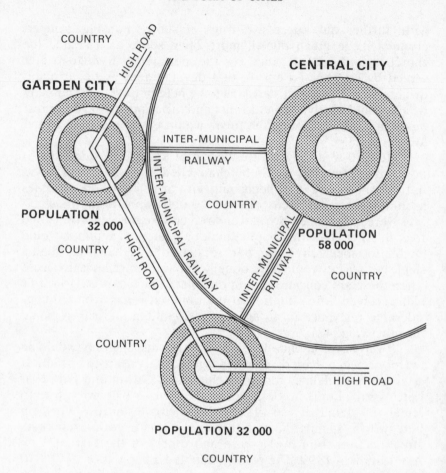

42   A portion of Ebenezer Howard's proposed 'social city', illustrating the 'correct principle' of a city's growth. (Courtesy Faber and Faber)

were set amongst tree-lined streets and recreational open spaces, a remarkable contrast with conditions in most colliery settlements at that time. In 1918 the Tudor Walters Committee, of which Raymond Unwin was a member, published a report which laid down minimum standards for public housing. Their recommendation of 12 houses to the acre was widely adopted when, the following year, the Housing Act made it possible for the first time for local authorities to undertake housing projects on a large scale (Chapter 1).

Work on a second garden city was begun at Welwyn in 1920. As at Letchworth the design is based on a single boulevard but this is of striking proportions and terminates in the kind of garden core which Howard envisaged in his 'diagram'. Welwyn is also noteworthy for the elegance of its 'Georgian'-style housing and for the control that was exercised over the layout of its shopping centre which is of unusual spaciousness. In 1948 Welwyn Garden City became one of London's New Towns and the town thus provides visible continuity between the aims of Ebenezer Howard and the objectives of post-World War II planners.

New Towns of the United Kingdom

When in 1976 it was decided not to undertake for the time being any more new town projects in the United Kingdom, work was already in progress on 32 such towns.* Fourteen of them had been designated between 1946, when the New Towns Act was passed, and 1950, and they may be regarded as the first generation of new towns. Only one site was added during the 1950s, at Cumbernauld in Scotland. The remainder, the second generation, have followed since 1960. Certain differences in approach to new town building are evident between the two main phases of designation which makes the division into two generations a valid one.

In 1944 the Abercrombie Plan for Greater London had proposed a ring of ten new towns in order to help solve problems of overcrowding and urban renewal in the capital. The idea of using new towns for this purpose was not entirely new. After the plagues of 1484-85 in Milan, Leonardo da Vinci had produced a plan which involved dispersal of some of the city's population to ten new towns, each designed for a population of about 30 000. He even anticipated Radburn principles of traffic separation by including high- and low-level roads in his plan for a rebuilt Milan. Following Abercrombie's report a committee under Lord Reith was appointed to advise on new town construction. This committee recommended that in order that new towns be more than mere satellites of the large cities, they should be built at a distance of at least 40 km from central London or 20 km from the centre of other cities. It was further suggested that their population should be not less than 20 000, considered to be the minimum necessary to support a certain range of services, and not larger than 60 000 in order that people could reach the countryside by walking and could walk or cycle to work. Many of Reith's recommendations were included in the New Towns Act. In the next few years eight new town sites were designated to serve principally as overspill centres

* At the same time the decision was taken not to proceed with another new town, at Stonehouse near Glasgow, in order to concentrate resources on urban renewal in Glasgow itself.

for London. Of the remaining six of the first generation, some, such as East Kilbride outside Glasgow, also had this role, but others were intended to act primarily as small growth poles in the commercially depressed 'Development Areas'. Cwmbran in South Wales and Aycliffe in Durham fall into this category, whilst Glenrothes in Fife and Peterlee in East Durham had a somewhat similar role but on what were thought to be expanding coalfields.

With one or two exceptions the first generation of new towns were designed to receive population until a total of around 60 000 had been reached, the upper end of the Reith 'optimum'. In a number of them the target has since been raised to over 100 000. Housing has taken the form to a large extent of short terraces, built either alongside the road or arranged around cul-de-sacs or courts, and overall densities are similar to those in the new housing estates of many existing cities. There are few tall apartment blocks. In the early 1960s the average amount of land consumed by the new towns was 22 hectares per 1000 persons. The proportion of housing that is rented, mainly from the Development Corporation, is higher than the national average, around 80 per cent, but varies from town to town. The degree to which sale of property and private development have been encouraged has also varied according to the political climate of the country as a whole. The plans of all the new towns included one or more areas set aside for manufacturing industry and employment policies have been successful insofar as most of them have job ratios of at least 100 per cent.

In addition to incorporating land use zoning, these early new towns were mainly built on the neighbourhood principle. This idea, though by no means new, was popularized in the early part of the present century by the American, Clarence Perry. Perry's interest in the neighbourhood arose from a study of the uses to which school buildings could be put out of school hours and in the holidays. He also lived in Forest Hills, New York, where he had experience of a wide range of community activities, and in 1929 he put forward his plan of the neighbourhood unit in a Regional Survey of New York (Fig. 43). At the centre of his neighbourhood was a primary school and this fixed both the population total of the neighbourhood—he thought a population total of 5000 would support such a school—and its areal extent since it was intended that all children should be able to walk to school (Perry, 1929). Recreational open space was attached to the school which would act as a community centre, and small play areas were dispersed through the neighbourhood. Shops were grouped at the edge, near

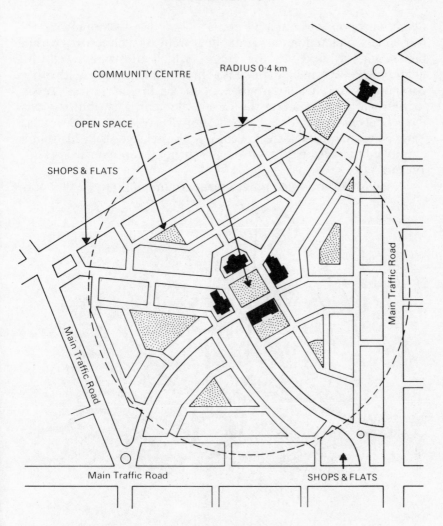

COMMUNITY CENTRE   RADIUS 0·4 km

OPEN SPACE

SHOPS & FLATS

Main Traffic Road

Main Traffic Road

Main Traffic Road

SHOPS & FLATS

43   Clarence Perry's design for a neighbourhood unit. (Courtesy Faber and Faber, *Homes, Towns and Traffic*)

traffic junctions, where they could serve more than one neighbourhood and sell higher order goods than one unit alone could justify. Siting the shops here would also reduce traffic within the neighbourhood and help to maintain what Perry described as the 'residential environment'. This was to be achieved further by using main traffic arteries to provide the boundaries to the neighbourhoods and by limiting heavy traffic within the neighbourhood to its own street system.

Perry's ideas were influential in the design of early new town neighbourhoods although his choice of site for a shopping centre was widely rejected in favour of a hierarchy of such centres within the neighbourhood. In Stevenage, which illustrates well the neighbourhood principle, there is a three-tier hierarchy, with other community facilities sited adjacent to the larger centres, and a 'corner shop' constituting the lowest element. Distributor roads have been used to demarcate the neighbourhoods, however, as Perry advocated, and different coloured street signs have also been employed to assist in creating neighbourhood consciousness (Figs. 17 and 44).

Neighbourhood size ranges from around 5000 to 12 000 per-

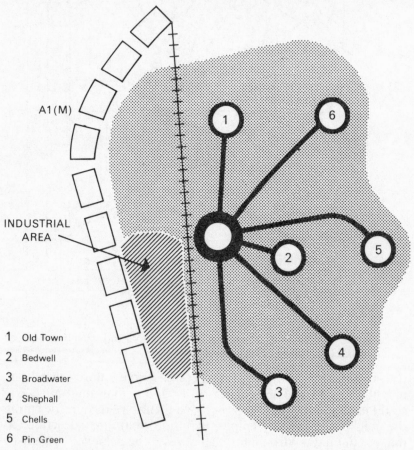

A1(M)

INDUSTRIAL
AREA

1   Old Town

2   Bedwell

3   Broadwater

4   Shephall

5   Chells

6   Pin Green

44   The neighbourhood principle as interpreted in the Master Plan of Stevenage, 1966. (Courtesy Stevenage Development Corporation). Examine in conjunction with Fig. 17

sons, related in part to the overall size of the new town. Their design has also been affected by the choice of architect to draw up the town's master plan. The use of sub-neighbourhoods has been favoured in some cases, the intention being at the local level to help create a sense of place and community, and at the level of the neighbourhood as a whole to bring about a degree of social mixing by creating a variety of living conditions. The planning of such units is also related to the hierarchical provision of educational, retail and other services.

All the new towns have a 'downtown', a main shopping and service centre. These incorporate traffic-free areas, although the principle of the pedestrian precinct was not invariably followed in the initial layout of the centre. Growth in the use of the private car was, in fact, generally underestimated in the design of the early new towns, and the greater mobility which the car affords is one of the main reasons why the neighbourhood principle has received less emphasis in the design of the second generation of new towns. It was soon shown, for example, that the main shopping centre was more popular than had been expected and that shoppers would bypass the neighbourhood centre to use it.

The neighbourhood idea was not used in the original design for Cumbernauld, the Scottish new town designated in 1955, although upward revision of the planned population total has necessitated a degree of residential subdivision. Cumbernauld has been built to a compactness and density which is unusual in British new towns but which may be said to reflect a Scottish tradition of higher density urban living. The design also made greater provision for the use of the motor vehicle than earlier new town plans had done. It incorporates, for example, a spine road running beneath a split-level town centre. Like Cumbernauld the succeeding second generation of new towns have also attempted to come to terms with the motor car and extensive use has been made of the Radburn principle involving separation of pedestrians and vehicular traffic.

Radburn, a small town in New Jersey, USA, had been planned by Clarence Stein and Henry Wright in the late 1920s. Main distributor roads enclosed 'superblocks', small neighbourhoods of 12-20 hectares within which the houses were built around cul-de-sacs. From the rear of the houses there was access to these service roads; from the front a system of footpaths linked by underpasses beneath the roads gave safe pedestrian access to shops and schools (Fig. 45). As a new town experiment Radburn foundered in the economic crisis of the 1930s which helps to explain why the traffic principles it incorporated were slow to be adopted

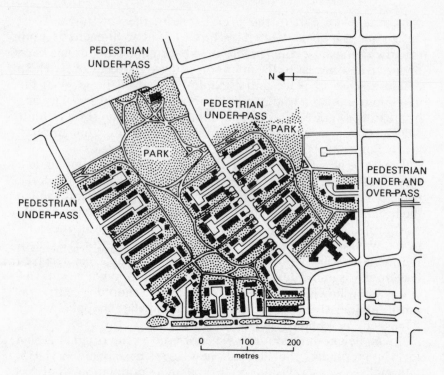

45   A portion of the town of Radburn, illustrating the principle of
     vehicular and pedestrian segregation. After Tetlow and Goss, 1965.
     (Courtesy Faber and Faber)

elsewhere. Yet in recent years attempts have been made to introduce pedestrian and cycle ways into even the older new town
neighbourhoods. The difference in road pattern between such a
neighbourhood and a more recent addition to the town is apparent
in the plan of Stevenage where the area known as Pin Green in the
north was built along Radburn lines.

   In spite of the obvious convenience of a linear design for
traffic movement, no new town in Britain has been built to the kind
of design which the Spanish engineer, Arturo Soria y Mata,
suggested as early as 1882. His vertebrate plan had a central
reservation for main road and railway with access from this spinal
column to residential, industrial and other functional areas of the
town, equivalent to the individual vertebrae (Fig. 46). A section of
'linear city' was built outside Madrid in the 1890s, but lacking as it
does a focus or centre it has never had the attraction of radial-
concentric plan or some variant of the latter. Yet elements of what
may be regarded as linear planning have been included in the

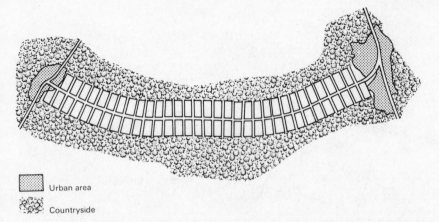

Urban area

Countryside

46   Diagram of a linear city proposed by Soria y Mata. (Courtesy
     Edward Arnold)

designs of several second generation new towns. The plan of Run-
corn, for example, includes an urban freeway in the form of a
figure-of-eight along which buses have reserved lanes. It constitutes a kind of urban spine yet its shape permits the town to be
served by a conventional 'down-town' which is at the central
crossroads.

   The projected population of several of the second generation
of new towns is well in excess of that contemplated when the earlier
ones were planned, reaching a quarter of a million in some cases.
Another difference lies in the choice of already quite sizeable
towns such as Northampton, Peterborough and Warrington for
expansion under the New Towns Act. Accompanying the growth
of interest in regional planning since about 1960, new towns have
also acquired a role in regional strategies. This is evident, for
example, in the government White Paper for Central Scotland
published in 1963 and in various reports on South East England:
the *South East Study* (1964), *A Strategy for the South East* (1967),
and the *Strategic Plan for the South East* (1970). Sub-regional
planning takes into account the effect which new towns have upon
each other and on other settlements nearby. Interest of this kind,
for example, has been focused on the Northampton, Peterborough
and Milton Keynes group of new towns in a part of eastern England
where there are, in addition to these three, a number of smaller
towns experiencing planned expansion under the Town Development Act of 1952. Such planning, which observes the complementary relationships between towns, is reminiscent of the
ideas which lay behind Howard's 'Social City'.

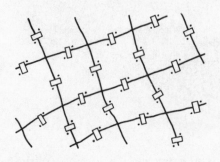

**POTENTIAL BUS STOP AND
ACTIVITY CENTRE LOCATIONS**

☐   Activity centre location

·   Bus stops

—   Main road

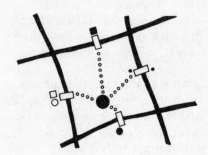

**ACTIVITIES WITHIN
WALKING DISTANCE**

●   Shops

■   Middle school

☐   First school

·   Bus stop

○   Local employment

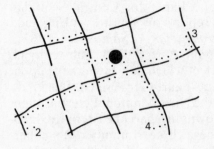

**ACTIVITIES WHICH CAN BE
REACHED BY BUS OR CAR**

1   Supermarket

2   Coffee bar

3   Health centre

4   Gardening club

47 'Activity centres' at Milton Keynes. After Evans, 1972. (Courtesy
    Charles Knight)

On a scale which comes even closer to that envisaged by Howard, the plan for Milton Keynes likewise makes use of the idea of complementary nodes (Fig. 47). The design of this new town, with a projected population of 250 000, is based on the assumption that service centres in the contemporary city are coming increasingly to exhibit complementary rather than hierarchical relationships (Chapter 4). Higher order services are thus to be provided from nodal points in different parts of the new town — a health campus, a higher education campus and so forth. Such an arrangement presupposes a good deal of cross-movement of traffic and to facilitate that the plan of the new town is based on a grid of distributor roads spaced at approximately 1 km intervals. This interval, it is considered, will avoid the danger of traffic congestion at intersections. 'Activity centres' offering shops and schools are situated, not in the middle of residential areas, but alongside these main roads in a similar way to that advocated by Perry in his neighbourhood plan. Pedestrian paths will converge at these points (Evans, 1972). The return to favour of the grid plan at Milton Keynes is interesting in view of its long history in town planning. But since the new town will extend over more than 60 sq km and have a net residential density of only 20 houses per hectare, care must obviously be taken in seeking too close parallels with the tradition represented by Miletus and Monpazier.

New towns in other countries

Western Europe
In selecting sites for new towns in the United Kingdom it has generally been policy to allow sufficient distance between them and the major cities to avoid undue dependence on the latter for employment and services. The desire for self-containment is less evident in other countries of Western Europe, however, where new towns are more often satellites of the city and are built as part of a plan aimed at metropolitan decongestion rather than decentralization. Vällingby, Farsta and Skärholmen in Sweden, Albertslund in Denmark and Tapiola in Finland are all within 10-15 km by road or rail from the centres of their respective capital cities. The five new towns under construction as part of the Schéma Directeur for Paris are similarly within a distance that allows for relatively easy travel to the city for work. Of the four provincial new towns in France, Lille-Est belongs to the 'satellite' category, but L'Isle d'Abeau (35 km south-east of Lyon), Le Vaudreuil (25 km south-east of Rouen) and Etang-de-Berre (built in connection

with the new industrial complex at Fos) have more in common with the British new towns. So too do the new towns planned at a distance of some· 40 km from the centre of Budapest.

A higher proportion of the dwellings are in the form of apartments in continental new towns than in British ones. In Sweden the proportion is as high as 85 per cent (Merlin, 1969), giving high densities but permitting easy access to the extensions of the underground railway system which links the new towns to central Stockholm. At Vällingby, for example, each of the four 'neighbourhood' units has tall flats grouped round a small commercial centre and these decrease in height to a distance of some 500 m, considered to be a reasonable walking distance from the railway station. There are individual houses beyond, but in general the Swedish new towns reflect what Merlin describes as 'the mastery by Scandiavian architects of the art of composing masses'. Scandinavian new towns also enjoy a high reputation for landscaping, none more so than the Finnish town of Tapiola which is renowned for its use of lakes and woodland.

Eastern Europe

In the USSR and Eastern Europe the most common reasons for establishing new towns have been economic ones: to house the workers engaged in some new manufacturing enterprise or in the exploitation of mineral or other resources, and to assist in bringing about a better economic balance within the country as a whole. They are not dissimilar from the motives that led to the siting of new towns in the British Development Areas and adjacent to the iron and steel works at Corby in Northamptonshire. A planned town was founded at Salzgitter in Germany as early as 1942 in connection with iron workings in the Harz Mountains and in recent years new towns have been built in a number of 'developing' countries, usually on the basis of newly found oil wealth, but also to accommodate the labour force of a major industrial project as at Cuidad Guyana (Venezuela) and Jamshedpur (India). The founding of Brasilia is in a tradition of planned capital cities that includes both Washington and Canberra, but the choice of site was also determined by the wish to bring about economic development in the interior of Brazil. Combined economic and political motives likewise influenced the building of Chandigarh, founded after the Punjab capital of Lahore became a part of Pakistan.

All of the eight new towns founded in Hungary before 1961 were built in connection with some form of industrial development. Typical of this phase are Dunaujvaros, 70 km south of

Budapest, which was founded in 1949 adjacent to an iron works, and Komlo, established soon afterwards on the Pecs coalfield to send coke to Dunaujvaros. The latter may be taken as representative of these 'socialist' new towns. It has been planned on the basis of neighbourhoods, each with a population of some 5000 and local services which include shops and a primary school. Housing is mainly in apartment blocks. As in other parts of the socialist world these were mostly of economy, five-storey construction at first, but taller ones have been built subsequently. Housing pro-.vision tended in the early years to lag behind the growth in employment and inward commuting from nearby villages, from which the population of the new towns was principally drawn, was common as was a dominance of men in the sex ratio of the population. The very low ratio of personal car ownership meant that little provision needed to be made for pedestrian and traffic segregation of the Radburn kind.

New towns were founded in Poland in the early postwar years for similar reasons to those in other socialist countries. Typical are Nowa Huta, associated with an iron-making complex to the east of Cracow, and Nowe Tychy in Upper Silesia which was intended to act as a focus of industrial development on the coalfield but which has tended to become something of a satellite to Katowice, having good rail connections with this city. Nowe Tychy was designated in 1950; it has a roughly rectangular plan, north-south and east-west axes dividing the town into neighbourhoods. In each of these the housing is mainly in the form of apartment blocks of three to five storeys, but rising to eight to twelve storeys near the centre of the town. The neighbourhoods separate an area of individual housing to the west from the industrial zone of the new town which lies to the east.

New town policies in the socialist countries have matured since the early 1960s. There is less exclusive concern with the promotion of major industrial projects and greater use of new towns as overspill or dormitory settlements, even as recreational centres. This shift in emphasis is apparent in the Hungarian National Plan of 1963 and the scheme for new towns outside Budapest to which reference was made above. Bulgaria, alone, now claims to have 66 new towns, ranging in size from Dimitrovgrad with a population of some 50 000 to several with only 2000 or 3000 (F. W. Carter, 1975).

USA
American interest in new towns dates from the visit of Clarence

Stein to Letchworth in 1920 and his subsequent experiments in
partnership with Henry Wright at Sunnyside (New York) and
Radburn. Government involvement dates from 1935 when, following the Depression, it was decided by the Roosevelt administration to create garden cities or 'greenbelt towns', to help solve the
housing shortage. Three such towns were built: Greenbelt in Maryland, Greendale near Milwaukee in Wisconsin, and Greenhills
outside Cincinnati, Ohio. They failed to attract industry, and
became little more than dormitory suburbs, but precedents had
been established both in the use of garden city principles and in
government participation. All, however, were sold to private
enterprise in 1949.

New towns built since the Second World War in the United
States are typically of the satellite kind, situated in most cases close
to the metropolitan fringe. They are the products of private enterprise to a much greater extent than is common in Europe. Promoters, for example, assume the responsibility for assembling sufficient land on which to build a new town and this has the effect of
imposing huge financial burdens from the start. Largely for this
reason the promoters of the new town of Reston in Virginia were
bankrupted in 1967. The Gulf Oil Company subsequently took
over the assets of the town and has continued its development since
that date. Revenues are obtained from commercial and industrial
properties, which are often rented, but in the absence of government pressure directing industry to the new towns, the promoters are likely to be dependent on commuters for their earliest
customers. Land for housing is resold by the promoters and
development undertaken by building societies and other organizations. In 1971 only 15 per cent of the working population of
Columbia (Maryland) were employed in the new town but the
proportion was expected to rise following General Electric's decision to open a large factory there. Merlin (1969) has suggested that
the desire for prestige rather than employment opportunities has
often guided the search for commercial and industrial under-
takings.

Both Reston and Columbia have attractive sites and as at
Tapiola good use has been made of woodland and lakes in the
layout of the new towns. Plans also make use of the neighbourhood
idea in an attempt to create a sense of community at the local level.
In Columbia, for example, housing — which includes short
terraces — is grouped in small neighbourhood units each of which
has a general store and an elementary school to serve as a focus.
Several of these neighbourhoods make up a 'village', each village

having a middle school and a variety of shops and other services. The new town is expected to have seven such villages when it reaches its planned population total of 110 000 in the early 1980s. The separation of pedestrian from vehicular movement is usual as may be expected where private car ownership is high, but American new towns have so far achieved little success in the use of public transport despite attempts in some cases to reserve space for such a system. The intention in Columbia was to have a fleet of minibuses that would operate continuously, but there was insufficient demand for the buses and after a time the scheme was abandoned in favour of something more nearly approaching a taxi service.

It would be unfair to dismiss American new towns as representing little more than middle class suburbs. In the use that is made of an overall plan they achieve more harmonious results than is common in many suburbs where development takes place on a piecemeal basis and the environment is cluttered with advertisements, hot dog stands and overhead wires. They provide an example of how urban development may be directed, even in the capitalist world. The criticism that they have contributed almost nothing to the urban housing problem was largely justified up to 1968 but following the Housing and Urban Development Act of that year (revised in 1970) efforts have been made to introduce subsidized housing to the new towns. There are also policies aimed at racial integration in the new towns.

The Act of 1968 has also had the effect of reintroducing government involvement in new town planning in the United States. Under this 'New Communities' legislation, promoters who can convince the government that the proposed new towns satisfy certain social and other requirements are entitled to federal assistance in order to purchase the necessary land and install basic services. Sixteen new communities had received government help by 1974 (Munzer and Vogel, 1974). Most of these are of the satellite type, but an exception is Soul City in North Carolina, built away from existing urban areas and sponsored by a black-owned enterprise. More typical is the development at Jonathan, 30 km from the centre of Minneapolis, where a town to house 50 000 in five 'village' neighbourhoods is being built on the site of the existing small town of Chaska. It is served by the main line railway to Milwaukee and Chicago. The development of Jonathan is paired with a major redevelopment scheme taking place in a portion of inner Minneapolis known as Cedar-Riverside. Pairing involves the exchange of advice and ideas, of services, and possibly also of homes as the respective populations' age and changing life styles make new demands. A parallel is suggested with the linking of certain of the British new towns with London boroughs, but this connection was established mainly for the purposes of directing population and industry and did not extend to complementary urban redevelopment projects. Cedar-Riverside has qualified as one of the sixteen schemes receiving government assistance. Munzer and Vogel describe it as a 'new town-in-town' enterprise. The same description could be applied to the plan for Le Mirail at Toulouse in France. Although not strictly speaking a new town, this project is being planned for an eventual population of 100 000. As at Cedar-Riverside the development will incorporate industry and higher order services, in this case the Faculty of Letters of the University of Toulouse, yet it is only 4 km from the centre of the historic city.

The colonial tradition

It is under conditions of colonization that planted towns have tended to assume their most stereotyped forms. This was particularly true of the Roman colonies (page 146) but is illustrated equally well by the urbanization of Hispanic America. Like the Romans, the Spaniards built towns to administer and exploit their extensive possessions; again like the Romans they employed a grid pattern which became increasingly formalized during the course of the sixteenth century until eventually rules governing this layout of towns were established in the Law of the Indies of 1573. In his study of early Spanish towns in the New World, Stanislawski (1947) sought to demonstrate the dependence of these rules on the writings of Vitruvius.

Mexico City was founded in 1522 on the ruins of the Aztec capital of Tenochtitlan. A plan was drawn up by the surveyor, Alonso Garcia Bravo, based on four avenues converging on a central *plaza* where the government buildings and cathedral were to be established. Thirteen blocks of streets were built in each direction from the centre, beyond which were the Indian quarters (Houston, 1968). Lima, on the coast of Peru, was founded in 1535 and also laid out according to a preconceived plan. This was a chequerboard, 13 building plots in length, 9 in width, separated by streets of sufficient width (40 feet) to permit the easy movement of armies and their equipment. At a later date the city was walled. It was not uncommon for coastal settlements to be fortified in this way but cities in the interior usually relied on strongly-built houses and churches for their defence.

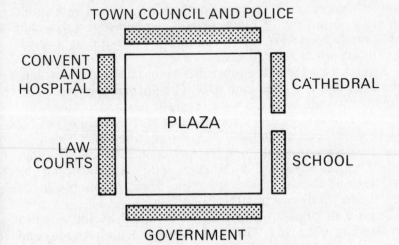

48   A planned town of Hispanic America

Mexico City and Lima were the major urban centres of Hispanic America. Many smaller towns were founded, and after 1573 their plan was carefully regulated by the Law of the Indies. The 149 ordinances of this law laid down standards which applied not only to the overall design of the town but also to such details as width of streets, size and form of the main *plaza,* location of public buildings, and subdivision of the building plots. Town layout in consequence became highly standardized. The town as a whole was divided into 25 equally sized squares or *cuadras.* Each of these in turn was subdivided into four *solares* within which were the actual house lots (Fig. 48). As the town's population grew and required more space, this could be achieved by adding to the basic chequerboard pattern. Centrally located and occupying the whole of one square was the plaza which was lined by public buildings, constituting a monumental town centre in the tradition of the Greek agora or the Roman forum. Residences of the Spanish population were located centrally, close to the plaza, sometimes occupying the storeys above shops on the ground floor. The Indian population, who supplied most of the labour required in the town, occupied the outer portions of the cuadras and were segregated on the basis of tribal origin. In those towns that had a somewhat less formal plan, the Indian quarters had narrower streets and the density of population was appreciably higher than in the Spanish residential areas of the inner city. Sometimes the Indian population was required to live outside the town in villages or in towns built specially to house them. Parallels may be found with the black townships of twentieth century South Africa. When extensions were made to the city of Lima towards the end of the sixteenth century the Indians were rehoused in a township of roughly gridiron plan known as the *cercado.*

Beyond the edge of the town also were slaughterhouses, tanneries and other offensive land uses. The Spaniards were health-conscious and such activities were carefully positioned downwind of the town. Swampy ground was avoided in the choice of site for coastal towns. The Law of the Indies also specified that each town should have two hospitals, one for non-contagious diseases that was to be built close to the church in the centre of the town, and one for contagious diseases away from the town, preferably in an elevated and windy position (Houston, 1968).

Despite its praiseworthy concern for good health, Spanish town planning in the New World invites criticism for its rigidity and lack of adaptability. It reflects a society which, preoccupied at home with its struggles against the Moors, had proved unreceptive

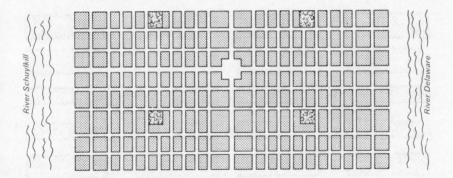

49   Planned layout of Philadelphia

to the ideas of the Renaissance that were penetrating other parts of Europe. Rules derived from early Mediterranean practice were followed with little attempt at improvisation to meet the needs of a different environment. Similar criticism may be levelled at colonial planning in other parts of the world but rarely was there the degree of formality and resistance to change represented by the towns of Hispanic America. The Portuguese in Brazil made little attempt at planning. Elsewhere the grid was widely adopted because of its convenience in allocating land for building, but town builders were generally receptive to new ideas and incorporated these in their plans. Such adaptability is well illustrated by experience in colonial North America where early plans tended to be as formal as those to the south, but in time came to reflect the changes taking place in Europe. Some, like the plan for Philadelphia, also displayed a measure of social awareness that was lacking too in the towns of Hispanic America.

The plan for William Penn's Philadelphia was the work of Thomas Holme in 1682. It was rectangular, extending across the neck of land between the Delaware and Schuylkill rivers and within it the streets were laid out on a chequerboard pattern (Fig. 49). The regularity of the plan was varied, however, by the inclusion of wide avenues and open spaces as was now the practice in Europe. Residential streets were of good width—50 feet—and tree-lined, and the still-wider avenues met in a large, central square, which was repeated on a small scale in each of the quarters formed by their intersection. Each of these smaller squares was to have a public garden and be dignified by the siting of churches and other imposing buildings around its sides.

Though formal in plan, Penn's city represents in its generous use of space and its inclusion of gardens and trees, an attempt to

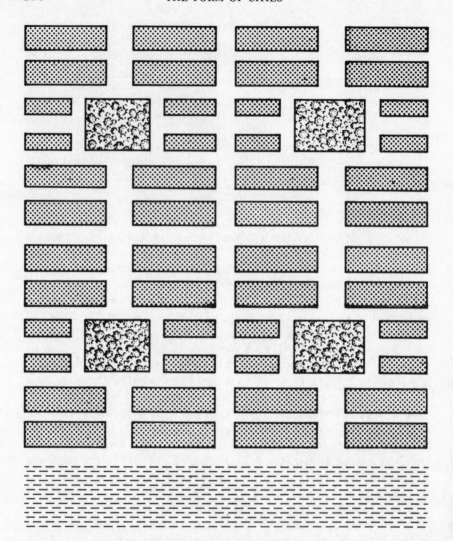

50 Planned layout of Savannah, Georgia

create an environment that was attractive and satisfying as well as
being unified and coherent. As such it also reflects the aspirations
of its socially-conscious Quaker founder, and the example it set
was followed in the design of other North American towns, especially in Pennsylvania.

Further south the city of Savannah was laid out by General
James Oglethorpe following the colonisation of Georgia in the
1730s. He, too, was socially motivated, envisaging his colony as
one for the rehabilitation of formerly-imprisoned debtors. The

plan of Savannah is not very dissimilar from that of Philadelphia by which it was probably influenced (Fig. 50). Broad avenues divide the town into four wards, each of them centred on an open space. One of these was to serve as the town market and the others would be flanked by public buildings. Generous provision was made in the allocation of plots for building houses. In part this was to reduce the risk of fire but it was also a measure of concern for the health of the population. Similar concern is to be seen in the preservation of a green belt on the edge of the town with, beyond it, five-acre (two-hectare) garden plots the cultivation of which it was considered would bring both economic—from the sale of silk and wine—and social benefits.

Savannah, like Philadelphia, helped to set standards in town design that were adopted elsewhere. This did not prevent the allocation on many town plans of specific parts of the town to different types of housing and thereby to different social groups. The social realities of colonial life were at least as strong as the philanthropic motives of town founders. Yet the strength of these founding ideals cannot be denied in the search for what was thought to be an acceptable urban environment. The War of Independence brought new reasons for town foundation. As settlement spread westwards many towns were laid out on a simple grid pattern which had more to do with convenience than idealism. In the east, creation of the new federal capital introduced showplace planning to the United States. L'Enfant's plan was an extended grid on which were superimposed diagonals, giving vistas of imposing buildings positioned at the intersections. With its oddly shaped building plots it was no more convenient to live in than Louis XIV's Versailles, but it set a fashion that was followed in state capitals and other cities where radial avenues were added to older chequerboard grids. If it did not make them more comfortable, baroque planning probably had the effect of making American cities a little more legible.

7

The Pre-Industrial City

Most of the generalizations concerning the form of cities have been based on observation of western examples. Amongst these, Chicago has received a disproportionate amount of attention (Chapter 2). By comparison the urban geography of the Third World has remained relatively neglected. Recent years, however, have witnessed a growing interest in the non-western city on the part of geographers, social anthropologists and sociologists, which is reflected in an expanding body of literature. Valuable contributions have been made towards the understanding of, for example, urbanization in the developing world (Weitz, 1973; R. Jones, 1975) and the nature of squatter (or spontaneous) settlements (Dwyer, 1975). But in spite of this progress, there is no model of the Third World city, and in the absence of a common frame of reference it is tempting to view even the most culturally diverse places in terms of their conformation with, or departure from, some western norms. International airports and the prestigious office or apartment complexes of capital cities, may indeed convey an impression of universal urban form, supporting Wirth's view that urban growth imposes its own universal stamp on society. Yet beneath the veneer of modernity there remains the possibility of a city that is an expression of the society and the culture that built it. The main object of this, and the two chapters which follow, is to investigate this possibility in the context of the non-western city.

Sjoberg's model

The most comprehensive view of the non-western city, at least in its more traditional form, is to be found in the work of Gideon Sjoberg (1960) relating to the 'pre-industrial city'. Sjoberg maintained that it was possible to identify three broad types of society within the wider compass of human society as a whole: a 'folk society' dominated by a rural, mainly subsistence, way of life; a 'pre-industrial' society; and an 'industrial' society characterized by an advanced technology and all the complexities of modern city life. His concern was with the pre-industrial society and its cities, which he regarded as quite distinct from industrial cities in social, economic and ecological terms. Examples of such cities were to be found in the earliest urban civilizations, in medieval Europe, and at the present day in all countries that were not highly industrialized. No allowance was made for diversity of cultural setting; the key was a simple technology and a 'feudal' society. According to Sjoberg, many of the cities in the Third World continue to be dominated by pre-industrial urban forms, whilst such characteristics are by no means absent from cities in the contemporary western world.

The pre-industrial city is· generally small—few exceeded a population of 100 000—and the growth of population tends to be slow and erratic. Technology is based on human and animal, rather than on inanimate, power, and there is little division of labour into skills. There is specialization, not by process, as in the industrial city, but by product, with a guild system to control both production and marketing. There is a rigid class structure and little social mobility. Literacy is restricted to a leisured elite. This elite, which is predominantly city-dwelling, unlike the rest of the population, dominates the political, religious and educational organizations, and within the city is clearly segregated from the lower class and outcast groups who perform most of the unpleasant physical tasks and provide the menial services. The upper class, in particular, maintains an extended family system, and the norms by which life is ordered are prescriptive rather than permissive.

The pre-industrial city is usually walled and, inside it, parts of the city are themselves sealed off from each other by further walls. The effect is to reinforce segregation, leaving what Sjoberg describes as 'little cells, or subcommunities, as worlds unto themselves'. The outer walls provide defence, but also control the movement of merchants and other visitors, and enable tolls to be collected. Those within the city give protection at night from thieves, as well as isolating what are thought to be undesirable ethnic minorities. The city is highly congested, although the houses of the elite are spacious and airy. People live where they work and, so far as social segregation permits, in close proximity to the facilities—markets, religious buildings, etc.—of the city. Most buildings are relatively low because of the constraints of technology and are crowded together. Streets are 'narrow, winding, unpaved, poorly drained' and, during the day, are filled with traders and the shops and stalls which spill out from the ground floor of the houses.

In addition to these general characteristics, Sjoberg pointed to what he described as three specific land use patterns.

1 Pre-eminence of the central area

The 'central area' is usually, though not invariably, coterminous with the physical centre of the city. Its pre-eminence is represented above all in the fact that it is the place of residence of the elite. Here, too, are to be found those imposing buildings which symbolize the political and religious power of the elite. Such buildings, commonly arranged around a central square, or at the end of a processional route, dominate the skyline. Streets converge on the central area, which is therefore a meeting place and a site of ceremonies and pageantry. It is also where the city's main market is usually held, taking advantage of the convergence of pedestrian movement, particularly on the religious buildings. But since economic activity is subservient to political and religious functions, the presence of the market does not give rise to structures which rival either palace or church in magnificence or symbolic importance.

Close to the centre are the homes of the ruling elite, often built around a central courtyard with blank walls to the street in order to ensure privacy and 'to minimize ostentation in a city teeming with "the underprivileged".' A central location affords easy access to the seats of power which are dominated by the elite; it is also safer in time of war, especially if protected by its own internal wall. Further out live the other groups, with the poorest sections of the population, the outcasts and those engaged in 'offensive' trades, living in the most distant suburbs or outside the city wall. Here some of them add to their meagre income by growing food for consumption in the city. Well beyond this zone one encounters the summer houses of the elite.

2 Differentiation along ethnic, occupational and kinship lines

Superimposed upon the above division, based on social class, are finer distinctions relating to ethnic groups, occupations and to kinship ties. Segregation on this basis gives rise to wards or quarters within the city, 'well-defined neighbourhoods with relatively homogeneous populations that develop special forms of social organization'. The three elements should not be regarded as mutually exclusive, however, and particular occupations may, for example, be associated with certain ethnic groups. Within each quarter there may be observed the kind of class differentiation that is to be observed in the city as a whole, with community leaders who make themselves responsible for anything that is distinctive in the religious, educational and social life of the group. Occupational segregation may be represented at the level of the whole quarter, but within such an area smaller districts or even individual streets are likely to be given over to specific trades, geographical concentrations being encouraged not only by simple forms of transport but also by the organization which the guilds impose.

Sjoberg notes two occupational categories which do not conform with the above pattern: the domestic servants and merchants. The former, though a low class or outcast element, will be found in upper class areas where they are separately housed by their employers. The latter are a wide-ranging group who include well-established business men upon whom the elite depend for commercial transactions and who therefore may be found living near the centre and, at the opposite end of the spectrum, foreign traders, who are compelled to reside on the edge of the city.

Family, or the larger kinship units, give rise to similar subdivisions within the quarter to the occupational sub-groups. They occupy a cluster of buildings, perhaps a whole street, and give rise to 'well-defined subsystems' within the social milieu of the quarter or city as a whole.

3 Absence of other forms of land use differentiation

In contrast with the segregation of social and occupational groups noted above, there is little differentiation of land use within the pre-industrial city. Buildings, and open spaces, serve several uses. This is strikingly apparent in the vicinity of churches, mosques or temples which are often used as schools and at the entrance to which the market is held. Domestic houses serve also as shops and as places of manufacture, the family living above or behind the workshop or saleroom. 'The ecological situation wherein a person may reside, produce, store, and sell his wares within the confines of the same structure has been a feature of pre-industrial urban life from the earliest cities in Mesopotamia down to the present day.'

Criticisms of the model

Criticism of what Langton (1975) has referred to as 'Sjoberg's monolithic ideas' has come from various sources, and particularly from students of the pre-nineteenth century European city. Wheatley (1963) expresses five points of disagreement:

1 Sjoberg's model ignores the fairly widespread occurrence of manufacturing for profit based on the control of natural forces such as wind and water, and the possible effects of this on the creation of workshops and even factories. Although he refers to the use of some inanimate sources of energy in 'later' pre-industrial cities, the emphasis is on human energy and animal power and upon the craftsman working at home.

2 Too great an emphasis is placed on the impossibility of upward mobility in society. In some cities, for example ports, the fragmented nature of society made progress from poverty to riches easier than Sjoberg imagined.

3 The division between rich and poor, elite and the rest, was in any case not always as sharply defined as Sjoberg suggests. Wheatley refers to the 'princely masons' of Ankor in support of his contention that merchants *were* in some cities members of the elite.

4 Sjoberg neglects to consider the relationship of pre-industrial cities to each other, particularly in the hierarchical sense.

5 His description of the city as one of 'houses jumbled together, forming an irregular mass broken at intervals by open spaces in front of a temple or governmental building' does less than justice to the formal layout of some early cities where wide streets divided the residential area into neat blocks. Wheatley considers Sjoberg's picture to be more appropriate to the cities of the Middle East and North Africa than to those of South and East Asia, where elaborate principles often underlay the design of cities, Chinese cities, for example, being laid out as an image of the universe.

Like Wheatley, Cox (1964) questions Sjoberg's emphasis on technology as the key determinant of social systems. Far from being wholly dependent on the prevailing level of technology, the city has acted as a centre of innovation, and improvements in technology have been brought about from within the city, products of the city's own institutions. This positive and constructive role of the city was later taken up more fully in Jane Jacobs' *The Economy of Cities* (1969).

Cox's main criticism, however, is of Sjoberg's failure to allow for the existence of different kinds of social system which are expressed in contrasted urban forms. 'The pre-industrial city type lumps so many disparate societal systems together that its value as an operational instrument seems nullified.' Sjoberg's pre-industrial city is a 'constructed type', one made up of social phenomena abstracted from a wide range of 'disparate cultural settings' and presented as a type. In support of his argument, Cox identifies forms of society that have given rise to markedly different kinds of city: society based on the concept of citizenship in the classical world; the non-feudal society of the medieval European city—progenitor of the modern nation; the caste system in India; and societies that have given rise to 'the multitribal, multiethnic, or multiclan aggregations common in China and in Mohammedan countries'. It is inconceivable that such diversity can be dismissed simply as sub-systems of a wider feudal society. Cox believes that Sjoberg has fallen into the trap, which has enslaved others, of placing too much emphasis on modern American society as a frame of reference.

Although no reference is made to the ideas of Sjoberg, criticism of the latter may be inferred from Vance's (1971 b) description of the 'pre-capitalist' city of medieval Europe and of the 'capitalist' city that succeeded it from the sixteenth century. In particular, the clear distinction which Sjoberg makes between the elite and poor, centre and periphery, is far less evident in Vance's scheme. The latter's pre-capitalist city is 'popular rather than patrician', the worker having the opportunity of attaining status and acquiring authority as a freeman of the city as a result of his membership of a guild. In this more fluid social system, government is in the hands, not of an aristocratic elite, but of civic leaders whose power is derived from trade. If the central market square is bordered by the imposing houses of these leading citizens, it is only because the guild merchants—historically the most prominent guildsmen and therefore likely to be civic leaders—find it advantageous to their business to live there. Civic leaders who happen to be drawn from other guilds will live in that part of the town appropriate to their profession.

Vance is more at one with Sjoberg in his account of 'occupation districts' within cities, not unlike the latter's 'quarters', although Vance lays greater emphasis on the role of the guild, which plays a social as well as an economic role. 'We tend today to cite the economic linkages that maintained the existence of these districts, but in the beginning they were considerably social in

origin.' This came about in part because of the strong association of
the guild with a particular parish church. There is clearly a greater
degree of social mixing within these trade or guild districts than is
envisaged in Sjoberg's model, with 'a strong tendency for those
who worked together to live together and to worship in common'.
Foreigners and other unorthodox groups were confined to their
own quarter in what was 'a many-centered city'. Noblemen, who
lived in the city for only part of the year, built their palaces in
various parts of it, having no reason to seek out a 'site of distinction' because of the status vested in themselves.

Change took place in the pre-capitalist city from the sixteenth
century, with the growth of long-distance trade and decline of the
guilds. Commercial organization was replaced by personal
advancement, competition and land ownership. The effect, according to Vance, was to create the capitalist city wherein land uses
became segregated and the 'house community' gave way to the
separation of the social classes. 'In place of the rather economic-
and class-undifferentiated medieval appraisal of land value, there
came the appraisal of the rent-productivity of land and a ranking of
location in economic terms.' A land-rent gradient appeared; merchants acquired sites in the centre for their shops and warehouses
and the impoverished craftsmen were compelled to move out,
perhaps to the industrial hamlets outside the town. High-income
residential areas emerged as class status became more closely
associated with the accumulation of wealth. In time 'there arose
the notion that the edge of the city was the most desirable area and
its core the home of the lower classes.'

Vance's association of change with the expansion of overseas
trade further undermines the validity of Sjoberg's pre-
industrial/industrial dichotomy. Langton (1975) goes so far as to
state that 'Sjoberg ignored the social and economic changes which
occurred in Western Europe, and particularly in its cities, between
medieval times and the Industrial Revolution'. Vance took
account of these, yet both his and Sjoberg's schemes are described
by Langton as 'ideal type' models. In his own research in
Newcastle upon Tyne, based on Hearth Tax Assessments and
other records, he found some confirmation of Sjoberg's thesis in
terms of the distribution of wealth, and of Vance's ideas in the
presence of a merchant clique who lived where their economic
interests were best served, and in the segregation of occupational
groups. But the pattern in this real situation was far more complicated than the model implies with, for example, conflicting
evidence of 'class zoning'. His conclusion points to the need to

interpret land use in pre-modern cities in terms of a wider range of variables. These may include the relationship between workplace and home, size and composition of households, and the nature of the housing and land markets.

Types of pre-industrial city

It is evident that, whatever its merits as a generalization, Sjoberg's concept of the pre-industrial city embraces a wide range of city types. Yet few attempts have been made to break it down into more acceptable sub-divisions. An exception so far as Europe is concerned is to be found in the classic work, *The City,* by Max Weber (Martindale and Neuwirth translation, 1962), who distinguished three types of 'pre-industrial' city: classical, medieval North European, and medieval South European. The distinction was made principally on the basis of their social and economic organization and the relationship between the city and the surrounding country, but differences in form arise from these organizational contrasts.

Employing slave labour, the classical city did not develop the guild system that characterized the medieval city. Instead of deriving from guilds, government was based on the control of tribal territories; thus city-based political organization extended well beyond the bounds of the city itself to take in the surrounding countryside. By contrast, the medieval city of northern Europe, markedly economic in character, was governed by its resident craftsmen, guildsmen who had risen to prominence by their own efforts. Under these circumstances city government did not involve control of territory outside the town. The southern European city was in many respects transitional between the other two forms. Here the ruling class owned land outside the city in the classical manner and on it built their castles, but they also maintained houses in the city, also fortified, against blood feuds or attack from the proletariat. The type is well described by Vance (1971): 'In the Italian republics the relative homogeneity of northern towns was missing, and along with that absence went a much less clear physical structure . . . with tower-houses seeking to provide a defensive site within the city . . . It represents the import into the city of a form of watch-tower which was very common in the countryside . . . this particular arrangement of city space was more the intrusion of the countryside and its way of life into the city than local growth.' The southern city lacked the obvious occupational districts of the northern one. It differed from the classical city, according to Weber, in its lack of the military associations that were 'the very foundations of the ancient city'.

Outside Europe, research into the nature of the pre-industrial Japanese city, the city as it was before the Meiji restoration of 1868, suggests a three-fold division into provincial capitals, temple or shrine towns, and postroad stages. Elsewhere the search for types of pre-industrial city has rarely proceeded beyond a distinction between 'native' and 'colonial' towns. These were termed cultural and administrative cities by Redfield and Singer (1954), the former referring to the settlement as it was before the advent of European colonialism, the latter to the, generally separate, township built by the colonial government. The importance of this distinction is stressed by McGee (1971), who sees the colonial city as a separate model. 'Perhaps the greatest fault of Sjoberg's twofold division of cities (pre-industrial/industrial) is that he has failed to take account of cities that have grown as links in the inter-action of two civilizations. Such towns were flourishing even in the pre-industrial society; for example, as a result of the contact of the Roman Empire and the North African cultures. Such cities are probably distinct enough to deserve a category of their own. They might be aptly titled "colonial cities".'

Greater problems arise when the attempt is made to distinguish categories of pre-colonial city (for which McGee retains the title of 'pre-industrial'). Few would dispute the fact that the city both reflects the cultural milieu in which it grows and, at the same time, influences the evolution of that culture. There is a mutual relationship, though the degree to which the city is an active or a passive agent remains a matter of debate. Where, however, is the line to be drawn between one culture realm and another? Figure 51 represents an attempt by Holzner (1967) to delimit world regions on the basis of processes involved in the relationship between cities and cultures. These he divides into seven groups: historical, economic, technological, demographic, religious, ethnic and political. Unfortunately, the paper is a brief one, and no explanatory key accompanies the map.

No such map is used as a basis for what follows. Rather is the attempt made to identify those elements of society and culture which are most clearly represented in the form of cities and which one day, when cross-cultural comparison in urban geography has proceeded beyond its infancy, may play a part in classification.

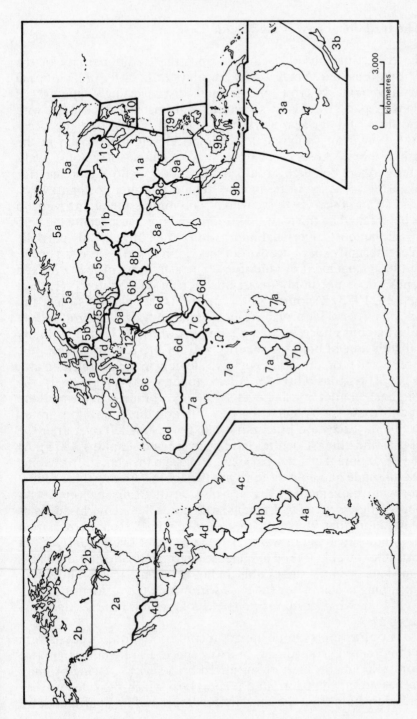

51 Holzner's (1967) system of 'functional world-regions in urban geography'. (Reproduced by permission from the *Annals of the Association of American Geographers*, vol. 57, 1967)

The traditional city of the Middle East

To the casual observer, the *madina,* the traditional city of the Middle East and North Africa, displays little order in its internal arrangement. Narrow alleys wind disconcertingly amongst a densely packed mass of structures and unsorted land uses, with mosques and shrines, workshops, *suqs* (bazaars) and the occasional *madrasa* (religious law school) closely interwoven in the urban fabric. Absence of open spaces, cul-de-sacs, house walls blank except for high, iron-grilled windows, and a tendency for even the mosques to be hidden behind unpretentious gateways, lend an air of secrecy to the whole. This impression of introversion is heightened by the nature of traditional dress, especially the veil.

Like most superficial impressions, the above is only partially accurate, and experienced observers claim to see logic, even order, in the arrangement of land uses. 'The syndrome of the "crooked lanes" does not imply disorganization in civic matters' (Ettinghausen, 1973). Another writer interprets the maze of streets and alleyways as a kind of built-in system of traffic control and an informal but effective zoning plan (Brown, 1973). Inaccessibility satisfies a need both for security and for privacy. In a sense, the streets and footpaths are a negative element in the overall land use; lack of responsibility for their upkeep has encouraged the encroachment of housing over the course of time, narrowing them and introducing irregularities of width and direction. Interpreted in this way, they are little more than the spaces left over after the houses and other structures have been erected (Lapidus, 1973). At the same time they are a perfect response to the climate, providing useful shade and helping to retain the cool night air, whilst reducing wind movement. They are also aesthetically pleasing. This observation is made by Lapidus, who notes the many closed vistas of not more than about 300 metres which make sections of a street 'easy and satisfying to walk'. Yet the sense of overall unity is not lost, since dwellings tend to increase in grandeur and importance as a mosque or some other public building is approached. This visual patterning accounts for the ease with which the resident finds his way about what, to the stranger, is a labyrinth of lanes and passageways.

Contrasting with the apparent confusion of the street pattern is the ordered arrangement of living space. Rarely more than two storeys in height, built of sun-dried bricks with a facing of mud, houses are arranged around a courtyard which provides privacy and protection from the sun. 'In the desert, nature at ground level is hostile to man, so he shuts his house entirely to the outside, and opens it instead on to an internal courtyard, or *sahn* . . . the cool night air collects in the courtyard and flows into the surrounding rooms, keeping them cool to a late hour' (Fathy, 1973). The courtyard and garden also afford relief from the noise and bustle of the streets outside. According to Fathy, this tradition in building was preserved, and therefore to some extent the form of the city as a whole, by legal sanction, the system of *waqfs*, which did not permit property to be sold. Public buildings display a similar degree of formality in plan, with functional units arranged about a rectangular courtyard. The traditional plan of the madrasa, for example, consists of four halls opening off the open court with students' rooms in the spaces between the halls.

The suqs, however congested they may seem, reveal a similar degree of order, both in the concentration of particular trades in their own bazaars and in the distribution of these activities in the city as a whole. Noisy or unconforming trades, like those of the blacksmith or tanner, are segregated from those of the cloth merchant, bookseller or perfumer, whilst livestock marketing and the wholesale functions of the caravanserais are most likely to be carried on near the edge of the city or even outside its walls. 'As a result of this "city-plan", the student in the madrasa, the pious at prayer in the mosque, or the shopper in the cloth bazaar could go about his affairs undisturbed by a constant stream of porters and heavily-laden donkeys . . .' (Brown, 1973). Expensive goods are most likely to be sold close to the centre where pedestrian movement is greatest (English, 1973), and booksellers naturally favour a site close to the leading mosque. In a study of Shiraz (Iran), Clarke (1963) found that although the segregation of trades was less than it had been formerly, there was still a clear tendency for the grouping of similar activities in the bazaars. Many of these had workshops as an integral part of the building. Goods sold in the bazaars were of the more traditional kind—clothing, carpets, metalware—with the retailing of modern articles (electrical, pharmaceutical, etc.) taking place in the shops of the 'new city'.

Looking at the city as a whole, a distinction can be made between those parts that are predominantly residential and those in which there is a more mixed pattern of commercial, religious and other activities. 'Speaking in the most general terms, one can say that the suq usually represents the main artery and urban axis from which secondary side streets with other shops and ateliers branch off.' Close to it are the 'other important buildings . . . around this area are the residential districts . . . minorities have their own quarter with their own places of worship, and civic needs, and altogether, there is a definite pattern of urban organization' (Ettinghausen, 1973). The contrast arises from the degree to which there is separation of public and private life in the Islamic city. Public life for the townsman involves a wide range of activities: prayer, learning, manufacture and retailing, public consultation. All these, according to Lapidus (1973), are part of an undifferentiated life style that demands the close proximity of mosque and bazaar, school and office, to permit easy movement from one to the other. But in the residential area beyond, life is private and largely confined to the home. There are few shops and little in the way of community institutions; public buildings may be limited to a mosque or shrine.

Typical of almost all Middle Eastern cities is the high degree of segregation of the residential area into quarters (*haras*). Within these quarters streets become even narrower and there are a great number of cul-de-sacs, adding to the privacy and facilitating control of the quarter by the appointed leader, or *shaykh*. The number of quarters varies, of course, with the size of city and the heterogenity of its population. Antioch is said to have had forty-five of them (English, 1973), Cairo fifty-three. Religion provides one of the main bases of division, Jews and Christians having their own quarters as well as the major sects or fraternities of Islam. There is differentiation according to ethnic origin—Greeks, Armenians and others living in separate districts—and to some extent on the basis of trade, even of village origin. Some cities possess internal walls separating one quarter from another, physical divisions reinforcing social ones, and assisting the Shaykh in his duties of maintaining order and collecting tax. Within the quarter itself there is evidence of clustering of closely related families. Blind alleys or cul-de-sacs are, at least in part, related to the grouping in this way of the houses belonging to members of an extended family.

Each quarter was permitted a large measure of autonomy, overall civic institutions being poorly developed in the traditional Middle Eastern City (Lapidus, 1969; Stern, 1970). 'These autonomous cells had their own civic and religious leaders, administrative organization, and even watchmen. The quarter was a common organizational principle of pre-industrial Muslim urban life' (English, 1973; Hourani, 1970). Under Ottoman control, the independence of the quarters became formalized in what was known as the *millet* system, the local communities being granted considerable freedom in political, religious and legal matters.

The traditional city, described above, conforms with the Sjoberg model in several respects, most obviously in the segregation of its population into quarters. But in others it differs. There is less emphasis, for example, upon the palace and the central market square. Some cities, such as Damascus and Aleppo, have a *qal'a* (citadel), but in others this feature is absent (Ettinghausen, 1973). Grabar (1969) has identified an early Islamic 'civic centre' which included an open forum, or *masjid*, in which communal activities took place, but in time a building, the mosque, replaced it. Decline of the civic centre would be encouraged by the poverty of municipal institutions to which reference has been made. Narrow streets and craft-type industries are typical of the pre-industrial city, but Sjoberg's model is clearly inadequate to account for those elements of the Muslim city which reflect the hold of Islam, not only on the religious, but on almost all aspects of the life of the population.

Although many Middle Eastern cities have pre-Islamic origins, it is the all-pervasive influence of Islam which, from the 7th century, has been principally responsible for moulding their character. Minarets tower above the generally low profile of the remainder of the city, introducing vertical elements to an otherwise mainly horizontal townscape, and affording unique landmarks. Bath houses, required for ritual washing, are one of the few 'public' facilities present in the residential areas. Clustering of mosque, schools and market in the city centre is suggestive of the way in which Islam regulates the legal, educational, commercial and political life of the community, and points to the organizing role of religious communities and the related schools of law. Hospitals and similar institutions owe something to the requirement to offer help to the stranger. Introverted house types mirror social customs, and above all the traditional attitude to women. Property is frequently held in religious trust, but since there is no protection for the street in Islamic law, houses encroach upon it, giving rise to the irregularities in profile and direction referred to above.

Sjoberg's model, with its emphasis on technology, fails to do justice to the strength of cultural tradition that derives from Islam, and von Grunebaum (1961) has suggested that the Muslim city, with its segregated quarters, intricate street pattern, convergence on the mosque, concentration of crafts in the bazaar, and lack of civic institutions, constitutes a sufficiently distinctive type to be regarded as a model itself. Pursuit of this typical Muslim city is not without problems, however, not least those posed by the traditionally unstable nature of Middle Eastern society and by a tendency for city populations to fluctuate widely over time. Over a long period of urban history, the fortunes of cities in the Middle East have varied greatly. Some have occupied the same sites for millenia; others have been refounded several times and even the 'old city' is composed of several nodes which represent these periods of renewal. Cairo, Fez and Jerusalem exemplify what Ettinghausen has called the tradition of adding·new cities to old. Attempts were made in some cases to plan the new towns. Baghdad was laid out to quite an elaborate circular design in the 8th century; it is thought to have reached a population of a million and a half in the succeeding century, but subsequently decayed. In spite of the unifying influence of Islam, there are many divisive elements in Middle Eastern society. Fernea (1969) refers to a 'persistent factionalistic tendency' which, in the absence of strong civic institutions to bind the population together, makes even the quarter's 'fragile institutions' subject to internal dispute. Instability must thus be regarded as a normal part of the Middle Eastern urban tradition, and allowance made for it in the search for the kind of model which von Grunebaum advocates.

India

It has been claimed that, at heart, Indian society is rural, village-based, and that the city is alien to this tradition (Bogue and Zachariah, 1962). Even when he becomes a townsman, the Indian does not easily give up his rural background, and many observers have drawn attention to the village-like character of large parts of Indian cities (Hoselitz, 1959). In these circumstances it becomes easier to understand why, in a study of urbanization in India published as recently as 1973, it was thought necessary to devote a whole chapter to 'defining "urban" in the Indian context' (Bose, 1973). The problem is not made easier by the variety of physical, economic and social conditions that prevail within India.

Indian cities have been described as lacking a basic unity of layout and function, as amorphous, loosely woven, and a collection of period pieces (Brush, 1962). 'La ville indigène peut être qualifiée d'amorphe: d'étroites venelles (alleys) s'entrecroisent sans directions privilégiées. La physionomie finale n'est guère, à une autre échelle il est vrai, que celle d'un village'* (Caralp, 1972). Though written thirty years ago, the description of the 'old' city by Spate and Ahmad (1950) retains much of its validity: 'In the Chauk—the area of the main bazaar—the adjoining streets are

---

*The native city may be termed 'amorphous': narrow alleys criss-cross without regard to priority. Although the scale differs, the end product in terms of form is not much different from that of the village.

wider than usual, the facades are modernistic (if hardly modern), with a lavish display of coloured concrete, and there is probably a clock tower, and perhaps a statue or two of doubtful political tact and aesthetic quality. For the rest the heart of the Indian city is a maze of narrow streets made narrower by the encroachment of open shop fronts and booths, the blocks of buildings traversed by narrow back lanes . . . Outward from the business centre, streets degenerate into ill-kept lanes and alleys. The outer fringe is . . . a chaos of mud or matting huts, market gardens, stables, cowsheds, muddy ponds, and waste-ground.'

Impetus to urbanization in India came with the Mogul invasions of the 16th and 17th centuries, which affected most strongly the towns of the northern plains (Agra was the Mogul capital) and Deccan plateau. Muslim influences may be invoked to account for the superficial resemblance between many 'traditional' Indian cities and those of the Middle East, but the parallel must not be taken too far. In an excellent summary of the morphological characteristics of Indian cities, Brush (1962) refers to the irregular pattern of narrow, crooked streets, usually lacking a pavement, on to which shops and stalls project, leaving little room for wheeled vehicles especially in the many side streets and alleys. There is little open space except for these lanes, the occasional market and the interior courts of some of the more important residences. Most buildings do not exceed two storeys 'although "lofty" buildings of three, four, or even six storeys may exist along the main streets . . . Historic palaces of Hindu or Muslim rulers often rise on a nearby hill or stand by the river. Sometimes the battlements and moats of the pre-British walled city survive. The domes and minarets and the pinnacles of temples are prominent features.' A similar picture is conveyed by Breese's (1966) description of the Old City area of Delhi.

The arrangement of markets and workshops has much in common with that of the 'old city' of the Middle East. The main bazaar shows the same clustering of related trades, with rather more specialized markets on separate, but nearby, sites. Those offering services—money-lending, letter-writing, various kinds of medical treatment—also find it profitable to be near the *chauk* (or *chowk*). Retailing extends along the main streets leading from the central bazaar in the larger towns in which there are likely also to be secondary bazaars. The manufacture and sale of pottery, brassware, and the products of other craft industries, are associated with particular streets. The pattern emerges in Singh's (1964) description of Bangalore: 'The town was divided into numerous *pettahs* or markets according to the commodities dealt in. For instance, Tharagupete was famous for cereals, Arlepet dealt in cotton, etc. The *Chowk,* or main bazaar, was at the crossing of the present Avenue Road and Chikpet . . . There were often bazaars or stalls lining the streets on a raised platform beside which the customer had to stand and purchase his articles. The shops catering for the same type of goods were found together.'

Residential segregation is as marked a feature of the traditional Indian city as it is in the Middle East. 'In pre-British India the city population was largely distributed geographically by religion, caste, and subcaste, and by occupational and regional groups forming social islands. These social characteristics had real meaning and developed such extensive exclusiveness that the groups often constituted cities within cities' (Clinard and Chatterjee, 1962). The term 'cellular' has also been used to describe this kind of city, in which the social life of the population is closely identified with particular neighbourhoods or wards (*mohallas*). Special importance is attached to the role of caste and Brush notes that, in conformity with Sjoberg's model, Brahmins and others of high caste usually live in the solidly built, *pucka* houses near the centre of the city, whilst the labouring castes and outcasts occupy mud-built (*kutcha*) dwellings on the periphery. Bulsara's (1970) description of Bombay serves to illustrate the significance of those factors, particularly religion and caste, which underlie residential segregation in the Indian city: 'it will be noted that the Upper Caste, or Advanced Hindus, live largely in Pacca built areas, whereas the Backward, or Scheduled Caste Hindus predominate in the Kaccha, or Hutment areas. The Banias and Jains cluster in the Bhuleshwar and Nana Chowk areas; the Muslims in the Nagpada area and in the Mori Road-Mahim and Mogra Road-Andheri hutments; the Parsis in Dadar and Nana Chowk, Grant Road; the Christians in the Bandra and Colaba areas; and the Harijans and Neo-Buddhists at Matunga Labour Camp and Clerk Road, Mahalaxmi. The Upper Caste South Indians are to be found largely in Matunga and Sion and the Backward class at Clerk Road and Matunga hutment area.'

The above description lends support to Cox's plea that caste be recognized as a distinctive social force acting on the form of the pre-industrial city. The same is true of tribalism in Africa. It is a theme to which we return in Chapter 9.

Nigeria

Over the greater part of Africa south of the Sahara, urbanization was initiated by the intervention of Europeans. Exceptions to this generalization, however, are to be found in the Sudanese area in the north, where trans-Saharan trade and contact with the urban cultures of North Africa led to the growth of such towns as Timbuktu and Kano, and amongst certain tribal groups living further south, of which the outstanding examples are the Yoruba of (what is now) south-west Nigeria and the Buganda of Uganda. Even when European towns were planted alongside the 'native' settlement, the earlier foundations continued to play an important urban role, as they did in the Middle East and India (Chapter 8).The rise of Mengo and the part it played in the evolution of modern Kampala has been described by Southall (1967), whilst the nature and functions of Nigerian towns have been fully documented in the extensive writings of Mabogunje (especially 1962 and 1968).

Many of the Yoruba towns were established between the 7th and 10th centuries by migrants from the north to serve as administrative and marketing centres; others were founded later as the centres of separate kingdoms. In common with most 'planted' towns, they exhibited order in the arrangement of their land use and Mabogunje stresses the symbolic and functional importance of the central area, conforming with Sjoberg's model. Here was the ruler's (Oba's) palace set in extensive grounds, probably with some kind of meeting place for the council of chiefs who assisted the crowned head in the administration of the town. The palace, perhaps with its own wall, was also the central feature of the Hausa towns of northern Nigeria and of the capital city of the Buganda. Southall suggests that this area of the city, which enclosed the Kabaka's palace, probably had a population of 3000 in the nineteenth century, whilst the 'native town' surrounding it housed at least 10 000. Close to the Oba's palace was the open space in which the principal market was held, with smaller markets elsewhere in the town similarly situated in close proximity to the residences of lesser chiefs and constituting sub-nuclei. The leading mosque (Islam was adopted as the religion of the Yoruba elite in the nineteenth century) also occupied a central position, adding to the prestige of the central area and to its attraction as a place of residence for the foremost families of the town.

Radiating out from the palace were the widest streets—up to 30 feet in the Yoruba towns, according to Mabogunje—which led

to gates in the city walls and continued beyond to provide links with
other towns (Fig. 52). Branching off from these were smaller
streets, up to 15 feet wide and exhibiting a rectilinear plan in the
early 'planted' towns, but tending to lose this formal pattern with
time, partly as a result of the destruction and rebuilding that
followed further invasions from the north. 'Yoruba towns today
show no discernible plan and streets are narrow and winding.'
Around these streets was grouped the population in 'quarters',
each under the authority of its own chief. Heterogeneity of population was greatest in the Sudanese towns where trade and periodic
invasion had introduced a wide variety of social types, but it was
evident also in the south where tribal, religious and occupational
differences all played a part in the residential differentiation of the
town. Merchants from other regions occupied separate quarters.
Associated with the occupational structure were contrasts in social
status, maintained, at least in the north, by a system of guilds.
Mabogunje describes how traditional skills were also jealously
guarded by the Yoruba and handed down through family lineages.
In addition to such lineage membership, which determined one's

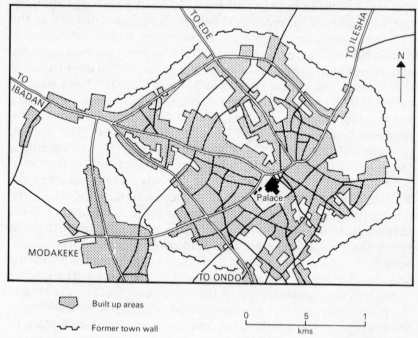

52   Town plan of Ile-Ife, a traditional Yoruba town. After Mabogunje,
      1962. (Courtesy University of Ibadan)

social status in the town, there was also status that derived from one's age group, particular age groups being accorded specific responsibilities with regard to, for example, administration or defence. Despite their great social and economic diversity, however, 'every quarter of the traditional Yoruba town presented the same appearance', and if for any reason the population was reduced by the emigration of a group of families 'the town would shrink in response but the structure would remain the same' (Lloyd, 1973).

The quarters of the typical Yoruba town were further subdivided into compounds, mud-walled enclosures, usually square or rectangular in shape and of single storey. The compound was the basic unit of settlement, housing a group of related families under the authority of a hereditary leader. Their individual dwellings took the form of rooms opening on to a central court, access to which was by means of a single entrance from the street. They ranged widely in size, from 40 persons to 340 in one quarter of Ibadan (Levine, et al., 1967), the larger ones being associated with minor chieftains. Mabogunje notes the tendency for the larger compounds, housing the nobler families, to be located near the centre of the town, the smaller, poorer ones being 'pushed towards the margin'. Except for a number of offensive trades or ones which required a stream-side location, most craft-type industries were carried on within the compound. It was also common practice for the inhabitants of the compound to own farmland outside the town with village settlements that were, in a sense, satellites of the urban compound. Between the two there was characteristically a good deal of coming and going and it was not uncommon for the town-dweller to spend portions of the year in the village, at planting or harvest time, for example.

Farmland was also to be found within the city wall—valuable at a time of war, and especially valuable for the northern, Sudanese cities which were subject to pillaging attacks from desert tribesmen. The open space maintained for cultivation is apparent from Barth's map (1851) of Kano (Fig. 53). This city had been visited earlier by the explorer, Captain Hugh Clapperton in 1824, who recorded the following impressions which sum up most of the characteristics of the 'pre-industrial city' in Africa: 'Kano may contain some 30 000 to 40 000 resident inhabitants, of whom more than one half are slaves . . . This number is exclusive of strangers who come here in crowds during the dry months from all parts of Africa, from the Mediterranean and the Mountains of the Moon, and from Sennar and Ashantee . . . The city is of an irregular oval

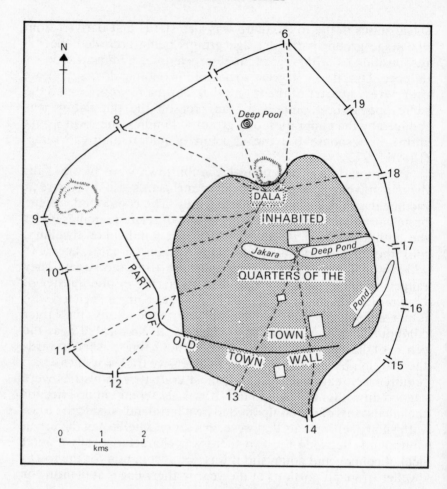

53   Kano in 1851 based on a survey by Barth. After Mabogunje, 1968.
     (Courtesy Hodder and Stoughton)

shape, about fifteen miles in circumference, and surrounded by a
clay wall thirty feet high, with a dry ditch along the inside, and
another on the outside. There are fifteen gates, including one lately
built up . . . Not more than one fourth of the ground within the walls
is occupied by houses: the vacant space is laid out in fields and
gardens . . . The houses are built of clay, and are mostly of a square
form, in the Moorish fashion . . . The governor's residence covers a
large space and resembles a walled village. It even contains a
mosque . . . The soug, or market, is well supplied with every
necessity and luxury in request among the people of the interior . . .
Particular quarters are appropriated to distinct articles . . . The

market is crowded from sunrise to sunset every day' (Denham, Clapperton et. al., 1826).

The foregoing paragraphs have attempted to present a picture of the traditional city by reference to those parts of the world where 'pre-industrial' characteristics could, and to some extent still can be most readily observed. But such areas have not remained wholly untouched by the forces of colonialism and of post-colonial modernization, and the effect of these other influences is the subject of the succeeding two chapters.

8

The Colonial City

Reference was made in the previous chapter to McGee's claim that the colonial city possessed sufficiently distinctive characteristics to justify its recognition as a separate type (McGee, 1971). To support his argument he distinguishes certain features of such a colonial city:

1   Social stratification. The colonial administrator or business man was alien to those he administered and there was virtually no entry to the ranks of administrators for the indigenous population.
2   The city was a collection of communities, each pursuing its own way of life.
3   Each community tended to group around the focus of its own activities. The governing elite lived close to the city centre which was the focal point of colonial administration, religious and business activities.
4   The occupation structure was characterized by a pronounced tertiary sector because of the emphasis on trade.
5   Despite their important political, commercial, and educational roles, colonial cities did not attract large numbers of rural migrants. Contrast in this respect the industrial cities of nineteenth-century Europe.

The closest 'fit' to McGee's model is probably to be found in the colonial city of South East Asia (below). Elsewhere the colonial city 'showed many variations in structure or form depending upon the form of colonial impact'. McGee goes on to make the important distinction between what he calls 'replica towns' and 'colonial cities'. The former were towns established on greenfield sites in, for example, Australia or North America, where there was no earlier indigenous settlement and the plan was usually inspired by planning ideals current in Europe at the time. The degree to which the towns of Hispanic America owed anything to earlier urban civilizations like those of the Aztec is a debatable point. But in view of the major part played in their design by principles like those set out in the Law of the Indies, they too, may be regarded as 'replica towns'. The characteristics of this particular kind of colonial settlement are examined in Chapter 6 which explores the nature of the planned town in general. McGee divides the 'colonial city' into three sub-categories:

1   A mixture of the pre-industrial and industrial cities in the sense that a colonial administrative town was 'grafted on' to an older indigenous settlement.

2   Mining settlements which were 'wholly industrial in nature'. McGee quotes Luanshya in the Zambian Copperbelt as an example. One is left to assume that these differ from 'replica towns' in their less-planned or unplanned nature.

3   Major ports which handled the trade of the colonies. They commonly outgrew all other settlements to achieve a position of primacy within the territory concerned. Within them 'long, ugly tin warehouses replaced the industrial smoke-stacks of the industrial towns of Europe'.

The dual city

Cities representing the first of McGee's three sub-categories are to be found in their most typical form in those parts of the world that formed the subject of the last chapter. In all cases the European plantation stood apart from the older, indigenous town, both physically and in plan. Nowhere was this more strikingly so, however, than in British India.

Brush (1961) contrasts the colonial town, laid out to a pre-conceived plan and possessing separate functional areas, with the confused and mixed land use pattern of the adjacent Indian settlement. 'The tree-shaded streets are broad, metalled or paved, and the buildings are set well back. Structures are almost exclusively pucka (of brick or stone, often plastered, and with a cement or tile roof), and many of them stand in the midst of large fenced compounds with much space devoted to trees and grass or landscaped in formal gardens.' The typical 'bungalow' was large, rambling, and usually surrounded by a wide, pillared 'veranda'. Separation of the two townships was, in part, a consequence of the need for space for the new settlement, but segregation of life-styles undoubtedly played a major role in maintaining it. The railway, too, played an important part in directing the growth of the European town, especially after 1850, a period of urbanization which Caralp (1972) has referred to as 'railway British'. Three types of colonial settlement were established in British India: the military cantonment, the civil lines, and the railway colony.

The cantonment, like military camps everywhere, was relatively self-contained with its parade grounds and rifle ranges, hospital, churches, stores and depots for equipment. Living quarters were for the most part regularly arranged blocks of barracks, with commissioned officers having bungalows set apart from the ranks. *The civil station* housed the officials who carried out the colonial administration and here, also, were the various offices and public buildings in which the work of government, at whatever level, was carried out. Although housing principally Europeans and their house servants, both the civil station and the cantonment had a small bazaar section — a replica in miniature of the indigenous 'old city' — from which goods of an everyday character could be purchased. Following independence, the civil station was taken over by Indian officials but Brush's description illustrates the degree to which European influence has lingered on. 'Public offices, often housed in strictly European-style structures little adapted to India, usually include the administrative (district magistrate's) headquarters, the tax collector's office and court, the law court, and the police barracks and jail . . . Post and telegraph offices, foreign banks, insurance offices, hotels, cinemas, colleges and secondary schools following English curricula, and stores carrying goods of European types and fashions, all of which originally served the needs of the British governing class, now cater to the Anglicized native population.' Public buildings of this kind have also spread to the former cantonments. During the colonial period top government officials and military officers would retreat in the hot season to a hill station. It was here, according to Brush, that a cultural landscape most nearly resembling that of the British Isles was created. Houses were spread out and roads winding, a consequence partly of the relief, but also of the style of living that was followed.

In sharp contrast with that of the hill station, the layout of the *railway colony* tended to be rigidly geometrical. Parallel rows of small, brick-built dwellings housed the various grades of employee, segregation taking place not on the usual Indian basis of caste, language or religion, but according to economic status in the company. Low-paid Indian workers, of whatever cultural background, would be housed in single room units closest to the rail depot or to the works used for the manufacture or repair of locomotives and other equipment. Those with greater responsibility lived a little further out in rather larger dwellings, possibly

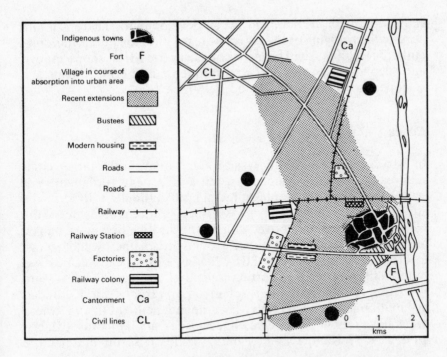

Indigenous towns

Fort   F

Village in course of absorption into urban area   ●

Recent extensions

Bustees

Modern housing

Roads

Roads

Railway   +―+―+

Railway Station

Factories

Railway colony

Cantonment   Ca

Civil lines   CL

54   Schematic diagram of a city of the Indo-Gangetic plain according to Caralp, 1972. (Courtesy the Editor of *L'Information Géographique*)

of two storeys, whilst the salaried managers and technicians, mainly British, occupied bungalows in their own grounds. Indian servants were usually housed in another row of small dwelling units nearby. Not only was segregation found on a Western rather than Indian basis but 'the system also differed from tradition in that the highest ranks would be found farthest out from the centre of town, usually on the opposite side of the railway tracks from the lowest ranks and the native bazaar. The commercial and industrial areas would be much less congested in a railway-owned settlement than in a typical Indian city. Broad streets were laid out, planted with trees alongside, and, if not paved with macadam, probably metalled with gravel and clay rolled hard.'

Streets were similarly wide and pleasant in the civil lines and the cantonment but without the rigid parallelism of the railway colony. In the civil lines they often focused on a central 'Mall'. Caralp has attempted to represent the arrangement of these different elements of the Anglicized Indian city in the form of a model (Fig. 54). What he refers to as the 'cordon sanitaire' which frequently separated the European settlements from the old city has

been filled with more recent urban development. There is a hint
here of the bridging of the two cultures 'with some public buildings
and offices, banks, and branches of European firms; shops appear,
and second-class cafes and bars frequented by both Indians and
Europeans' (Spate and Ahmad, 1950).

Africa

In Africa a similar duality was brought about in the larger cities
such as Ibadan and Kampala when a European settlement was
established close to the older, indigenous settlement. In form the
addition was comparable in many respects with the civil lines of the
Indian city described above, with administrative buildings, banks,
hospitals and shops etc. grouped around broad, uncrowded streets,
forerunner of the modern CBD. Ibadan's European nucleus was
built to the west of the Yoruba town and associated with it were
five reservations of houses set in large gardens for European
occupation. Since the country became independent in 1952 these
areas have tended to receive Nigerians 'of similar status' (Mabogunje, 1968). Kampala, like Rome, is built on 'seven' hills and the

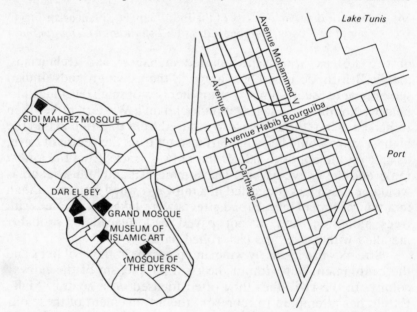

55   The old and new cities of Tunis. After Brown, 1973. (Courtesy
Darwin Press)

first colonial settlement was established in 1890 on Kampala hill to the north of the Bugandan capital on Mengo hill. A new, and larger, European township was laid out on Nakasero hill to the east of what is now known as Old Kampala in 1903. Southall (1967) describes the social ecology of Nakasero which has remained a distinctive part of modern Kampala, the location of the CBD. Near the top of the hill was the European club and around it the houses of the colonial officials, each with its spacious garden and quarters for African servants. Below this residential zone were the government offices and many other public buildings, the European commercial premises and, finally, near the foot of the hill, the Indian bazaar.

Duality and the juxtaposition of old and new in North Africa is strikingly illustrated in Brown's sketch plan of Tunis (Fig. 55). In Cairo, the ruler Ismail built a 'colonial-style' city in imitation of Haussmann's Paris in the 1860s. This was added to by the British from 1882 and Azbakiyah - Ismailiya remained for many years quite distinct from the old city of Al-Qahirah, what Abu-Lughod (1973) has described as 'an undissolved lump of European urbanism'.

Colonial foundations in South-East Asia

With the exception of Bangkok, all the major cities of South-east Asia may be regarded as colonial in foundation. That is not to say that all of them were laid out on greenfield sites. Some, such as Singapore, were, but others were established on or close to the sites of older settlements. In the latter instances, however, it was a case of the cuckoo quickly growing to fill the nest, and the pre-colonial nucleus failed to retain the functional importance of the old cities of, say, India or Nigeria.

Even the earliest urban settlements appear to have owed their origin to outside influence, mainly from China and India. McGee (1967) recognizes two types of 'pre-industrial' city: the 'market cities', coastal or riverine and living by trade, fore-runners in a sense of the great nineteenth-century ports; and the 'sacred cities', agrarian-based cities of the interior which flourished especially during the second half of the first millenium. Angkor in Cambodia provides the classic example of the latter, but Mandalay in Burma was established as a royal capital as late as 1857.

During the early centuries of colonial involvement in South-East Asia the indigenous market cities continued to serve the trading needs of the Western powers and, with the possible addition of a fort and administrative buildings, pre-industrial city forms persisted. Exceptions were to be found in the Spanish Philippines where a policy of town planting was implemented, and occasionally elsewhere. Batavia, for example, was laid out in imitation of a Dutch canal town, a 'replica town' in McGee's terminology. The nineteenth century brought rapid and striking changes. This period saw the emergence of the primate, port city —which for many exemplifies the South-East Asian city — but also witnessed the rise of a number of inland towns as centres for administration, mining or the despatch of agricultural products. They played an essentially complementary role to that of the major ports and, in the present century, some, such as Hanoi and Kuala Lumpur, have grown to considerable cities in their own right.

Amongst the leading cities of the colonial era only Bangkok resisted the impress of colonial domination. Elsewhere cities expanded, mostly in gridiron fashion, the extensions over-shadowing, if not totally obliterating, traces of the older nucleus. Most served as administrative centres, but their principal function was undoubtedly commercial. As McGee put it, 'the colonial city was the "nerve centre" of colonial exploitation. Concentrated here were the institutions through which capitalism extended its control over the colonial economy — the banks, the agency houses, trad-ing companies and the insurance companies'. Characteristic of all of them was the racially-diverse and immigrant nature of their population, though within the city the different groups remained highly segregated both residentially and in terms of occupation. Indeed segration was incorporated into city planning. 'The Euro-pean community of the colonial city was as closed and tight-knit as any Asian village. The spacious residences of the European com-munity, their clubs, the golf and racecourses, remain a permanent feature of the morphology of the contemporary city. The alien Asian communities of the cities were no less segregated, both residentially and occupationally, although they tended to mix much more in the market places.' The indigenous population, if they were drawn to the city at all, would live in semi-rural (Kampong-type) settlements on the urban fringe, engaging in casual and unskilled labouring jobs.

Despite the universality of many features of the South-East Asian colonial city — the European commercial quarter, the Chinese shophouse district, and the market gardens on the fringe — McGee suggests a division into three types, largely on the basis of the degree to which European influence dominated the form of the city:

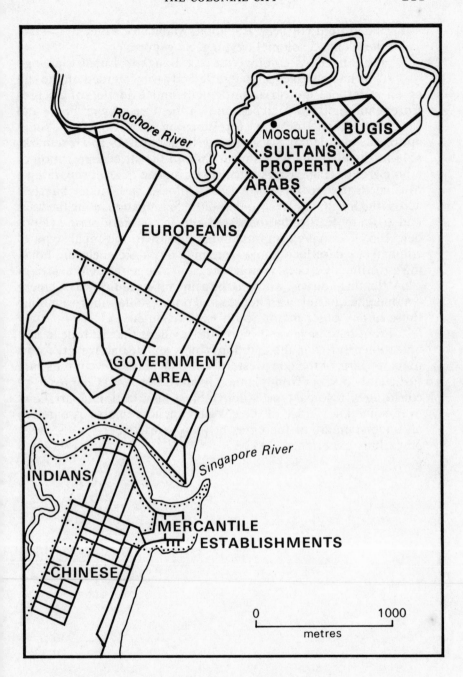

56   Distribution of ethnic groups in the plan of Raffles for Singapore,
     1828. After McGee, 1967. (Courtesy G. Bell & Sons)

1   the grafted city, e.g. Rangoon, Mandalay, Hué;
2   the planned colonial city, e.g. Singapore;
3   the indigenous 'colonial city', e.g. Bangkok, Luang Prabang.

As its name suggests, the grafted city was founded on the site of an older pre-industrial settlement and evidence of its pre-European origin is still to be found in the form of what Spate and Trueblood (1942) describe for Rangoon. as 'fossil areas'. Singapore was founded by Sir Stamford Raffles in 1819 and is remarkable for its planning which incorporated the strict segregation of ethnic groups (Fig. 56). A spacious European quarter separated a Muslim district to the north from Chinese and Indian quarters across the Singapore river to the south. Segregation along the lines laid down by Raffles has persisted into the modern period (Hodder, 1953). Bangkok approximated closest to the 'dual' type of colonial city described above, retaining its palace enclosure housing government offices, temples etc., and a large residential area of Thai 'floating houses', whilst at the same time acquiring its Chinese commercial quarter, warehouses and port installations resembling those of any other major South-East Asian city.

From the above description it is evident that European colonization resulted in the addition of new and distinctive city forms to many parts of the non-western world. Whether or not these are sufficiently distinct from planned forms elsewhere (Chapter 6) to constitute a 'colonial type' is debatable. Classifications apart, however, some knowledge of the colonial impact remains essential to an understanding of the cities of those areas where it was most powerfully experienced.

9

Modernization and the Non-Western City

Is contemporary urbanization, in a highly interconnected world, creating essentially similar city forms, or are the processes that underlie change so culture-specific that modern cities are increasingly divergent, rather than convergent, in structure and layout? Berry (1973) opts for the latter view, claiming that twentieth century urbanization may be seen to have taken a number of different paths. 'We are dealing with several fundamentally different processes that have arisen out of differences in culture and time, and these processes are producing different results in different world regions.' McGee (1971) appears to be moving towards a similar conclusion when he states that, 'Although the form of the urbanization process in the Third World may appear to be the same as that which characterized the West, the different *mix* of the components of the urbanization process in the Third World suggests that this factor is of such importance that at least one element of Western theory should be discarded when investigating the Third World city. This is the view that the city is an inducer of change ... Rather, the city must be seen as a symptom of processes operating at a societal level.' Wheatley (1963) goes still further, introducing the concept of the 'ethnocity'. He and Landay (1971) argue that no single city model provides an adequate tool for comparative study of the highly diverse social systems found in different parts of the world.

Observers who disagree with the above view have emphasized the forms which cities have in common, seeking to account for these in terms of what Berry refers to as underlying technological imperatives of modernization and industrialization. For Sjoberg the catalyst to change was industrial technology. Others, whilst prepared to admit the problems that arise from the attempt to equate industrialization with modernization, are nevertheless broadly in agreement. Harvey (1975), in a review of Berry's *Human Consequences of Urbanisation,* sees Third-World urbanization, for example, as no more than a localized manifestation of a global urbanization process. 'The different manifestations of urbanization in different regions are to be interpreted as parts of a whole rather than as separate processes which can be treated as isolated objects for study and comparison. It is doubtful if it makes any sense even to consider urbanization as something isolated from processes of capital formation, foreign and domestic trade, international money flows, and the like, for in a fundamental sense urbanization is economic growth and capital accumulation—and the latter processes are clearly global in their compass.' Johnston (1972 b) is expressing a somewhat similar point of view when he considers it possible to relate 'the spatial form of the city to ongoing social processes, notably the development of middle classes and their attendant housing-choice behaviour.'

An evolutionary view-point

It is a fairly easy step from the views expressed by Harvey and Johnston to the recognition of a sequence of stages through which the city passes as it submits to international forces of modernization. A sequence of this kind has, in fact, been suggested by Schnore (1964; 1965 b), largely on the basis of evidence collected in the cities of North and South America. He dismisses the cultural variable as something that does little more than invest certain areas of the city with 'non-rational' values. 'There seems to be no intrinsic reason for expecting an inordinate amount of culturally induced variability in the use of space.' Thus, instead of representing two culturally quite distinct types of city, the traditional 'pre-industrial' city of Latin America and the contemporary city of North America are at opposite ends of a spectrum where change is brought about by economic development and related shifts in social values. Five stages and one variant case are suggested, beginning with the pre-industrial city which exhibits what Schnore describes as a 'reversed-Burgess' pattern of social areas:

1 'Reversed Burgess' or Latin American pattern. High status groups live in the city centre and the poor on the periphery.
2 Similar to 1, except that the lowest status groups are more evenly spread through the city.
3 An intermediate type. The highest and lowest status groups are concentrated in the centre. A 'middle class' has emerged and lives in the suburbs.
4 An 'almost Burgess' city which differs from 5 only in the concentration of the very highest status groups in the centre.

5   The Burgess pattern. Low status groups are over-represented in the central city and high status groups in the suburbs.
6   A type differing from 5 in the relative suburbanization of the low status groups.

General support for Schnore's evolutionary hypothesis can be found in the distinction which Vance makes between the 'pre-capitalist' and 'capitalist' city. As choice of residence becomes determined by income rather than by traditional status, movement takes place of the better-off towards the edge of the city (page 188). Johnston (1972 b), whilst not questioning the need for an evolutionary view-point, offers a number of criticisms of Schnore's scheme. In particular it fails to take into account (1) the known sectoral development of socio-economic areas in many cities, (2) the survival of high-class areas near the centre of the city, and (3) the phenomenon common to many Third World cities of the squatter settlement or shanty town. Johnston proposes instead a model which introduces a stage between the 'pre-industrial' and 'industral' situations which he terms one of 'industrial take-off'. During this phase the city experiences a large increase in population, and more sophisticated division of labour takes place. A middle class emerges, engaged in tertiary occupations and enabling interaction to take place between specialized producers. Strongly marked communities tend to persist only at the upper and lower ends of the class spectrum. Residential patterning becomes based on wealth, although this does not preclude the survival of the 'urban village' type. Sectoral development of high-status areas is initiated. Other groups obtain housing by, (1) taking over dwellings vacated by the high-income groups; (2) paternalistic construction on the part of an employer; (3) speculative building by capitalists; (4) self-help construction. The first method is principally employed by the middle classes, the others by the 'working classes'.

Johnston's city in 'take-off' represents an interesting attempt to bring together in a single model what is known about the developing cities of nineteenth-century Europe (factory villages etc.) and those of the Third World at the present day (shanty towns). This stage is followed by one of 'continuing modernization' which is marked by expansion of the middle class, with suburbanization of the kind usually associated with the modern industrial city. Spatial community may remain amongst certain groups, however, notably the very poor or very wealthy, and in a number of ethnic societies.

Writing some years after the publication of *The Pre-industrial City,* Sjoberg (1965), like Johnston, introduces an intermediate stage between the pre-industrial and industrial types. This he terms the 'transitional city'. It is a stage which, as Johnston does in his 'take-off' phase, makes allowance for the large-scale rural to urban migration currently taking place in many Third World countries and for the phenomenon of the squatter settlements. According to Sjoberg, newcomers to the city do not behave as independent individuals but rather identify themselves with earlier migrants. The latter may be from their own village or region, or be of the same class, ethnic or occupational grouping. Enclaves arise within the city, corresponding with these common-interest groupings, and comparable with the immigrant communities typical of United States cities in the early part of the present century. 'Through these subsystems the migrant from the village or another city is orientated to the new urban milieu.' Their existence serves to maintain rural traditions and, by return visits, knowledge of the city is taken back to the village. According to Sjoberg, the survival of these subsystems tends to slow the rate of industrialization because of their 'orientation to a pre-industrial way of life'.

In assuming the merits of any evolutionary thesis of the kind outlined above, recourse must be made to the criticisms already presented of the conventional models of urban form and to accounts of urban residential structure (Chapter 3). The evolutionary models, however, represent an attempt to examine the city on a cross-cultural basis and thus incorporate features such as the shanty town, hitherto associated not so much with the Western city as that of the Third World. It is logical, therefore, to consider next whether this latter phenomenon can be fitted into any generalized interpretation of the city.

Spontaneous settlements

The squatter settlement is no recent addition to the urban landscape. Describing the ancient Mesopotamian city of Ur, Sjoberg (1960) observes that 'near the city's periphery resided the poorest people, as evidenced by hovels of mud and reed'. And Turner (1966) quotes a contemporary description of sixteenth-century London which, language apart, may well pass for comment on the barriadas of modern Lima. ' . . . both sides of the street be pestered with cottages and alleys, even up to Whitechapel Church, and almost half a mile beyond into the common field . . . But this common field . . . is so encroached upon by building of filthy cottages, and with other purpressors, inclosures and laystalls . . . that in some places it scarce remaineth a sufficient highway for the meeting of carriages . . . which is no small blemish to so famous a city to have so unsavoury and unseemly an entrance or passage thereunto.' Such settlements are not unknown in the cities of Europe at the present day, *bidonvilles* housing foreign workers having caused quite as much anxiety to the authorities of Paris in the 1960s as did Stow's 'suburbs without the walls' to the rulers of Elizabethan England. And the legal and other problems caused by squatters' occupation of vacant property continue to arouse regular correspondence in the British press.

It is, however, the massive increase in population which has taken place in the cities of the 'developing world' in the last few decades that has given rise to the squatter phenomenon as it is generally understood. It is not uncommon to find a third, sometimes more, of the population of some of the world's largest cities now living under such conditions. One-third of the population of Mexico City, representing one-and-a-half million people, were squatters in the mid-1960s. Fewer than 5 per cent of Lima's population lived in the *barriadas* in 1940; by 1966 the proportion was one-quarter and, extending these growth trends into the future, it is possible that three-quarters of the city's expected population of 4 500 000 could be living in squatter settlements by 1990 (Turner, 1966). In many cities in the Third World the population of the squatter settlements is increasing at a faster rate than that of the city itself, and the latter figure may well be over 6 per cent per annum. Nearly a half of Ankara's population live in the *gecekondu,* and in South-East Asia 'squatters now comprise between a quarter and a third of the total population of most of the region's capitals' (Jackson, 1974). Even higher proportions are recorded in some of the smaller cities that are experiencing rapid urban growth but missing the investment in housing which is channelled into the primate cities. The proportion of the city's area occupied by squatter settlements is also increasing noticeably. Jackson observes that, in 1969, squatter dwellings accounted for 13 per cent of the municipal area of Kuala Lumpur. Turner records what is probably still rather an extreme example, that of Kinshasa, where the *villes extracoutumiers* have an area that is greater than that of the remainder of the city.

Squatter settlements are defined by Dwyer (1975) as 'makeshift housing areas erected by the poor in Third World cities'. He, himself, prefers the term 'spontaneous settlement' because of the

legal implications of the word 'squatter'. Most spontaneous settlements originate by illegal occupation of private or publicly
owned land, but it is common for the occupants to seek later to
legitimize their position, and Dwyer considers the term 'squatter'
prejudicial to this aim. The phrase 'shanty town' is commonly used
in the sense of squatter or spontaneous settlement and is descriptive of the appearance of many of these makeshift housing areas.
Dwellings are constructed of whatever scrap materials can be
found—packing cases, galvanised iron sheets, cardboard etc.—
together with local building materials if they can be obtained. In
Medellin, Colombia, the principal materials used are *adobe* (mud
bricks) and *baharaque,* made from animal dung and the stumps of
sugar cane (Stadel, 1975). Where income permits it, individual
dwellings are likely to be improved over the course of time. Dwyer
describes the *ranchos* of Caracas: 'Wood may gradually be
replaced by brick, stone or cement; the earthen floor covered with
concrete; interior partitions in the houses transformed into internal walls, and ultimately extra rooms, and even sometimes a second floor, added.' It may be thought that 'shanty town' does less
than justice to this improving movement.

The word 'slum' conjures up too great a range of mental
images to be of much value in definition or description. For some it
is associated with the conditions that are encountered in inner city
tenements, in the *chawls* of Bombay for example, but also in the
inner city ghettoes of some Western cities. Slum-like conditions
also prevail in many shanty towns where streets are unpaved, there
is no lighting, the water supply is limited, water-borne sewage
disposal is rare, refuse collection is non-existent and where, in
consequence, there is a constant struggle against disease. From an
analysis of slum conditions, Stokes (1962) makes a distinction
between what he calls 'slums of despair' and 'slums of hope'. The
former are most likely to be encountered in the inner city, though
not necessarily only in the decaying tenements. The latter term
applies most appropriately to the improving kind of squatter settlement, commonly found on or near the urban fringe. Turner's
reference to 'the inner-city tenements and slums of the very poor,
the interstitial shanty towns, and the peripheral squatter settlements' is suggestive of a typology but he, like Dwyer, appreciat-
ing the problems that arise from the use of any of these terms for
what is in effect a wide range of types and conditions, prefers to
introduce a more general phrase: 'autonomous urban settlement'.
By that 'we mean urban settlement, whatever its duration or expectations may be, that takes place independently of the authorities

charged with the external or institutional control of local building and planning.' In parenthesis it should be noted that the phenomenon of the spontaneous or autonomous settlement has given rise to a variety of local or regional terms, often descriptive of the conditions represented there. Thus the Turkish *gecekondu* means 'built during the night'; others used include *barrios paracuidistas* (parachutists' quarters) in Mexico, *callampas* (mushrooms) in Chile, *villas misarias* in Buenos Aires and, indicative of changing attitude towards the squatter settlements, *pueblos jovenes* for what have long been known as *barriadas* in Peru.

Spontaneous settlements may be found in any part of the city and they range widely in size. Unquestionably the main factor affecting their location is the availability of vacant land or property; after that, access to a place of work is of importance, especially to the newcomer to the city who cannot afford the cost of public transport and is anxious to obtain casual or unskilled work in the CBD, the docks, or perhaps on the newly established industrial estate on the urban fringe. Frequently sites are those physically unsuited to more normal forms of housing development: steep hillsides, wadis and river valleys subject to flash flooding, swampland, railway embankments, garbage dumps, or the pavement. Dwyer notes that 'in Latin America there seems to be a tendency for spontaneous settlements to sprawl over larger areas than elsewhere. In Africa this feature is not nearly so marked, perhaps because urban populations as a whole are generally small, while in monsoon Asia the city is often surrounded by intensely cultivated land which tends to restrict sprawl.'

Some attention has been given to the search for a model relating to the formation of spontaneous settlements. Generally speaking it may be said to be based on the assumption that migrants to the city will first seek living space and employment near the centre and that later, possibly after marriage (migration often being sex-selective) and on securing permanent employment, they will seek to move out to the periphery, establishing a peri-urban squatter settlement. Eyre (1972) found evidence of this kind of migratory movement in his study of Montego Bay, Jamaica, and the theory has received a good deal of support from other work carried out in Latin America (Mangin, 1967; Morse 1971). Johnston (1972 b) explores the theory, applying the terms 'slums of despair' and 'slums of hope' respectively to the inner city and peri-urban settlements. He sees a close parallel between this migratory cycle and the suburbanization movement of less-well-off Americans to peri-urban trailer parks or of young New Zealand families (the 'suburban peasantry') to state-financed housing developments on the edge of the city. The differences are ones of degree (of poverty, state involvement etc.), not of kind.

Johnston also refers to the distinction made by Turner (1968)

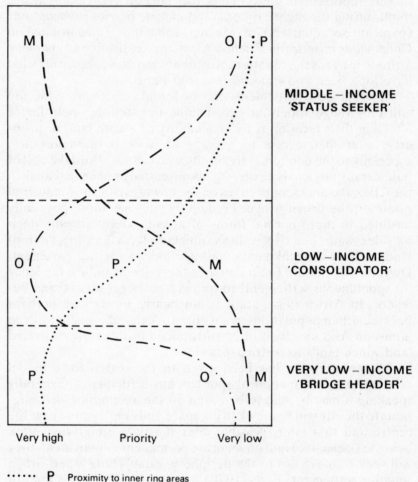

MIDDLE – INCOME
'STATUS SEEKER'

LOW – INCOME
'CONSOLIDATOR'

VERY LOW – INCOME
'BRIDGE HEADER'

Very high   Priority   Very low

······ P   Proximity to inner ring areas

–·– O   Permanent ownership and residence

– – M   Modern standard of amenity

57 Housing aspirations of different sections of the population in Third World cities according to Turner, 1968. (Courtesy the Editor of the *Journal of the American Institute of Planners*)

between 'low-income bridgeheaders', 'low-income consolidators' and 'middle-income status seekers'. Bridgeheaders are the migrants from the country who live first in the inner city; consolidators are those who, having established themselves, move out to the fringe in order to satisfy their aspirations, especially for better housing conditions; whilst the status seekers are ones who have achieved economic security and are able to move to a part of the city which affords them increased social status (Fig. 57). These sub-divisions can be linked to a developmental model, and Turner makes a distinction between what he calls cities in early transition, mid-transition and late transition. In the first phase there are few migrants to the city; during the second phase there are large numbers of in-migrants who crowd into the central city (the situation in Mexico City, for example, in 1950); in the third phase in-migration is slowing and movement is mainly outwards from the city centre to peripheral locations prompted partly by rising living standards, by high rents and insecure tenure in inner-city tenements and by commercial development of the central city (Mexico City at the present day).

It is significant that the evidence in support of the above ideas is drawn principally from Latin America and it must not be assumed that spontaneous settlements originate in precisely the same way in all parts of the world. Dwyer comments, 'The same tendency (for migrants to proceed first to inner-city areas) undoubtedly exists in both Asia and Africa, though whether the proportions of migrants currently successful in finding inner-city accommodation are as high as in Latin America is perhaps more doubtful. It would seem that in most African cities the opportunities for residence in inner-city areas would probably be proportionately fewer than those in South America because of a lesser development of multi-storeyed tenement areas, while in south and eastern Asia such inner areas have for long been very much more densely peopled than those in Latin America and already they may well have approached their limits in terms of human carrying capacity.' Even where movement is typically to the inner city and then outwards, it need not be assumed that all peri-urban squatter settlements are peopled exclusively in this way. Once established, such a settlement is certain to attract rural migrants who, obtaining information from relatives visiting the village from the city, move there direct.

Support for this latter view lies in the extent to which city-dwellers do return, for short or longer stays, to their village of origin—a feature of urban life in Africa in particular—and in the

clustering of people of similar origin within the spontaneous settlements. Kinship ties appear to play a key role in determining
where migrants live, newcomers settling near relatives who help
them to find accommodation and also work. Evidence for such
grouping has been found in different parts of the world: in Tripoli
(Libya), for example, by Harrison (1967); in Monterrey (Mexico)
by Vaughan (1970); in Libreville (Gabon, West Africa) by Lasserre (1958); and in Baghdad by Phillips (1958). Turner (1966)
notes that in Ankara settlement patterns are closely related to
village origin, whilst Jackson (1974) draws similar conclusions in
South-East Asia: 'Generally newly arrived migrants seek the assistance of relatives, friends or fellow villagers already in the city and,
in large measure, this determines where they settle and, to a lesser
extent, the occupations they enter. These spatial clusterings are
perpetuated partly through the continual arrival of new migrants
and partly through the strong preference for ethnic endogamy.
Usually, the migrants retain close links with their home village,
making regular visits for ceremonial and other occasions, remitting
cash and, in the case of young males, frequently returning to marry
a village girl who they then bring to the city.'

Closely allied to the idea of bridgeheaders and consolidators is
that of self-help, the view that squatters, far from being lawless,
immoral, frustrated revolutionaries, are in fact conservative by
temperament and, provided they are not hounded by the government, able to improve the quality of their settlement by their
own initiative and labour. Again the strongest evidence is from
Latin America, Turner drawing for his concept of consolidators on
such examples as the Cuevas *barriada* of Lima (Turner, 1967). Of
Rio de Janeiro it has been said that 'the forced intimacy of the
urban slum breeds conflict but also a variety of simple forms of
organization to deal with common problems. Though the petty
crime and violence of the *favela* fill the front pages of Rio's more
sensational press day after day, a great many *favela* families are
relatively stable, have fairly regular employment, and are even
rigidly conventional by middle-class standards' (Bonilla, 1961).
The most common form of self-help involves improvements to the
home by the individual or his family, but communal organizations
are also formed with responsibilities that range from the building
of roads and schools to the organization of police protection and
the provision of credit facilities. Communal action may even
extend to the actual layout of the settlement.

With the exception of Latin America, evidence of self-
improvement in the squatter settlements is largely confined to the

cities of Turkey and North Africa. Of India and Pakistan, Turner (1966) writes: 'We have no information, so far, to show that *bustees, jhonpris* or *jhuggis* tend to develop into anything approaching an acceptable modern environment'. And Dwyer observes that 'it is possible to set against the improving parts of the Lima *barriadas* the generally static experience of the *bustees* of Calcutta, for example, and most east Asian squatter areas seem to conform more to the Calcutta pattern in this respect than to that of the improving parts of the Lima *barriadas*'. Squatter settlements may generate small-scale industries, especially of the workshop kind. There are many such trades in the *bustees*. But self-improvement on the Latin American scale appears to take place according to Turner, only 'where industrialization has made a significant start'.

The success of self-help schemes depends to a large extent on official attitudes towards the spontaneous settlements which, in turn, are likely to be governed by the political power exercised by the squatters, including their right to vote. Numerous are the examples of squatter settlements that have been bulldozed because they were an eyesore, or to make way for an urban redevelopment scheme. In some cases they have been replaced by blocks of flats that are little more than an expensive showcase. Dwyer quotes the example of the superblock programme in Caracas which, far from solving that city's housing problem, added to it. More migrants were attracted to the city, whilst bad design and failure to control sub-letting resulted in a high degree of social disorder. A major problem confronting most governments contemplating a house- or apartment-building programme is the inability of most of the potential occupants to pay anything approaching an economic rent. Few can afford to follow the example of the government of Hong Kong who achieved considerable success with a massive programme of low cost apartment housing. Jackson reflects on the application of these methods in other parts of South-East Asia: 'Elsewhere, as in Kuala Lumpur and Singapore, official efforts at a solution hinge on the provision of low-cost housing, mostly in the form of high-rise flats. Yet, even when rent concessions are allowed, these schemes have had varied success. There are doubts about the appropriateness of multi-storeyed housing for recent rural in-migrants and in any case with only 10-15 per cent of their incomes available for rents, many squatters cannot afford even the low rates chargeable. Moreover, with continued in-migration, resettlement often does little to reduce the total squatter population.'

The alternative to this kind of programme is the encouragement of self-help, the impetus towards which has so far largely come, as we have seen, from Latin America. Such encouragement is likely to involve provision by the authorities of a site and services, possibly of some basic building materials, and the rest is left to the individual or to groups. The method has also been employed in New Towns, for example in Cuidad Guayana, Venezuela, where the planning authority has reserved sites for squatter occupation, assisting them with advice on construction methods and with loans for the purchase of materials. Granting of security of tenure is closely linked with the promotion of self-help. It was on the basis of what was seen to be happening in *barriadas* like that of Cuevas that the Peruvian government introduced legislation in 1961 which enabled official recognition and security of tenure to be granted to existing *barriadas* and provided funds for the provision of services and of loans for self-help construction. Dwyer notes that most schemes involving the legitimization of tenure in Lima have been on public land and he wonders whether it will prove possible in the future to arrange the transfer of land from *private* ownership to the inhabitants of squatter settlements, both here and in other parts of the Third World.

The granting of security of tenure to existing sites is not invariably the right answer. Squatter settlements usually have such a haphazard distribution throughout the urban area that to formalize all these locations would be seriously to impede future planning of the city. Furthermore, the sites which squatters have been able to occupy are often unsuitable for long-term occupation, whilst the internal arrangement of the settlements may be so chaotic as to make any kind of improvement very difficult. The obvious alternative is the provision of suitable greenfield sites but this, in turn, raises other planning issues, not least that of access to work or to public transport.

The problem of housing the population of world cities such as Calcutta would appear to be almost insuperable and to be getting worse. Help on an international scale seems to offer the only possibility of reducing, at least in the short term, the misery of disease, starvation and early death. Where the problem is of lesser dimensions one may find encouragement in the inherent resourcefulness of man. A final example will suffice, that of the Plaka settlement on the northern slope of the Acropolis in Athens and described by Turner as 'probably a "provisional" squatter settlement when it started life some 130 years ago. It is now a delightful area where accommodation is sought by writers, artists, and, even, by architects.'

Latin America

In at least two respects, the commercialization of the central city and the suburbanization of the wealthier section of the population, the larger cities of Latin America are coming to resemble those further north. Towering office blocks, department stores and fashionable hotels, newly-widened streets and traffic interchanges are as obvious a part of the urban scene in Caracas or Mexico City as they are in Houston or Toronto. Partly in response to the pressures arising from these commercial developments, and partly also to the opportunities provided by increased mobility, the wealthy have shown a strong tendency to move away from the formerly elite areas of the central city towards high-status suburbs. Here there is clearer air; there may be a good view; and they are well separated from the inner city slums, the crowded tenements with all the social problems associated with fast-growing urban populations. Such movement usually follows a sectoral path but is influenced by local topography. The outward migration of the wealthy has been well documented for a number of Latin American capitals—Bogota, Quito, Santiago and Lima—by Amato (1970 a, b), and for Rio by Morris and Pyle (1971). In Quito, for example, a city situated at an average height above sea level of 2800 m, the movement has been to slopes which receive the warming influence of the afternoon sun and the city now extends for a distance of 18 km from north to south, but only 2-4 km from east to west (Bromley, 1974). In these fashionable suburbs there is considerable diversity of house style, as Odell and Preston (1973) observe: 'In the middle and upper class suburbs the house style is more heterogeneous than in Anglo-America or Europe. Colonial-style homes (built after 1960) that would not be out of place in Beverly Hills California, stand cheek by jowl with rococo extravaganzas looking like gingerbread castles. Gleaming, daring, modern plateglass houses stand beside copies of Anglo-American ranch-style houses.' In a detailed study of Bogota, Amato (1968) found that architectural style had a good deal of status significance and was closely bound up with the suburbanization process. Morris and Pyle reach the more general conclusion that the 'self-interest of the upper classes (remains) a dominating factor in urban development in Latin American cities'.

Evidence in support of the suburban movement noted above

has been derived principally from observation of the largest cities in Latin America and it would be premature to suggest this trend was universal and that the elite had everywhere abandoned their central city residences. Beyer (1967) points to several factors which have had a restraining effect on suburbanization and which, together, serve as a reminder of what may be termed 'the cultural constraint'. One of these is related to landownership and, in particular, the tendency to keep land 'in the family'. 'Historically . . . landownership has been the source of political power, economic sustenance, and social prestige. In part, this emphasized trait was inherited from Spain, but it has been further strengthened by a general lack of further investment opportunites for capital. The early disinclination to sell land has continued, and much land, in some cities, is leased or converted to other use rather than sold.' Another restraint is to be found in the traditional form of dwelling, 'The centering of family and social activities around inner patios has caused an indifference to the existence of nearby commercial and even manufacturing activities.' The inward-looking dwelling also helped to isolate the wealthy from the poor clamouring in the street outside. Beyer also refers to the legacy of colonial planning and to the rebuilding or relocation which has, in some cases, followed earthquake damage.These have, in different ways, kept the central area 'as much suited for residential as for other use'.

A consequence of the only-partial abandonment of the central area by the wealthy is, according to Beyer, that 'land use throughout the cities shows a high mix with manufacturing and commerce and professional and other services scattered more or less haphazardly, and with little segregation of exclusive residential areas from other activities'. Where they have been abandoned, the mansions of the elite, with their many rooms arranged around a central patio, have lent themselves to conversion into small, single-room apartments. Known variously as *vecindades, conventillos, corticos,* or *callejones,* these tenements house both 'middle classes' and some of the urban poor.

The extent to which economic progress has led to the emergence of a middle class is a matter of debate; equally questionable is the degree to which valid comparisons can be made between the residential behaviour of such a group and that of the middle classes in a Western industrial city. The debate is central to the problem of whether or not Third World societies are undergoing 'modernization'. From his studies in the four capital cities, Amato observed that middle-income groups are to be found both in the central areas 'discarded' by the elite and, further out, in buffer zones between the residential areas of the rich and those of the poor. On the basis of this and other evidence, Johnston (1972b) moved to the more general conclusion that 'In Latin American cities . . . as in New Zealand and, probably, North America too, the sectoral residential districts of the elite are being outflanked by middle-class developments. Having pioneered the move to suburbia, the upper-class are now finding themselves in the same position as their counterparts in New Zealand. Whether they, too, will become stable in their neighbourhood location, while middle-class developments extend the city further still, only occasionally containing a pocket of 'better' quality residences, will determine whether a general process common to the cities of both cultures can be identified.' Johnston's views are easier to accept if one is able to interpret the peripheral squatter settlements as 'slums of hope', as incipient middle class suburbs occupied by 'consolidators'. As we have seen, the evidence of self-help and improvement in these settlements is derived to a large extent from Latin American experience. Public housing constitutes another variable. Fox's (1969) work in Mexico suggests that when there is a limited supply of public housing it is usually taken by middle class families who can afford to pay the rent, or, where property is sold, to obtain a mortgage. If this is generally true, the location of such housing will direct the 'out-flanking' movement, as appears to have been the case in New Zealand.

There is still a big gap in Latin American society between rich and poor and in these circumstances the appropriateness of using the term 'middle class' will remain in question. Large numbers are certainly employed in low-grade tertiary occupations—what C. G. Clarke has referred to as 'refuge activities'—but the better kind of white-collar jobs are often in short supply or, in the poorer countries, are taken by outsiders e.g. foreign businessmen. Social contrasts are mirrored in the fabric of the city: in the proximity of squatter huts to the skyscraper or the modern factory, of ranch-style houses on their hill-top to the shanties in the ravine below. If the rate of population growth in these cities were comparable with that in Western Europe one might, with some confidence, look forward to the emergence of middle class suburbs; in present circumstances one hesitates to forecast what form they will assume by the end of the century.

The Caribbean

Caribbean cities resemble those of mainland Latin America in their close intermingling of modern and traditional forms. 'Colonial grid patterns are surrounded, and dominated, by a variety of geometrical and haphazard layouts. The location of multiple stores in city centres, the replacement of old office blocks with high-rise buildings and the rapid growth of shopping precincts in the suburbs, are outgoing signs of the importation of the American way of life. But in small towns, shops are often lock-up sheds, and concrete and neon are appearing only slowly . . . There is a continuum between small traditional communities and large urban centres which is reflected in fabric, land use and ecology' (C. G. Clarke, 1974). Clarke observes that some of the smaller towns still exhibit a social gradient which declines from the centre to the periphery but that in larger centres there has been 'a partial reversal of the original sequence'. There has been a move to the suburbs as 'upper-income groups leave their old-fashioned homes to inhabit ostentatious properties which reveal more conspicuously their superior status and life-style'. Social differences remain very great, however, and there is still a colour-class hierarchy. There are government-financed housing estates, most of them on the edge of the city, but Clarke notes that in spite of their use of modern designs and layout, these areas of public housing are often 'as socially deprived as the inner sections of the city'.

Squatters make up a lower proportion of the total city population in the West Indies than is common in much of Latin America, rarely accounting for more than 5 or 6 per cent of the population of any one town. The explanation of these low figures lies in the use which is made of other forms of accommodation. Central city tenements are minutely sub-divided, single rooms being let off to families, whilst rent yards are available in some cities. These are plots which are leased to tenants who build their own dwellings—mostly simple wooden sheds. Where squatting takes place there is some evidence of the outward movement of 'consolidators' from inner city tenements to 'improving' shanty towns (Eyre, 1972), and there are a number of government-sponsored site-and-service schemes, notably in Jamaica. But since squatters form a relatively small proportion of the urban population, and therefore constitute a weak political pressure group, it has been more common for individual governments to ignore their needs or even to seek to remove them. Thus, although there are exceptions to the generalization, Clarke's conclusion is that 'conditions in the (squatter) settlements rarely improve over time either through government help or individual initiative'.

The Middle East and North Africa

The most striking feature of the contemporary Middle Eastern city is the close juxtaposition of old and new, of the traditional and the modern. It is as obvious at the scale of the single street as it is in the contrast between the alleyways and courtyards of the madina and the boulevards and squares, public buildings and apartment blocks of the twentieth-century city. Abu-Lughod (1969 a) refers to a 'time-technology' dimension in Cairo, where 'side by side stand the modern factory and the primitive workshop, the bank and the turbaned moneylender, suggesting the persistence of a vital residue from yet another variety of urban living.' The wider differences are described for Iranian cities by Clark and Costello (1973) who note the influence of Western styles on the form of the modern city: ' . . . the end result of suburban development in the larger cities has been to create cities which have a dual personality and form with what might be called Western and non-Western parts, broadly similar to the pattern in India, south-east Asia or West Africa, or to those in other Middle Eastern countries. The smart houses, broad tree-lined avenues, *maidans* (roundabouts) and modern retailing facilities of the new parts of Iranian cities contrast with the dense jumble of houses, pathways and cramped bazaars of the old. But while the traditional parts of Iran's cities are idiosyncratically Persian, Islamic and personal, the new too often conform to the mediocrity and vulgarity of Western commercial culture in planning, architecture and life styles.'

The persistence of traditional activities, even in the more modern parts of the city, is brought out in Khalaf and Kongstad's (1973) study of the Hamra district of Beirut, a cosmopolitan area of the city which became popular as a place of residence of an emergent middle class following the establishment of the American University in 1866. 'Market analysts, systems engineers, and public relations experts still coexist with the self-employed middleman or traditional brokers. Supermarkets have not as yet displaced the small shopkeeper or the grocery store. Nor have shopping centres for ready-made clothes and mass-produced shopping goods driven the tailor, carpenter, or traditional black-smith out of business. In much the same way, the traditional moneylender and idle rentier still coexist with bankers, heads of investment firms, and real estate agents. Finally, eating stalls and street vendors continue to derive a viable existence despite the proliferation of self-service restaurants and sidewalk cafes. In short, much like the mixed character of its land use pattern, Hamra

continues to display a dualistic and mixed occupational structure.'
The authors conclude that the duality which they observe is
unlikely to disappear in the near future.

Adding to the confused picture that arises from the close
intermingling of life-styles are the effects of rapid population
growth, both by natural increase and by city-ward migration.
These are to be seen in changes taking place in both the old and the
new parts of the city; they express themselves also in the form of
peripheral squatter settlements and, where resources permit, in
public housing projects. Abu-Lughod (1969a) suggests that the
clue to understanding the contemporary Middle Eastern city lies in
the recognition of three contrasted life styles: rural, traditional
urban, and modern. 'The Middle Eastern city is not all of one
piece; it is not simply a special "urban type" which differs from
western cities by virtue of its unique Islamic heritage or by virtue of
the particular culture in which it grows. Although these are important factors,they are not the only ones. Cairo contains within it the
contrasting lifeways of the peasant village, the pre-industrial city
and the modern metropolis. As such it comprises a mosaic of
subcities which exemplify each of these models. To the observer,
these subcities present striking visual contrasts and seem at times
to represent separate social worlds which co-exist without inter-
penetration.' From her studies of the social ecology of Cairo based
on factor analysis (Abu-Lughod, 1966; 1969b) she concludes that
the variables which best express these life-style differences are
literacy, age at which women marry, fertility, and household over-
crowding. 'Modern' family characteristics are confined to the
higher classes able to enjoy the benefits of modernisation.

Migration to the city, whether it be to the crowded quarters of
the inner city or to peripheral squatter settlements, is strongly
influenced by the place of residence of kinsmen or of earlier
migrants from the same village. This congregation of ex-villagers is
brought about, not only by the need for security and perhaps for
help in finding a job and place to live, but also through the work of
formal associations which offer various kinds of aid to their members. There were already more than a hundred village benevolent
associations in Cairo in the mid-1950s (Abu-Lughod, 1961). By
settling close to relations and friends, migrants serve to perpetuate
the socio-cultural characteristics that have made the quarters such
a distinctive feature of the traditional Middle Eastern city. They
also ensure that such differences are built into the newer parts of
the city. In 1960 the *sarā-if,* squatter settlements, of Baghdad were
made up of eleven tribal groups. 'They were established so that the

members of each group were clustered together. Their shaykhs continued to exercise their authority by adjudicating disputes and maintaining guesthouses. While tribal codes of conduct and indemnification were maintained, they were adapted somewhat to city conditions and problems such as the one created by the operation of motor vehicles' (Gulick, 1969). The same author notes similar grouping based on village-of-origin in the *gecekondu* of Ankara and Istanbul.

The portion of the city in which migrants settle is also influenced by the direction from which they have travelled and by proximity to point of arrival (cf. similar conclusions from Western cities, Chapter 3). Both Abu-Lughod in Cairo and Gulick (1967), in his work on Tripoli (Lebanon), note the importance to newcomers of the bus station which provides a link with the home village. When settlement began this may have been on, or close to, the edge of the then built-up area of the city. Marital status also affects choice of residential location, unmarried males generally gravitating to a more central location. In Iran, at least, there is evidence of the two-stage migration process, first to the inner city and then outwards, which was noted above in connection with Latin America. 'First stage migration to cities such as Isfahan and Mashad is that of non-established migrants from rural areas to central areas of the old town. The map of males per 100 females for Isfahan shows concentrations of males around the old central bazaar. Many of these are known to be migrants not yet well enough established to bring in their families; they live in the caravanserais and lodging houses of the old town centre or with relatives and fellow villagers. Second-stage migration is that of better connected or longer established families from other small, urban areas to the new suburbs or from the centre of the old town to the peripheral suburbs' (Clark and Costello).

The old city, the madina, though still displaying many of the characteristics described in Chapter 7, has not remained unaffected by population growth and by the pressures exerted by the motor vehicle and the blandishments of 'Western commercial culture'. Khalaf and Kongstad describe the crowding of migrants in the houses of the central city vacated by middle- and upper-income groups moving out to modern apartments on the urban fringe or to detached residences in the suburbs. Former courtyards are filled in with new constructions, and extra storeys added to existing houses in an attempt to accommodate the influx. Those who fail to find space in the central city have to resign themselves to life in squatter camps on the periphery. Similar crowding of the old city is observed by Dethier (1973) in Morocco. Removal of the better-off has resulted in the creation of what Dethier describes as 'proletarian or sub-proletarian ghettoes within the old walls'. The madinas become 'reservations' for an uprooted population and for 'a proletariat living in often appalling conditions'. In some cities, however, notably in Fez which attracts large numbers of tourists, attempts have been made to improve the quality of life in the madina through expenditure on sanitation and other public services, on the restoration of historic buildings and the revitalization of selected craft industries.

Clark and Costello refer to the destruction of older residential and commercial property in the centre of Iranian cities in response to the demand for higher-order central area functions, and J. I. Clarke (1963) describes the segmentation of the old city of Shiraz in order to accommodate the motor vehicle. But in those parts of the old quarters untouched by such developments there is the same crowding of population and general poverty of services as in other cities of the Middle East. Kermanshah may serve as a model: 'The old city lacks facilities and services, has a high room occupancy and acts as a reception area for many of the poorer migrants coming from nearby small towns and tribal areas. Many of the newcomers are accommodated in sub-divided houses now vacated by the more successful members of the urban community while others are found in caravanserais and other commercial premises now functionally outmoded as their centrality has declined' (Clark and Costello). The old cities not only display higher population densities than the newer suburbs, but have higher rates of natural increase and lower levels of literacy. Abu-Lughod (1961) also found that low levels of literacy picked out some of the inner areas of Cairo where newcomers cling to rural tradition to the extent of, in some cases, building village bread-ovens on the top floors of their urban dwellings.

Contrasts between the old and new portions of Middle Eastern cities are striking despite the intermingling of forms noted at the beginning of this section. They are observed for Shiraz by J. I. Clarke: 'New Shiraz is middle and upper class, educated, literate and wealthy; old Shiraz is working class or unemployed, still largely illiterate and poor . . . in new Shiraz we find all the cinemas, the main hotels, the three major hospitals, and the University, as well as all the principal industrial sites and military areas'. Such bi-polarity may be observed throughout the Middle East and North Africa with the frequent, though not invariable, addition of squatter camps, some self-help settlements (*trames sanitaires* in

Morocco) and government housing schemes. To what extent does this represent modernisation? Drawing her evidence from what she describes as the 'grey areas' of Cairo—lower middle class districts where 'typists and clerks, mechanics, electricians, and machine operators live side by side with and even within the same extended family households as petty proprietors, minor bureaucrats and simple workmen who follow older ways of making a living', Abu-Lughod (1969 a) is in little doubt that a new society is emerging. Here are 'the crucibles in which the Cairo of tomorrow—maturing beyond the ethnic fissions and class extremes of yesterday—is being forged'. Others are less sanguine, seeing resistance to change in the 'urban villages' of both the old city and the new settlements, and the persistence of divisions even in the wealthier suburbs. Of the Lebanese middle class, for example, Khalaf and Kongstad suggest that although it possesses the earning capacity and life-style necessary for the reception of new ideas and patterns of behaviour, it is nevertheless weak as a social group—more employed than 'employing'—lacking the 'cohesion and self-consciousness which characterized the growth of the middle class in other (Western industrial) societies'. Gulick (1969) also expresses doubts, drawing attention to the survival of elitism: 'Mobility into and out of the elite is considerable, but the existence of the elite is a constant factor.' Other observers have noted the rise of new forms of factionalism in place of the traditional ones. Of these, politics is perhaps the most powerful, its strength reinforced by revolutionary movements. Thus, 'in Baghdad you can quite clearly determine which is the Ba'athist area, which is the "Iraq-first" nationalist area, and which is the Nasserite area' (Lenczowski, 1969). Some of these factions coincide with older tribal, ethnic or religious divisions in the city; sometimes there is no such connection. For Landay (1971) the problem is to determine how the values and institutions of Islamic culture provide continuity between traditional patterns of society and transformations to the modern.

Africa south of the Sahara

Studies of African towns, particularly those by social anthropologists, have also been concerned with the extent to which ethnic ties are either weakened or reinforced as a result of urbanization. It was fashionable at one time to emphasize the 'detribalizing' influence of the town, but later work has pointed to the survival, at least amongst a large section of the urban population, of traditional groupings and loyalties. On the basis of studies in Addis Ababa, Shack (1973) concludes that 'African towns are not "melting-pots" for rural Africans with diverse tribal backgrounds. Even after living in an urban environment for periods of up to a generation or more, Africans in town retain their tribal identity and membership in the rural society. . . . African townsmen generally do not lose their ethnic traits and tribal characteristics after several decades of active participation in the social, political, and economic spheres of urban society. . . . separation from tribal life and entry into urban life, far from weakening the bonds between tribal members, on the contrary greatly strengthens them . . . . Urban associations and ceremonial cults based on ethnic membership both express and reinforce ethnic solidarity, which is commonly connected with competition for employment or trade.'

Other writers likewise point to the maintenance of tribal bonds and the value of these to the urban newcomer. Of migrants to the towns of Zambia, Mitchell (1967) notes: 'People in rural areas are apt to take their tribe for granted, but when they come to the town their tribal membership assumes new importance.' Similar comment is forthcoming from Rouch (1956) who observes that in Ghana 'ethnic ties are greatly strengthened by separation from one's home, residence in an urban area, and job competition in a free market situation'. Southall (1967) concludes his study of Kampala-Mengo with the comment that 'the African townsman brings a lot of cultural and tribal luggage with him to town, on the strength of which he fabricates new relationships to meet urban needs.' And of African towns in general, Spengler (1967) says: 'Movement into cities does not, of course, produce agglomerations of "detribalized" and disorganized individuals, but rather organizations, deriving from tribal affiliations or emerging *de novo,* which relate individuals to other individuals and to the city and thus cushion the impact of city life on those newly settling there.' The range of such organizations is great, embracing trade unions and political parties as well as associations aimed at providing social and financial security. And their strength is not easily undermined. Looking at local government in the contemporary Yoruba town, for example, Lloyd (1973) finds that 'ward and constituency boundaries often follow those of the compounds and quarters, and various local rivalries often develop into political factions and form the basis of membership of rival parties'. Commenting on Shack's views (above), Banton (1973) considers that 'urban tribalism' or ethnicity is most likely to be projected into the

labour market under conditions where economic growth is relatively low and employment does not require advanced technical
skills. In Southern Africa, opposition to a European-owned company may serve to unite diverse groups who, when there is no
commonly-observed threat, divide along traditional lines.

Maintenance of ethnic ties is assisted by the extent to which
the African townsman retains close links with his home village, and
examples of town-based benevolent associations can be found, the
aim of which is not to help assimilate the immigrant into town life
but to improve the lot of rural kinsmen (Shack, 1973). The degree
to which the townsman is involved in both urban and rural affairs is
governed in large measure by distance of the town from the rural
home and the nature of the transport services between the two
(Mitchell, 1973). In the case of the Yoruba, where groups of
townsmen hold lands outside the town, the links are very close.
Bascom (1963) has described the Yoruba as 'commuters, not from
their places of work in the city, but from their city homes to the belt
of farms which surrounds each city', and according to Lloyd (1973)
'some men spend most of the year in the hamlet, returning to the
town only for the major religious feasts or for important funerals',
whilst 'craftsmen or clerks may visit their farms at weekends or in
slack periods of work.' P. Mayer's (1962) study of the Xhosa in
East London affords a detailed picture of a group which maintains
a high degree of rural orientation, recreating in the town the 'moral
and cultural atmosphere of their own (rural) homes'. Labour migration is another factor which serves to maintain a cultural bridge
between town and country in many parts of Africa (Mitchell, 1961;
Prothero, 1964). Involving some five million Africans a year, it is
brought about by the needs of agriculture as well as mining, periods
of residence in the town ranging from weeks to several years.

It may be, as Dwyer (1975) suggests, that the stability of town
life in Africa is increasing. But evidence of the kind referred to
above is not indicative of rapid change, and the persistence of
ethnic divisions remains apparent in the form of the contemporary
African city. In those cities of pre-colonial origin there is a similar
contrast between old and new to that observed in the Middle East
and North Africa. Overcrowding of the old town has brought about
what Mabogunje (1968) has described as the 'fission of the compound', whilst open spaces like the palace grounds have been
subdivided to make way for the offices of local or regional
administration (Fig. 58). 'The walls have crumbled, and the earth
from the ramparts has been taken to build the new houses which
are extending beyond the former limits of habitation. As the old

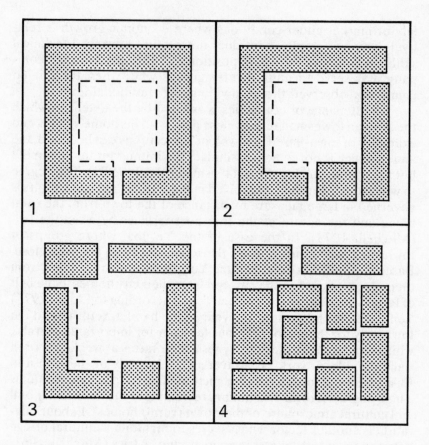

58   Stages in the 'fission' of a traditional Yoruba compound according to
      Mabogunje, 1968. (Courtesy Hodder and Stoughton)

courtyards grow derelict they are replaced by single- or two-storey
houses which increasingly tend to face the newly constructed
roads. Shops and gas stations spring up around the main market
and the new truck parking lots' (Lloyd, 1973). Yet despite this
veneer of modernity, the Yoruba town, with its electoral divisions
reproducing the old quarters (above) 'is still far from possessing
those features usually attributed to the urban area'. The market
remains a vigorous institution and certain forms of retailing that
are common in the Western city, e.g. grocery and butchery, have
no formal existence in Nigerian cities (Mabogunje, 1968). The
break-up of the compound may be a product of social change as
well as of the pressure of numbers, but the extended family remains
a strong force as Morris (1960) and Aldous (1962) have demonstrated.

In a description of the newer residential districts of Ibadan, Mabogunje (1968) distinguishes three types of suburb: those to the east of the old city mostly occupied by young families moving away from the crowded compounds; those to the west where the population is largely immigrant and housing is of poorer quality (single-storey, often mud-built); and the high-quality districts which include the 'reservations' built for Europeans and occupied since the country became independent by Nigerian administrators and businessmen. The three-fold division may serve as a crude model of the residential structure of many African towns at the present day, though it may be necessary to add a fourth element to allow for the semi-rural, squatter-type settlements on the periphery occupied by recent arrivals to the city (the *zongo* of Ghana and the *sabongari* of Nigeria).

Of the immigrant areas, Mabogunje (1967) says: 'The morphology of this half of Ibadan reflects the ethnic and racial differences among the immigrant groups; the date of arrival of the earliest substantial section of each group; the prevalent idea of housing and architectural design; the incidence of land apportionment and sales; and increasing social and economic differentiation in the city.' Brand (1972) similarly stresses 'migration status' as a major influence on the differentiation of residential areas in Accra. There are concentrations of locally-born, and others made up of groups of foreign-African migrants. Brand also refers to the 'tradition-bound poor' found both in the central city and in rural-type conditions on the periphery. The significance both of ethnic status and of length-of-stay is also brought out in Lasserre's (1958) study of Libreville. Here in the late 1950s there were 22 African 'villages', all outside the European 'town'. Immigrants from other African countries occupied 'villages' nearer to the centre and within each village there was grouping of families on the basis of ethnicity (Fig. 59). The most recent arrivals to the town were to be found in the peripheral 'villages', the newest of which resembled real villages in appearance and in the continuing importance of agricultural activities.

In Africa, as elsewhere in the Third World, the degree to which modernization is replacing traditional ethnic divisions by something approaching a Western class structure remains an open question. In relation to the better-off it may be necessary to distinguish between a small elite— inheritors of a colonial tradition, largely engaged in government service and imitative of European life styles—and an emergent African middle class made up of, for example, skilled workers and businessmen whose lifestyle is less

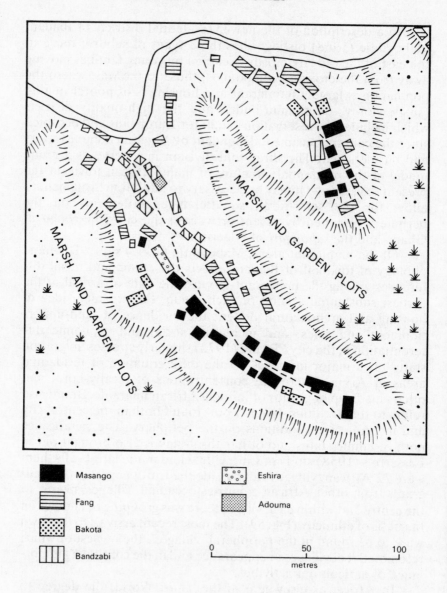

59 Distribution of ethnic groups in an 'urban village' of Libreville. After
Lasserre, 1968. (Courtesy *Fondation Nationale des Sciences Politiques*)

ostentatious and who, granted the economic opportunity, will gain
increasing influence in African society in the future. Nigeria has
long had such a middle class. But where resources for economic
development and education are lacking, and where tribal divisions

persist, changes other than those resulting purely from the concentration of population are bound to be slow.

Republic of South Africa

Generalizations concerning the nature of the African town must take into acount the peculiar conditions created by the presence of a sizeable White minority population practising apartheid in the cities of South Africa, and of an Asian community both here and in many parts of eastern Africa. In South Africa 'group areas' legislation has had far-reaching effects on segregation, confining non-white groups to peripheral townships and creating 'border strips' to ensure visible separation (Lemon, 1976). Only 'Coloureds' and Asians live together to any significant degree. African townships—small, box-like houses arranged in serried rows in new housing estates (Pollock, 1968) — are often at a considerable distance from the town centre and, therefore, from the main centres of employment. Distances are made greater by the requirement that one racial group should not pass through the residential area of another on its way to work and this, in turn, has affected the layout of the city. R. J. Davies (1963) has proposed a model of the South African town with 'semi-independent African and, where necessary, Indian and Coloured townships segregated in one or two outskirt localities separated from the remainder of the residential fabric by vacant buffer strip land. Where possible these townships could be developed also in sectors fringing large industrial areas which then act as a buffer for European residential areas'. It has been government policy to separate as far as possible tribal groups into different townships, encouraging the retention of rural ties. The success of such a policy may be judged by the tribal disturbances which flare up in the larger cities such as Johannesburg and by the survival of traditional attitudes among such groups as the 'red' (tribal) Xhosa to which reference was made above. But the demand for labour is so great that it has also led to the creation of townships such as Soweto to the south-west of Johannesburg which already had a population of half-a-million in 1965. Here the population is of mixed tribal background and of varying length of residence in the city. It is from such a melting pot that one looks for the social characteristics of the emergent urban African.

India

'Recurrent', as opposed to permanent, migration is a feature of urban life in India as it is in many parts of Africa, although it appears to be less common in the south of the country than in the north (Rowe, 1973). The practice of returning to the village for long or short visits has not, however, prevented the accumulation of population at high densities in urban areas and the creation of what are probably the worst examples of poverty and deprivation encountered in any of the world's cities. Urban slums take many forms and masquerade under a variety of names: *katras, lanes* and *chawls* (single or multi-storey tenements), *bustees, ahatas* and *cheris* (squatter settlements, of mud and thatch and whatever other materials are to hand, on the edge of the city or wherever there is vacant land). A survey of Hyderabad-Secunderabad carried out in the 1960s revealed that in none of the city wards did residential densities fall below 100 persons per acre—64 000 persons per square mile—and in three wards the density was in excess of 300 persons per acre. 70 per cent of the city's households—average size 5.6 persons—were living in one- or two-room tenements (Alam and Khan, 1972). Singh (1964) describes the squatter-type slums of Bangalore '. . . small patches of poor mud huts roofed with anything from straw to mutilated kerosene tins, being scattered in low ill-drained areas in contrast with the surrounding finer residences of the fairly wealthy people'. They concentrate around tanks as the main source of water supply, and are also drawn to areas of industrial employment although Singh notes that the larger firms, whether public or private, often provide housing for their workers and this checks the development of spontaneous settlements.

According to Clinard and Chatterjee (1962), housing pressures are resulting in residential desegregation, the demand for space making it less easy for people with similar characteristics, be they of caste, region of origin or occupation, to form exclusive groups in any one area of the city. They conclude that caste as a social force appears to be declining in the cities at the present time. This view conflicts with that of Rowe (1973) who points to the importance of migration in maintaining traditional attitudes and concludes that 'caste, kinship, and place-of-origin have remained solid bases for the choice of residential area (*mohalla, pura, patti,* etc.) within the city. It may be less evident in parts of the old city, for the reason suggested by Clinard and Chatterjee, but caste communities have been re-created in the newer portions of the

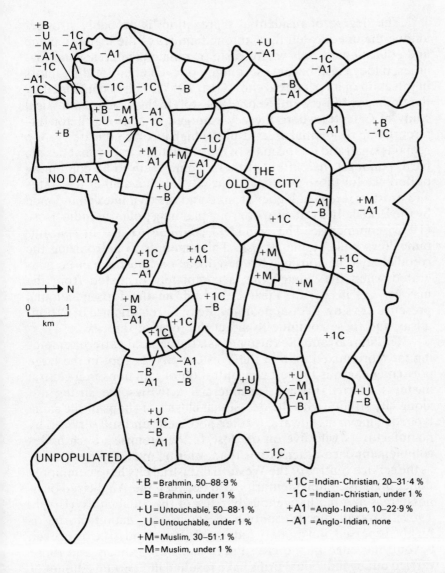

+B = Brahmin, 50–88·9 %
−B = Brahmin, under 1 %
+U = Untouchable, 50–88·1 %
−U = Untouchable, under 1 %
+M = Muslim, 30–51·1 %
−M = Muslim, under 1 %

+1C = Indian-Christian, 20–31·4 %
−1C = Indian-Christian, under 1 %
+A1 = Anglo·Indian, 10–22·9 %
−A1 = Anglo-Indian, none

60 Degree of ethnic and caste segregation in the wards of Greater Bangalore. After Gist, 1957. (Courtesy the Editor of *Social Forces*)

city. In the case of Bangalore 'caste communities moved as the city grew' (Fig. 60). The formation of caste associations to promote the welfare of their members has contributed to this phenomenon. In their welfare and related functions these associations are similar to the organizations which in like manner sustain traditional ties in the cities of the Middle East and Africa.

The degree of residential segregation 'is probably stronger among the uneducated than among families of the higher income and educational levels where caste or religious interests and loyalties, if they exist, become secondary or even unimportant factors in selection of a residential site' (Gist, 1957). This is confirmed by the findings of Berry and Rees (1968-69) in their factor analytical study of Calcutta where literacy emerged as a strong factor differentiating residential areas. But the high income educated group remains small and for the mass of the population traditional ties die hard. Amongst the better-off there would seem to be continuing preference for those portions of the city that have inherited status and prestige, areas of higher ground and the civil lines abandoned by the British. In a criticism of urban planning policy in India, Bose (1973) comments: 'The Ministers continue to live in spacious bungalows built by the British. This amounts to patronizing the colonial style of housing. No new ideas on housing can be generated when the ruling elite is completely insulated from the masses.' As in Africa, ideas derived from the former colonial presence are slow to disappear in spite of the emergence of nationalism, and these continue to affect the form of the city.

Traditional land uses also persist, the general pattern remaining far more mixed than in the Western city. Except in the large port cities there is limited concentration of functions in a central business district. Instead, commercial activities are strung out along city streets, with the occasional cluster of shops of the same type, dealing in metalware, leather-goods etc. and still serviced by manufacturers who live on or close to the premises. Such nodes complement each other rather than offering overlapping services as the service centres of the Western industrial city have commonly done; there is complementarity also between the Anglicized business areas and the indigenous bazaars of the 'dual cities' (Brush, 1962). Overall the distribution of small-scale manufacturing is highly dispersed, but modern industrial plants tend to be on or even beyond the edge of the city. Public housing projects and those carried out by individual firms have resulted in a certain amount of residential development on the urban fringe, but in the absence of more comprehensive slum clearance and housing programmes there is a large amount of commuting outwards by bus, bicycle and even train from the city which retains the sharp edge between town and country that has long been a feature of most Indian cities (page 47). Berry and Spodeck (1971) recognize the 'limited suburbanization' that is taking place in larger Indian cities but leave unanswered the question as to 'whether the emerging forms are converging on the model of the industrial metropolis, or whether some new synthesis of traditional and modern will emerge'.

South-East Asia

The city in South-East Asia exhibits striking contrasts between its westernized CBD and the 'alien' commercial quarters; between modern industrial estates on the fringe and the cottage industries of the inner city; between densely crowded shophouses and the comfortable residential areas of the middle class; between squatter settlements which retain many of the characteristics of rural villages and the high-rise apartments of government housing projects. The contrasts emerge clearly in McGee's (1967) model of the spatial structure of a large South-East Asian city (Fig. 61).

In many respects the South-East Asian city is not unlike other cities of the Third World. There is the same proliferation of petty services ('shared poverty'), residential segregation along ethnic lines, and the housing and other problems posed by cityward migration and by natural increase of the already-resident population. But there are differences too, not least those related to the strength of the inherited colonial European tradition, and those which arise from a situation in which urbanization first involved migrant communities, and the arrival of the 'host population' in the cities has been a much more recent phenomenon. The closest parallels with this latter situation are to be found in East Africa where Asians and Europeans provided the initial impetus to urban growth (Dwyer, 1975), and the effect upon the city of this sequence of development has been well documented for a typical example, Kuala Lumpur in Malaysia, by Sendut (1965) and McGee (1971).

McGee (1967) refers to the 'transitional nature' of the economic structure of South-East Asian cities in which a *'bazaar-type* economy coexists with a *firm-type* economy'. The former is represented by the commercial quarters of the Chinese and Indian 'towns' in which the population still live and work in the same premises, by markets scattered throughout the city, by the small shops and eating places found strung out along the roads in the principal residential areas, and by the market gardens which surround the city and provide it with fresh food. The latter is to be found in the port—where the city is coastal—in the European-type business district with its offices, banks, stores etc., the areas devoted to garages and car-sale lots, and in modern manufacturing

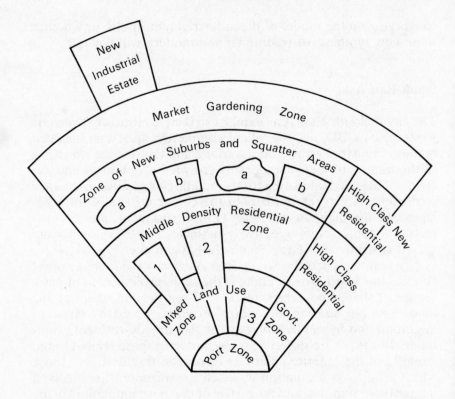

1   Alien commercial zone

2   Alien commercial zone

3   Western commercial zone

a   Squatter areas

b   Suburbs

61   McGee's (1967) land use model of a large South-East Asian port
city. (Courtesy G. Bell & Sons)

plants on the edge of the city. Yet the boundaries between these
land uses are in many cases far from clear-cut and by comparison
with the city in the West a 'mixed and seemingly chaotic distribution of land use prevails'.

The strong tradition of ethnic segregation inherited by
South-East Asian cities from their colonial past has been reinforced by rural migration. It is further sustained by the tendency
for occupational structure to be closely related to ethnic background and by cultural preferences for certain types of housing.

McGee (1967) makes the latter point in relation to Kuala Lumpur where Chinese and Indians were willing to occupy multi-storey apartments near the city centre, but Malay resettlement had to take place some distance from the city because of their preference for detached dwellings in small lots for growing fruit and vegetables.

Population growth has resulted in intense overcrowding of the inner city tenement quarters occupied by Indians or Chinese, and in his graphic description of Upper Nankin Street in Singapore, Barrington Kaye (1960) has illustrated the degree to which concentration can take place in such areas. Under these conditions there is little space available for the development of spontaneous settlements; otherwise squatters may be found in any part of the city and also on its fringe where they compete for space with th' market gardens. Floating 'squatter' settlements on the rivers are not unknown. Within these settlements there is a tendency, comparable with that observed in many other parts of the world, for population of similar rural origins to cluster together (Dwyer, 1968). McGee suggests that close links are maintained with home villages, at least in the early stages of city life, and he finds a certain amount of evidence of self-help (improvement) taking place where security of tenure has been granted (1967).

As a proportion of the total population, the middle class in most South-East Asian cities remains a small group, although its presence is evident in the smart suburbs occupying attractive hill sites and in the government housing areas with their large numbers of those who service the bureaucratic machine. Here there is some ethnic mixing of those who share common social aspirations but it is on a sufficiently modest scale for McGee (1967) to conclude that 'the move towards Western urban patterns of life is only just beginning'. Middle class suburbs and squatter settlements have added new elements to the form of the colonial city without transforming that older pattern. Rich and poor are to be found in both the inner and outer parts of the city. In his search for some meaning in this pattern, and for any comparisons that may be made with the Western city, McGee tentatively suggests that it could 'represent some transitory phase which is developing between the patterns of pre-industrialism and industrialism'. As in other parts of the Third World, further projection comes up against the imponderables of economic and social change.

Japan

Emerging from feudal rule and from a state of political and economic introversion little more than a century ago, Japan presents a good opportunity for studying the effect on city growth both of the forces of modernization and of a strong, underlying cultural tradition. Urbanization in Japan has been rapid, especially in the present century. As recently as 1920, only 18.8 per cent of the population was classified as urban; by 1965 the proportion had risen to 68.0 per cent. At this time Tokyo alone had a population of some 10 millions and very nearly half the country's population was crowded into the cities of the 'Tokaido megalopolis' which extends for some 600 km from Tokyo/Yokohama through Nagoya to Kyoto, Osaka and Kobe. The most lasting impression created by Japanese cities is one of milling people. Economic progress is represented by huge industrial corporations, high rise office blocks, suburban housing estates, fast trains and elevated urban motorways. Accompanying social change has depressed the birth rate, following a postwar 'baby boom', to around one per cent per year (Kornhauser, 1976). Yet despite the obvious manifestations of 'modernization' and the adoption of western styles, Japanese society retains a strong respect for the past, and city forms can only be fully understood by reference to inherited patterns of town layout and building. Of particular significance is the traditional structure of the *jŏka-machi,* or castle towns.

Early Japanese town-building was influenced by the checkerboard pattern of the Chinese city but with one or two exceptions, Nara being the obvious example, this tradition is not represented very powerfully in the modern city, although Kornhauser claims to observe it in the streets of the CBD 'which are rather uniformly rectilinear'. The castle town was the key element in the administrative structure of Japan during the Tokugawa period of military rule which lasted from 1603 to 1868, and it is the layout of this town that has left its mark most obviously on the city at the present day. The internal structure of the castle town has been described by Tanabe (1970) and by Yazaki (1963; 1973). A number of distinct sub-areas could be recognized (Fig. 62). Surrounding the castle itself, the residence of the feudal lord, were the dwellings of the ruling military caste, the *samurai.* These were arranged according to the retainers' status, the highest military class living closest to the castle and the lowest class further out where they could undertake the defence of the city. Noble families also lived in the inner city where there was, in addition to the residential zones of the

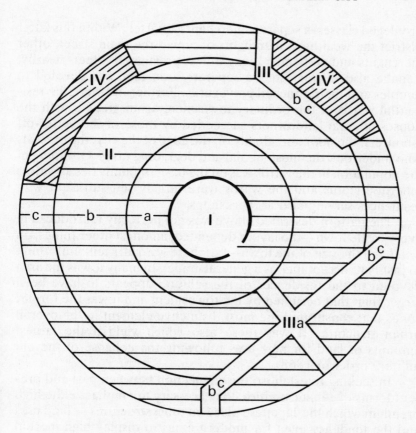

I	Political and military area
IIa	High-class residential area
IIb	Middle-class residential area
IIc	Lower-class residential area
IIIa	Commercial area
IIIb	Light-industrial area
IIIc	Workmen's residential area
IV	Green-belt

62 Schematic diagram of a Japanese castle town. After Tanabe, 1970. (Courtesy Association of Japanese Geographers)

privileged classes, a separate merchants' quarter. Within this latter district the wealthiest merchants occupied the main street, other merchants and craftsmen living in less prestigious streets nearby. Tanabe also distinguishes a separate area that was devoted to temples and their attached graveyards. Further out were the residential wards of the ordinary townsmen, again graded, with the houses of rural landowners succeeded by those of the better-off labourers, the poor and, finally on the edge of the city, the outcasts who undertook the most menial and degrading tasks. Grouping of the population in the wards was on the basis of family ties as well as inherited status and the wards were largely self-sufficient with residences serving also as workshops.

The pattern described above was not perfectly reproduced in every castle town—the layout depended, amongst other things, on relief and the size of the town—but there was sufficient uniformity to justify its acceptance as a general model. In many towns the area devoted to the residences of the samurai appears to have been larger than that occupied by the townsmen, and it was the former zones that constituted the most distinctive element in the overall urban structure. It was these also which yielded the largest amounts of land for new uses following the collapse of the old military order in 1868.

In seeking to establish the connection between past and present forms of Japanese cities it is necessary to emphasize the high premium which the Japanese place on relict structures or land uses and the tendency even for modern cities to display high inertial values (Ginsburg, 1965). Yazaki (1963) claims the survival of feudalism and of old culture traits, concluding that 'to understand the reason for the emergence of the modern Japanese city, or the changes or present state of its social structure, a historical and cultural approach is extremely important.' Within the former castle grounds, sloping land has commonly been retained as parks or used for shrines whilst level sites have attracted public buildings and government offices, schools and barracks (Yamori, 1970). The castle moat, at first used for rice cultivation, was later filled in for housing or to provide part of the route for an inner ring road. The spacious quarters once occupied by the samurai were also turned over to cultivation but as industrialization proceeded the size and relative cheapness of sites available in these portions of the city proved attractive to early factory builders. Other industrial nuclei grew out of the old handicraft districts. Factories did not take over the whole of the former warriors' quarters, however, some parts retaining their status as a high-class residential area for the new elite of political and industrial leaders. Continuity has also been traced between the former merchants' quarter and the modern shopping and financial centre. After railways were built — the main line network was established between 1872 and 1907— the tendency was for the commercial core to be drawn in the direction of the railway station. In other cases a new commercial focus grew up in the vicinity of the station and the two centres were rivals for the expanding retail trade of the city. Kornhauser (1976) notes the effect of the railway in creating multiple nuclei of commercial activity and of corridors of such enterprises linking them. In a model which also introduces new residential and factory districts, Tanabe (1970) has tried to illustrate the spatial connections that can be found between several of the elements of the old castle town and the modern city that has succeeded it (Fig. 63). Yazaki (1963) might be describing such a diagram when he observes that 'the traditional land use pattern and the new pattern overlap and a similar culture pervades the whole, so that the functional differentiation of areas in terms of industrialism and groups with different cultural backgrounds is not so distinct as in America.'

Having escaped colonial rule and all its consequences, the population of Japan is racially, culturally, and also socially, more homogeneous than that of most other countries in the world. This means, not only avoidance of ethnic segregation of the kind so widely encountered elsewhere, but also blurring of the edges between 'social areas'. Although social segregation undoubtedly exists, there is probably a greater mixing of income groups than is common in the capitalist West and it is not easy to distinguish one residential area from another. This is not to say that community-consciousness and sense of territory are necessarily lacking in Japanese cities and, indeed, a number of authors have drawn attention to the role that is still played by *chōnaikai,* area organizations which once had a local government function but which are now more likely to act as pressure groups for the improvement of public services in their section of the town or to arrange social functions (Dore, 1958; Nakamura,1968).

Difficulty in distinguishing visually one part of the city from another can be ascribed in part to a strong cultural tradition in housing. There is considerable uniformity in house type throughout Japan and this extends beyond design and materials used to include also dimensions of the individual room and its furnishings. Wooden houses of one, possibly two, storeys are still typical. Even in Tokyo with its high-rise apartments the average height of struc-

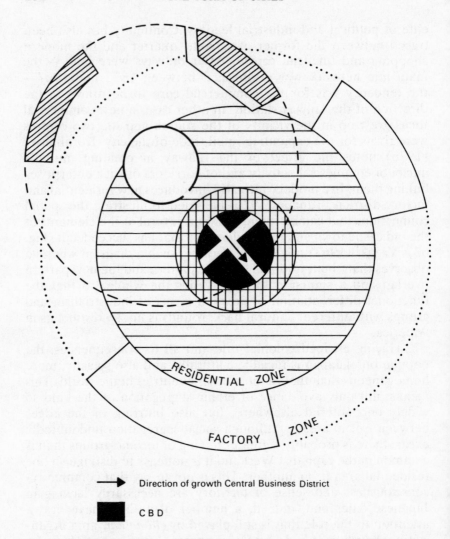

63 Relationship between the castle town and the modern Japanese city according to Tanabe, 1970. (Courtesy Association of Japanese Geographers)

ture was only 1.9 storeys in 1966. The skyline over large areas is low and flat, punctuated in the past only by the occasional Buddhist temple or castle, but increasingly now by modern office buildings or blocks of flats (Fig. 8). The threat of earthquakes, and also of fire in a country where wood is a traditional building material, has acted in the past as a further brake on the spread of high buildings. The effect as cities have grown has been urban sprawl of the worst kind. Cities give the appearance of having no plan, the irregularity of their outlines increased by the construction problems posed by an often highly accidented relief and by the need to conserve the best wet padi land. The apparent lack of order in the city is in sharp contrast with the regular and controlled appearance of the rural landscape.

Electrified railways have played a major role in bringing about suburbanization in the larger cities. In Tokyo the necessity of changing from suburban to main line railways has also resulted in commercial decentralization and the development of nodes of shopping, recreational and other activities around these exchange stations which may be four or six kilometres from the centre of the city. Elsewhere clusters of housing were built around the railway stops and in time many of these have grown into *danchi,* housing estates, which are built by public housing authorities, private agencies, or a combination of both. Although the railways, and to some extent main roads, have guided the pattern of suburbanization, the spread of new housing has also been strongly influenced by the search for low-priced land. Indeed in some cases it is even possible to observe an inverse relationship between accessibility and the preference for a place to live, the advantage of accessibility having driven land prices so high as to repel development. In extreme cases this means that sites midway between the railway stops may be more attractive than ones close to the station, and one observer has referred to the 'turbo-cornutus', or shell-like, growth of the city (Tanabe, 1970). Outward growth assumes a vortex-motion: outward expansion in one direction raises land values to a level which retards further growth; at this point residential development is compelled to take a different direction; this in turn increases the value of land there, and so it goes on (Fig. 64). The effect of this search for cheap building land and the associated leap-frogging effect of urban development has been further sprawl and additions to the already large amounts of time spent travelling to and from work. Some of Tokyo's housing estates are 30 km, even 50 km, from the city centre, and journeys may take as long as two hours in each direction.

In contrast with the long-distance commuters are the employees of major industrial corporations, many of whom are housed by the company and live in close proximity to the factory. The location of these major industrial plants has thus acted as another significant influence on the growth pattern of the modern Japanese city. Their effect on urban development is further enhanced by the tendency for smaller firms, suppliers of parts or services to the big

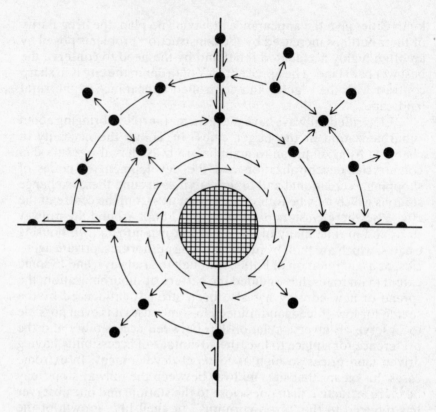

64 'Turbo-cornutus' growth of the suburbs of a large Japanese city.
   After Tanabe, 1970. (Courtesy Association of Japanese Geographers)

corporations, to cluster like satellites around the leading employer.
It is seen, for example, in the concentration of sub-contracting
firms in the automobile industry around Toyota City.

The inter-war years, when the *Zaibatsu*, or giant corporations,
were virtually a law unto themselves, saw the establishment of
close-knit company towns away from the main cities. Under a
changed regime it has become more common for industrialization
to take the form of new 'estates' or 'parks' on the edge of the
metropolitan area, but these still include areas of housing for the
employees together with the provision of many kinds of services:
schools, medical facilities, and so on (Kornhauser). This close
involvement of factory management with the life of its workers
remains a characteristic of industrial Japan. Employees commonly
spend their whole working life with a single firm with whose
fortunes there is close personal involvement. In turn, the company

assumes responsibilities for the well-being of its staff which extend far beyond the level expected in the industrial West. Yazaki finds here further evidence of feudal custom, and Abegglen (1958) refers to the industrial corporations as 'in a very real sense clans'. The latter author sees in Japanese factory organization and group loyalty, not merely a survival of older customs, but a system that is consistent with the traditional customs and attitudes of the Japanese. 'If a single conclusion were to be drawn from this study (of the Japanese factory) it would be that the development of industrial Japan has taken place with much less change from the kinds of social organization and social relations of pre-industrial or non-industrial Japan than would be expected from the western models of the growth of an industrial society.' When considered in relation to that of the West, Japanese industrialization is still comparatively recent and it may be that another generation or two of industrial experience will further dilute, or even destroy, traditional social relationships. But meanwhile the fact that such relationships survive at all in an industrial situation as technologically advanced as that of Japan, must lead one to pause before accepting the idea of an economically-directed path to universal urban form.

Convergent or divergent forms?

It is not possible to provide an unequivocal answer to the question posed at the beginning of this chapter. In an age when not only big business but also town planning and the construction industry are international in scope, it is tempting to look for spatial forms that are common to all cities. Yet social and cultural traditions are strong and, as in Japan, continue to influence the evolution of cities even in the rich and technologically advanced nations. In cities of the Third World, beset with problems of poverty and of unchecked population growth, the urban milieu is scarcely conducive to modernization, either economic or social. Culture traits inherited from a rural past survive little changed or are adapted to urban conditions. The authorities, faced with the immensity of urban problems, are more inclined to seek solutions in terms of self-help and compromise than of wholesale redevelopment. There is also the force of nationalism to be taken into account. Building in Third World cities has often been imitative of European styles, even in the post-colonial period. But as self-confidence or self-assertiveness grows it is more likely that attempts will be made to create cities that reflect the national image. Herein lies a fruitful avenue of research, and perhaps an eventual answer to the question.

10

The Socialist City

At first sight it is less easy to justify the concept of a socialist city than it is that of, say, a Middle-Eastern or Japanese city. Socialist policies are carried out by governments that are not socialist (in the sense of communist), and one could therefore expect any differences that there might be between socialist and non-socialist cities to be ones of degree rather than kind. Comparisons are often made, for example, between new towns in the West and those that have been built in Eastern Europe (Chapter 6). Yet the extent of control that is exercised by the government, not only over planning but over all the main city-forming processes, is so much more total and comprehensive in the socialist than it is in the non-socialist world, that there would seem to be some likelihood of discovering fundamental contrasts in physical form. Such is the view of Dawson (1971) who considers that the differences in spatial organization are sufficient to support a model of the socialist city (Fig. 65).

Contrasts in land use as between one part of the city and another are reduced in the socialist world. There is greater uniformity, less areal specialization than in the 'capitalist city' where market forces operate powerfully and segregation of land uses comes about through competition for desirable sites. The sorting effect of land values and of rents is of much reduced significance in the socialist city, if indeed it is permitted to operate at all. Other factors are also at work ironing out differences within the city. The tendency towards greater equalization of incomes than is common in the West leads to greater homogeneity in the demand for housing and for goods and services. Reduced consumer preference is also likely to be brought about by low rents charged for accommodation and by standardization of rates charged on public transport, the decision over where to live being based on less complex considerations than in the West. The needs of the family and access to work are likely to have most bearing on what choice there is. Uniformity also results from the application of planning norms by the State which acts as developer as well as planner. The enormous

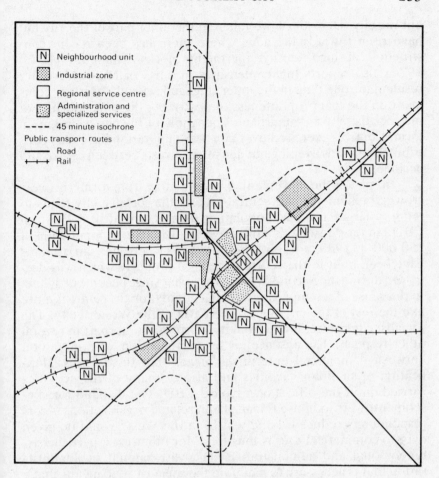

65   Schematic plan of a socialist city according to Dawson, 1971. (Courtesy the Editor of *Tijdschrift voor Economische en Sociale Geografie*)

demand for new housing created by wartime destruction coupled
with a high birth rate and rural to urban migration after the Second
World War, led governments to introduce cheap, mass-production
methods of dwelling construction and this has had the effect of
creating visual conformity over large areas of the city.

A consequence of reduced areal specialization in the socialist
city has been the creation of a density gradient which differs from
that of the typical Western example with its central 'crater' and
diminishing curve from inner to outer suburbs. Dawson (1971)
observes a substantial weakening of this gradient in Warsaw and its
replacement by an intermixing of high and low densities through-

out the city. Densities have fallen in the inner part of the city but
have risen towards the edge where there has been recent construction of high-density apartment blocks. Hamilton (1973;
1976) also reports higher densities in parts of Moscow's outer
residential zone than in the inner ring, and several observers comment on the inappropriateness of describing the outer portion of
the socialist city as 'suburban'. The whole of the city is 'urban' in
form. Controls exercised over city-ward migration have also contributed towards evening out density contrasts between centre and
periphery.

In spite of the movement of people away from formerly overcrowded tenements, the central area of the socialist city tends to
retain a larger resident population than is typical of a Western
CBD. Inner Moscow is still expected to have a population of
250 000 in 1980, and both here and elsewhere new apartments
have been built in the centre to replace property which was destroyed during the Second World War or has since become obsolete.
In this sense of retaining a residential population the centre is more
like the rest of the city than is the CBD of the Western city. The
socialist city centre differs from its Western counterpart in several
other respects. The absence, or severe reduction, of competition
between commercial enterprises means that there is less duplication of shopping facilities and also of many of the activities
carried on in the offices of a typical CBD. The demand for skyscraper towers to house financial and related organizations is cor-
respondingly reduced. Land which, in the West, would be given
over to commercial uses is thus freed for other uses, particularly,
recreational and administrative. The vast amount of administration that is necessary to maintain the socialist state means that a
large area is given over to offices of central and regional governments, of party institutions and of international political organizations. Hotels are built to cater for foreign visitors and some at
least of the shops are maintained for purposes of prestige and for
tourist needs. Dawson suggests that central Warsaw 'has become
an area of specialist and prestige shops — the department store,
antique, second-hand book, and souvenir shops, and shops catering for tourists'.

In a study of Zagreb, Fisher (1963) describes the planning of a
new 'socialist' centre focusing on a square with a predominance of
buildings serving administrative and cultural purposes together
with clustered blocks of apartment complexes. The older city
centre retains its commercial role but is expected to do this on a
reduced scale serving, in time, not the whole city but only its largest

single concentration of population. Fisher refers to the new focus, Proleterskih Brigada Street, as the Yugoslav manifestation of the accepted socialist concept of a city's centre which he defines as 'having a political-cultural-administrative character'. A typical element in any such urban reconstruction scheme is likely to be the impressively broad street or wide square where parades can be held on the First of May and on appropriate national occasions. The parade ground syndrome is not limited to the socialist state. It is to be seen in Haussman's Paris, and tends to appear whenever the state has sought to glory in its achievements. In this sense the socialist city is following in a long tradition.

It is an essential part of socialist doctrine that class distinctions be abolished. The effect has been to reduce considerably the socio-economic differences between sections of a city which are so apparent in the West. It has not, however, prevented the retention, or emergence, of desirable residential areas for the elite of party officials, scientists and other intellectuals. These aside, the trend is towards greater uniformity in residential areas. In Prague, Musil (1968) can find 'no close correlation between the size of income and the quality of dwelling inhabited by the households . . . there is no massive concentration of population groups with lower incomes in dwellings of poor quality.' Rents do not vary according to the location of dwellings within the city as they do in the West so that this economic constraint leading to social segration is removed. Turnock (1974) observed 'mixing of professional and working class elements' in new housing estates in Bucharest, but the absence of social area studies prevented generalization for the city as a whole. Allocation of new housing in the socialist city is generally on the basis of family needs so that it is stage in the life-cycle, rather than socio-economic characteristics, that most commonly differentiates one residential area from another. Musil notes in Czechoslovakia a close correlation between age of dwellings on the one hand and both age of their inhabitants and average size of households on the other.

Contributing to the uniform appearance of residential areas are regulations which, in many socialist states, govern the allocation per person of floor area in new housing projects. Equally important is the stereotyped layout and the industrial construction methods used in the building of the almost universal apartment blocks. In the early postwar years, when resources were in short supply, a widely preferred form of construction was the 5-storey block of apartments. Built often of prefabricated concrete panels, and without a lift, this kind of building was cheaper to construct than either small houses or tower blocks that would have required a strong frame and the incorporation of lifts. Reduction of ceiling heights helped by shortening the building as a whole and reducing the number of stairs required (Frolic, 1963-4). Some of these apartments were set amongst gardens and play areas; many were built in monotonous rows, lining the streets to which they gave a dull and canyon-like appearance. More recently as resources available for housing have increased and as new ideas in planning and architecture have been adopted, there has come somewhat greater variety in apartment design. Blocks of from 9 to 16 storeys have been widely built in the outer part of Moscow since 1965 (Hamilton, 1976), and Turnock refers to blocks of up to ten storeys in Bucharest, although here standardization in design continues to give 'an impression of stark regimentation'.

Socialist city planning has made widespread use of the neighbourhood concept in the design of new residential areas. The *microrayon* has been an approved form of residential unit in the Soviet Union since 1958 (Osborn, 1966). The number of people housed in these neighbourhoods ranges from about 5000 to 20 000 and they incorporate hostel-like blocks of flats for single people as well as family apartments. It is intended that they should be largely self-contained with their own shops, schools, recreational facilities and services, and with employment nearby. They are also considered to be convenient units for the administration of various kinds of community services, for example helping in the kindergarten, but they do not serve as local-government administrative units. Fox (1963) notes the role of formal, local associations in fostering neighbourhood ties in the Soviet city of Odessa. He also makes the point that in a country where most women go out to work, the time available for shopping is limited and the role of the neighbourhood shopping centre therefore enhanced. 'The absence of a wider range, a different selection or lower prices elsewhere are strong disincentives to shop away from the neighbourhood unit.' Daily needs are also satisfied by shops distributed throughout the residential area. Overall, however, the pattern of service provision in the socialist city tends more to the recurrence of centres of similar type than to the kind of hierarchy beneath a dominant CBD that has been typical in the West.

Postwar emphasis on industrial production required the setting aside of many sites for new or expanded industries. Manufacturing zones have been established in close proximity to new residential areas and to these have also been directed industries relocated from inner city areas of redevelopment, as in the West.

Siting of the industrial zones is influenced by the strong desire to achieve a balance at the neighbourhood level between employment and population and to limit the time spent travelling to work. The continuing commuter problem in major cities such as Moscow suggests that there is some way to go before this aim can be achieved. A further factor in the choice of site for individual factories has been the need to maintain linkages with other manufacturing plants so that directional bias may be apparent in the pattern of moves. In some cases dispersal of industry has been to satellite towns (Russian *sputniki*) beyond the main built-up area.

Public transport plays a proportionately greater role in the socialist city than in most Western cities, where individual car ownership is generally much higher. Sectoral growth is encouraged by radial routeways and the outline of the city is likely to assume something of a stellate form in response to the overwhelming use of bus or rail. Wedges of open space have been preserved between these radials to a greater extent than is common in the West where use of the private car has brought about infilling of the interstices of the 'spider's web'. Ringroads have been built in the larger cities, e.g. Moscow's Garden Ring, and the effect is to make these spaces more accessible. But offsetting this is the desire to maintain access to land for recreational purposes.

Generalizations concerning the nature of the socialist city must take into account the significance of patterns inherited from the past and also the possibility of contrasts that arise as a result of following different national paths to socialism. With regard to the latter, Turnock considers that 'although the "socialist city" has been construed as a distinct model it is difficult to isolate aspects of form, as distinct from decision-making processes, which are intrinsically socialist once national and local characteristics have been considered.' Hamilton finds evidence of areal specialization in Moscow which derives both from nineteenth-century patterns of capitalist development and from the need, under any economic system, to preserve a degree of clustering of linked activities. Notwithstanding the creation of a 'socialist' city centre, Fisher can find little evidence of change in the residential class-structure of Zagreb and comes to the conclusion that the 'capitalist heritage is too strong a factor for the socialist planners to overcome'. Dawson, too, makes a distinction between the USSR and the countries of Eastern Europe where 'perhaps it is too soon . . . to evaluate the effect of socialist control upon cities whose internal structure is, as yet, still dictated by a considerable legacy of, buildings, streets and transport facilities from an earlier, free-market economy.' Such views as these suggest that, in spite of the trends outlined above, pursuit of the 'socialist city' may still be premature. When the information is available, it will be interesting to compare Soviet and East European cities with those of China and other communist regimes in South-East Asia.

11

Future Urban Forms

It is no longer realistic, in the final quarter of the twentieth century, to study the city as a single aggregate of people, buildings and activities. Perhaps it never was, yet theories of urban spatial structure have traditionally taken as their starting point the unicentred city, assuming that, although the city has contacts with the world outside its own boundaries, these were insufficient to affect to any significant extent the internal arrangement of land uses brought about by competition for a central location or by other locally operating economic and social forces. But whatever the validity of such a standpoint in the past, modern transport and communications make it increasingly untenable at the present. Jet travel and fast inter-city trains enable the businessman to keep appointments in several cities during the course of one day; instructions are flashed to clerks who work in the offices of an 'expanded town'; the wealthy fill deep-freezes from out-of-town hypermarkets and weekend in 'second-homes'; lordly estates have become safari parks as their owners cater for the demands of mass leisure; factories are re-sited on estates near the motorway and the inner city dweller becomes a 'reverse-commuter'. Observing the rise of what he described as 'interlocal interests', Martindale (1958) concluded that 'the modern city is losing its external and formal structure. Internally it is in a state of decay while the new community represented by the nation everywhere grows at its expense. The age of the city seems to be at an end.'

Cities that are increasingly interdependent may be thought of as components of an urban system. 'The cities and urban regions of a modern industrial economy constitute a set of interrelated sub-systems nesting in a complex hierarchy of increasing scale upward from individual urban areas to a national urban system' (Bourne, 1975). The structural properties of such a system are not difficult to define, constituting the movements and linkages that unite the individual urban elements making up the whole. Representation of its spatial characteristics in the form of a model is less easy to

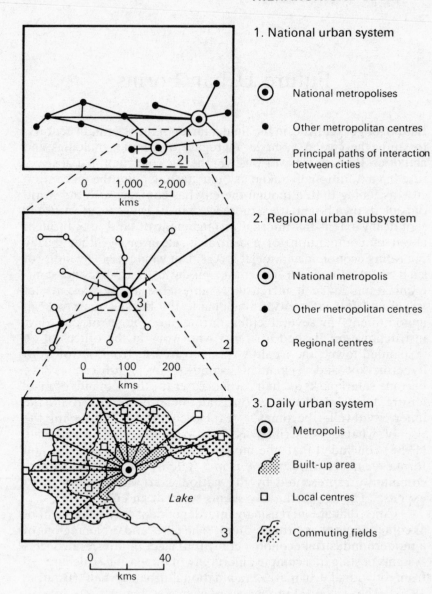

HIERARCHICAL LEVEL

1. National urban system

National metropolises

Other metropolitan centres

Principal paths of interaction between cities

0   1,000   2,000
kms

2. Regional urban subsystem

National metropolis

Other metropolitan centres

Regional centres

0   100   200
kms

3. Daily urban system

Metropolis

Built-up area

Local centres

Commuting fields

Lake

0   40
kms

66   Schematic representation of three levels of an urban system according to Bourne, 1975. (Courtesy Oxford University Press)

achieve, particularly having in mind the changes that may take place over even quite a short period of time (Fig. 66). In his 'Broadacre City' Frank Lloyd Wright (1958) saw the future as one in which any distinction between urban and rural was finally removed and settlement became more and more uniform over a region. Clarence Stein's (1964) 'Regional City' is, by contrast, one of evenly-dispersed clusters; Lynch (1974) describes it as an 'urban galaxy'. Both these glimpses into the future have an element of unreality, of the utopian, about them, however, and better clues to the form of the dispersed city are to be found in the studies that have been carried out in recent years on Megalopolis and other highly urbanized regions of the world. Gottmann (1961) introduces his detailed analysis of interrelationships and land uses in the north-eastern seaboard of the United States with the statement that 'the area may be considered the cradle of a new order in the organization of inhabited space. This new order, however, is still far from orderly; here in its cradle it is all in flux and trouble, which does not facilitate the analyst's work. Nevertheless, a study of Megalopolis may shed some light on processes that are of great importance and interest.'

Since publication of *Megalopolis*, the same term has been applied, sometimes rather randomly, to areas of closely-packed cities elsewhere in North America, in Japan, and in North-West Europe including Britain. Observations have not always been backed up by the careful attention to processes which Gottmann advocated. It has been suggested, for example, that the cities which make up an urban system will tend to assume an increasingly specialized role, concentrating on manufacturing, administration, a dormitory function, and so forth, but in practice this is difficult to prove. It may be necessary to envisage different processes operating at different scales. Friedmann and Miller (1965) have employed the phrase 'urban field' — confusingly in view of its more general use — for what they describe as 'a new element of spatial order' and 'a community of shared interests'. Their urban field extends outwards from a core SMSA (Standard Metropolitan Statistical Area of the US Census) of at least 300 000 people for a distance equivalent to 2 hours' driving on modern highways, assumed to be about 100 miles. This is considered to be the approximate limit of commuting and also of intensive weekend and seasonal use for recreation. Interdependency will not be limited to these forms of association, however, and it is suggested that 'the present dominance of the metropolitan core will become attenuated as economic activities are decentralized to smaller cities within the field.'

Although more evident now than in the past, the inter-dependence of cities is not a wholly new phenomenon. As early as 1915, in *Cities in Evolution,* Patrick Geddes used the term 'con-urbation' to describe the closely linked cities that make up such industrial areas as West Yorkshire ('this natural city-alliance'), South Lancashire ('Lancaston') or 'Clyde-Forth'. He, and later writers including Sargant Florence (1948) in the West Midlands, recognized the strength of the economic ties uniting these towns and anticipated, to that extent at least, the later work of Gottmann and others. Friedmann and Miller's core-dominated region was likewise anticipated by Mackinder (1902) who, at the beginning of the century, wrote: 'In a manner all south-eastern England is a single urban community . . . A city in an economic sense is no longer an area covered continuously with streets and houses . . . The metropolis in its largest meaning includes all the counties for whose inhabitants London is 'Town', whose men do habitual bus-iness there, whose women buy there, whose morning paper is printed there, whose standard of thought is determined there.' Mackinder's words had an even more modern ring about them when, sixty years later, it was proposed in the South East Study (1964) that new and expanded towns be sited at a distance of 100-120 km from the capital.

The urban fringe

Processes of change operate both within the city and outside it, but evidence of an approaching 'new spatial order' is probably easiest to recognise in the urban fringe. This is not to say that resistance to change is absent from the fringe (Chapter 1), but that overall the forces of inertia are less strong when change is from rural to urban land uses rather than from one kind of urban use to another. In a conurbation the fringe of one city may well be the fringe of several others and decentralization is likely to be speeded up in the belief that a site in the fringe can be used to serve several cities. Thus Megalopolis becomes cradle to the new order.

There is no universally accepted definition of the urban fringe. The United States Bureau of the Census refers to it as 'that portion of a census Urbanized Area that lies outside the central city'. Less legalistically, Johnson (1974) describes the fringe as 'the zone at the edge of the city into which urban growth of various kinds is extending' and 'the area in which suburban growth is taking place and where rural and urban land uses are mixed together to form a transitional zone between town and country'. It is possible to quibble over the precise meaning of 'urban growth', and some may seek a statistical measure of the degree of conversion from rural to urban land uses, but it is unlikely that a better general definition can be found of a zone which by nature is subject to constant change in land use and which rarely has any obvious spatial limits.

Certain land uses have always characterized the urban fringe (p. 13), whilst the presence of others is a more recent phenomenon (below). On the basis of studies carried out in the metropolitan fringe of London, Pahl (1968; 1970) has also suggested that certain population groupings are represented to a greater than average extent in the fringe. He distinguishes eight such categories, and it is possible to recognize forms of residential land use associated with them:

1 *Large Property Owners* It has long been the practice for wealthy townsmen to acquire estates outside the city on which they can spend part of the year and indulge their taste for farming and recreational pursuits such as hunting and shooting. Some have been owned by the same family for many generations and resistance to change may bring about the 'closed village' situation described in Chapter 1. In recent years, taxation and death duties have resulted in the sale of some of these estates which have been bought by major companies, trade unions and other organizations as conference, training or convalescent centres.

2 *The Salariat* Pahl describes this group as business and professional people who aspire to a certain style of life and tend to buy 'period' properties in locations which offer both space and seclusion. Wooded areas may satisfy these needs but rustic settings can also be created and Gottmann found that in Megalopolis the amount of woodland as a proportion of total land use was increasing in response to urban demands. The Bagshot country west of London is such 'stockbroker' territory. Sandy heaths interspersed amongst the woodlands afford good golf courses and if they also attract military training grounds this is convenient for the top military personnel whose life-style conforms with that of the salariat.

3 *Spiralists* Almost a sub-category of 2, these are people who are required to make frequent moves as their career advances. Since they are unlikely to remain in one place long, they are more likely to be attracted by a convenient location than by a particular

kind of house or setting. Pahl suggests, however, that the group as a whole is now sufficiently numerous to make up 'communities' in the fringe belts of larger cities, for example that of Cheshire south of Manchester. Clustering is attributable partly to the desire for rapid social integration which it is believed will follow from living with similar career-minded people.

4 *Reluctant Commuters*   These are typically young couples with small children who have moved out of town because of the high cost of land and housing (Chapter 3). The inconvenience of a long journey to work is outweighed by the possibility of obtaining a mortgage on a house they can afford to begin buying. This is likely to be on a newish housing estate in some 'open' village where a high proportion of the population is at a similar stage in the life cycle.

5 *The Retired*   The thought of living in the country has a romantic attraction for some couples approaching retirement. A thatched cottage is where they picture themselves living, but many will opt for the convenience of a modern bungalow. The latter is an extravagant form of housing where land is expensive and is therefore relatively more common in the urban fringe than in the city itself.

6 *Rural Working-class Commuters*   Most of these people grew up in the village and are the sons and daughters of categories 7 and 8. The local authority — until 1974 the Rural District Council in England and Wales — has an obligation to provide housing and many are therefore council tenants. Since there is little employment available locally, they are obliged to travel to the city for work. Small housing estates are attached to most villages in the fringe, and are sometimes large enough to constitute a council 'end'. Occasionally the development goes further, as at Berinsfield in Oxford's Green Belt, where the local authority has built what may be described as a miniature 'new town' on a disused airfield. It is no more than 8 km by main road from the car assembly works on the edge of Oxford's built-up area where many of the residents are employed.

7 *Farmers and Farm Tenants*   A self-explanatory category.

8 *Local Tradesmen*   Together with the farming population, this group makes up what Pahl also refers to as the 'traditional ruralists'. It may be extended a little to include owners of local

businesses, often of the repair kind, and those who serve the rural community as vicar, schoolmaster etc.

Population segregation in the urban fringe is encouraged by the fact that both private developers and local authorities tend to build housing in blocks for similar socio-economic groups. In the combination of segregation and transience, the latter represented by the 'spiralist' group, Pahl sees some parallel between the fringe and the inner city 'zone in transition' with its long-term residents and newcomers seeking a foothold in the city. Bearing in mind the concept of the fringe as a zone of growth, the point is also worth making that house-building does not proceed there unin-terruptedly and without competition. In a study of the fringe belt of Glasgow, Whitehand (1974) examined the relationship between land use changes and the building cycle. As may have been expected, potential building sites such as country estates were shown to be most vulnerable to the developer during and immediately following the peak of the cycle. But in the troughs of the cycle, various kinds of institution in the fringe were not only able to hold their own in the market against housing but actually extended their sites.

Out-of-town shopping

Amongst the land use changes that have characterized the urban fringe in recent years, those brought about by the appearance of the hypermarket and other forms of out-of-town shopping centre, have been perhaps the most striking.

The trend towards out-of-town shopping has come about in response to a variety of factors. They include increased use of the motor car and growth in the number of families owning more than one car; reorganization in the retail trade and the emergence of large, competing companies; innovations in the processing and packaging of food and its storage at home; and changes in patterns of domestic activity which involve spending less time shopping and more on do-it-yourself projects. These latter are based, very often, on the purchase of discount, 'cash-and-carry' goods. The reasons are common to all the advanced industrial countries, yet there are considerable variations in the degree to which out-of-town centres have been permitted to compete with older-established business districts in the city centre and suburbs. Planning controls largely account for the differences, and in the United Kingdom there has been much greater resistance to change than in several other European countries. Opposition arises from the desire to protect existing commercial interests, usually those of smaller traders, and also from the fear of losing revenue in the form of rates, especially where there has been expensive investment in inner city redevelopment schemes, as for example in Nottingham's Victoria Centre, (780 000 square feet of retail space) opened in 1972. There is opposition, too, on aesthetic grounds. 'Of the many trendy things rearing their ugly heads today the out-of-town supermarket or hypermarket is the ugliest . . . If "convenience shopping" is put to the newly married woman she will vote for it every time . . . Yet if you want to know which single thing can contribute better than any other to the decline and fall of the gracious city, it is the out-of-town supermarket' (Heap, 1975).

In North America a distinction is made between different kinds of planned shopping centre on the basis of the range of functions offered and the number of people served. A 'regional' centre will normally serve a population of at least 100 000; a 'community' centre between 20 000 and 100 000, and a 'neighbourhood' centre from 7000 to 20 000 people (J. A. Dawson, 1974). The terminology corresponds with that of Berry's classification of intra-urban service centres (Chapter 4). Not all planned centres are built out-of-town, however; many of the smaller ones are suburban in location, and interest so far as the urban fringe is concerned focuses principally on the large, regional centres. The first such regional centre, the Country Club Plaza in Kansas was opened in 1923. Only seven had been built by 1950, but rapid expansion came in the 1950s and now there are several hundred such centres in North America. They offer all types of general merchandise, clothing, furniture and indeed almost the whole range of retail facilities that are usually available in the CBD (National Economic Development Office, 1971). The amount of gross selling space may exceed 1 million square feet, the average for all out-of-town shopping centres in the United States being 400 000 square feet with an average of 4000 car parking spaces. Some 45 per cent of the rentable area is taken up by department stores (C. S. Jones, 1969).

In 1960 there were no comparable regional centres in Europe and, according to the N.E.D.O. report, only 16 in 1970, but it is certain that the number will increase. Each of the sixteen had more than 200 000 square feet of selling space and at least one department store of 35 000 square feet or more of selling space to act as a magnet to shoppers. Applications to build this kind of centre in the

United Kingdom have, until recently, been refused planning permission. Typical is the experience of the company wishing to build an out-of-town centre at Pear Tree farm in Oxford's Green Belt. This would have provided 330 000 square feet of shopping space and parking for 2150 cars but refusal of permission by the Department of the Environment followed a public enquiry held in 1971. Still more ambitious was the project for a shopping centre at Haydock Park in Lancashire, turned down in 1971. At the time it was estimated that the scheme would result in Manchester and Liverpool losing 12 per cent of their existing retail trade, smaller towns in the vicinity even more. In March 1976, however, what is claimed to be the first regional shopping centre in Britain, the Brent Cross centre, was opened in North London. It is close to the junction of the MI and the North Circular Road at Staples Corner, Barnet, and is, therefore, more correctly described as edge-of-town rather than out-of-town. There are 790 000 square feet of gross selling space on a 20-hectare site which also has parking for 3500 vehicles. The population catchment area is estimated at between 1 250 000 and 1 500 000. If Brent Cross proves to be successful it will add to the pressure for similar centres in other parts of the country.

The freestanding superstore, known also as the hypermarket or consumer market, is a much more common form of out-of-town shopping centre in Europe than the 'regional' kind. As its name implies, the superstore is under the control of a single company although adjacent sites may be let to a number of smaller and specialist retail firms in order to add to the attraction of the centre as a whole. The superstore has many departments and is able to offer a wide range of merchandise including food. There are also ones which specialize, for example, in the sale of furniture. They usually have at least 50 000 square feet of selling space and may exceed 200 000 square feet. Superstores have been built mainly since 1960 in Europe and are most common in France, Germany, Belgium and Sweden. There are a number in the United Kingdom, for the most part on edge-of-town sites.

A major attraction of the superstore lies in its prices which are lower than average, the benefits of bulk purchase being passed on to the customer. This is done often in combination with an aggressive marketing policy. Cut-price operations are also typical of the discount store. The latter is a less precise kind of out-of-town development than the regional centre or freestanding superstore, mainly because of the variety of premises employed. Hardware, furniture and domestic appliances are sold rather more commonly than clothing or food. Some discount stores are purpose-built but many of them occupy premises that were formerly used for other purposes, warehouses, factory buildings or corn mills, for example. By using existing buildings the discount company reduces its capital outlay; it has also tended to find local planning authorities more sympathetic to applications which involve change of use rather than the development of greenfield sites. Short circuiting opposition to other forms of out-of-town retailing in this way, the discount store has in recent years become a feature of the urban fringe in Britain.

The re-use of old premises is a process of change in the urban fringe which it is easy to overlook or to underestimate. Sites that, in wartime, served as airfields or ordnance depots have similarly become available for commercial, industrial or even residential (Berinsfield) use. Colonization of such sites by research institutions of various kinds has been a feature of the urbanization of Oxford's fringe belt since World War II (Scargill, 1967). The nuclear research establishments at Harwell and Culham, for example, were both built on former military bases. An ordnance depot at Didcot has provided the site for a large, coal-fired power station, and another depot at Milton is now a trading estate, mainly for firms engaged in storage and distribution. For the latter a location in the urban fringe has strong attractions provided that it is well served by road.

Sites close to major highways are also preferred for what is still largely a North American phenomenon, the out-of-town office park. In some cases these are combined with a regional shopping centre, possibly also with motel and recreational facilities (Daniels, 1974).

Green belts

Irregularity of urban development in the fringe may be attributed in part to differences in the planning policies of local authorities whose boundaries meet in this zone. Even when the administrative limits of the city are outdated and anomalous, having been overtaken by suburban growth, the fringe may still be crossed by the boundaries of several 'rural' authorities. Reorganization of British local government in 1974 did not do more, in some places, than group former Rural District Councils into the new District Councils. In Oxfordshire, for example, the City District of Oxford retains the same boundaries as the former County Borough, whilst

portions of the city's urban fringe are administered by each of the
remaining four District Councils which make up the County. Local
planning remains the responsibility of the District Councils and it is
perfectly possible for one such Council to pursue a housing policy
which involves the concentration of new housing, so far as possible,
in a number of selected villages, whilst a neighbouring Council
prefers to see this distributed evenly over all the settlements in its
area. In the United States there has been some grouping of cities
and counties into new 'city-region' units of local government, as at
Jacksonville, Florida in 1967, or regional councils have been set up
to deal with a particular range of problems. A Regional Council
was set up for the twin cities of Minneapolis — St. Paul and surrounding counties in 1967 and similar arrangements have been
adopted for Atlanta, Georgia and Seattle, Washington. But progress with schemes of this kind is always slow, encountering many
vested interests, and the fringe of most American cities is likely to
remain a zone of conflicting pressures.

Some degree of unity is given to planning policies in the urban
fringe when that zone, or a portion of it, is designated a 'green belt'.
The idea of such a belt is not new. In 1580, Queen Elizabeth I
forbade new building within three miles of the city gates of London, the intention being to protect the city's food supply and to
reduce the risk of plague. In the present century, the idea of
providing London with a green belt of agriculture and recreational
open space was revived when the Greater London Regional Planning Committee was set up in 1927. But it was not until 1938 that
the Green Belt (London and Home Counties) Act was finally
passed. The Town and Country Planning Act of 1947 permitted
the belt to be widened to between 10 and 15 km and it has
subsequently been extended further (D. Thomas, 1970). The 1947
Act also made it possible for other local authorities to designate
green belts but it was not until the mid-fifties that they began to do
so.

Three reasons for establishing a green belt were set out in a
circular sent to local authorities by the Ministry of Housing and
Local Government in 1955. These were:

1   to check the growth of a large built-up area;
2   to prevent neighbouring towns from merging into one
     another; or
3   to preserve the special character of a town.

Green belts have been established around the major English
conurbations principally for the first of these reasons. The green
belt between Gloucester and Cheltenham falls into the second

category; those around Oxford, Cambridge and York can be seen to satisfy the third reason.

It was never supposed that green belts could, or indeed should, inhibit all urban development within the area so designated. The same Ministry document stated that forms of development were permissible which do not interfere with the 'open character of the land'. These were listed as buildings for sport or recreation, hospitals and similar institutions standing in extensive grounds, cemeteries and mineral workings. In addition, a number of selected sites could be reserved for future housing needs. Thus Oxford's green belt, for example, included ten 'inset villages' where applications for housebuilding were to be considered more sympathetically than elsewhere (Fig. 67). That the policy has had some success may be judged by the fact that population growth in these settlements was 27 per cent during the 1960s compared with only 4.6 per cent in the remaining parishes which make up the green belt. The same villages have acquired a number of functions that have moved out of the city centre; they include branches of county administration and the headquarter offices of the district police and electricity services (Scargill, 1975).

Many green belts have been slow to receive formal government approval. It was not until 1975 that such approval was granted to Oxford's green belt and then only to the outer part of it. Failure to give approval has made them rather more vulnerable to development pressures than was perhaps envisaged in 1955. Yet local authorities have usually treated the 'proposed' green belts as though they had formal government backing, and green belt strategy must, therefore, be counted amongst the factors influencing the urbanization of British fringe belts.

Recreation and second homes

Rising standards of living in the wealthier countries of the world have created a rapidly growing demand for recreational and other leisure activities. Golf courses are a well-established form of land use on the edge of the city but to these have now been added country clubs, sports and garden centres, and the Country Park. Reservoirs, from which the public were once excluded, are today used for fishing and sailing. Sites are required for caravans and for camping. With the exception of pressures that arise from the need for housing, the pursuit of leisure is probably the greatest single factor leading to land use changes in the urban fringe. Such changes

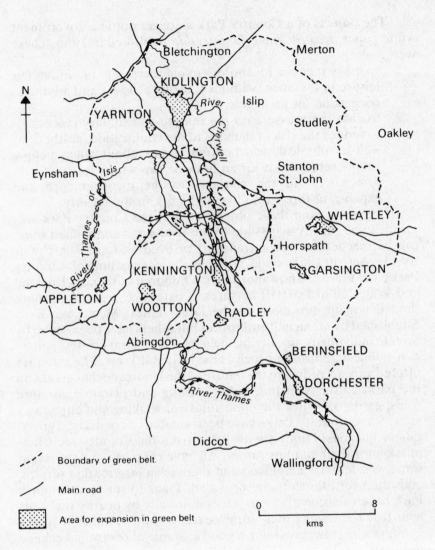

N

Bletchington
Merton
KIDLINGTON
Islip
River
YARNTON
Studley
Oakley
River Cherwell
Eynsham
Isis
Stanton
St. John
River Thames or
WHEATLEY
Horspath
KENNINGTON
GARSINGTON
APPLETON
WOOTTON
RADLEY
Abingdon
BERINSFIELD
DORCHESTER
River Thames
Didcot
Wallingford

- - - Boundary of green belt.

/ Main road

Area for expansion in green belt

0   8
kms

67 Oxford's green belt and its 'inset villages'

are not, of course, confined to this zone. The motorway system
ensures that large numbers of urban dwellers can spend their
weekend in a National Park. But for the less dedicated motorist,
the schoolboy with half a day, the retired enjoying an afternoon
outing, and many others, the fringe has the greatest attraction
because it is near home. The need to satisfy this local demand is
well illustrated by the creation in England and Wales since 1968 of
Country Parks.

The objects of a Country Park were set out in a government white paper, *Leisure in the Countryside* published in 1966. These were:

1 to make it easier for those seeking recreation to enjoy their leisure in the open, without travelling too far and adding to congestion on the roads;

2 to ease the pressure on the remote and solitary places;

3 to reduce the risk of damage to the countryside, aesthetic as well as physical, which often comes about when people simply settle down for an hour or two where it suits them, somewhere 'in the country' to the inconvenience and expense of those who live and work in the locality.

It is clear from these objectives that the Country Park was meant to be readily accessible to the townsman and indeed some can be reached by public transport or even on foot. The Countryside Act of 1968 made possible the designation of Country Parks and there are now more than a hundred of them in England and Wales all at least 10 hectares in extent. A high proportion, though not all, are close to the larger cities. Most have been established by municipal authorities but others have been set up by private individuals, usually the owners of ancestral estates, and by non-public organizations such as the National Trust. The activities offered vary according to the nature of the landscape that makes up the park, and may include riding, sailing and swimming, nature trails, gardens, or just the opportunity of walking and enjoying a view. Some Country Parks have been created out of disused gravel pits or quarries. Funds are available from the Countryside Commission for their administration. All have car parks and toilets; in some, wardens are employed and there is an information service, and often refreshments are provided. Plans to set up a Country Park have occasionally been resisted, usually by nearby residents who fear the loss of their rural peace, but the number of parks continues to grow, providing a good example of controlled change in the urban fringe.

Less controlled is the extension of second-home ownership into the fringe. This phenomenon, formerly part of the way of life only of the very wealthy, has become increasingly common as contraction of the farm workforce has made dwellings available for purchase by townsmen and as road improvements have added to the distances that may be travelled in an hour or two's driving on a Friday evening. Some country properties are visited only at holiday seasons, but many are used at the weekend and it is in connection with the latter that travel time has most bearing on the decision to purchase. Clout (1974) quotes French evidence which suggests that the 'weekend suburbs' of Paris extend to a distance of 160 km or 3 hours' driving time from the capital. For cities of up to a million inhabitants the corresponding limit of weekend travel is reached at about 100 km, and for those with a population of under 100 000 the radius is reduced to 50 km. Within these limits there are roughly concentric zones of decreasing intensity of second home ownership. In a study of second home ownership around Toronto, Wolfe (1966) found, not unexpectedly, that such zones also corresponded with income groups. But there was segregation too on other grounds, notably between Jews and gentiles, the groups clustering in their own weekend resorts. Wolfe sees this as representing 'the zonation of the city . . . extended to the country'. More generally, Clout concludes from his studies of the distribution of second homes in France that 'a new type of settlement geography is developing around the major cities of France and, one suspects, elsewhere in the world . . . '

Urban influence on agriculture

Proximity to a large urban market is no longer a dominant influence on the location of agricultural production. London's daily milk supply is brought from the furthest western counties of England, and the production of fruit and vegetables is as likely to be affected by the policies of freezing and canning companies in Grimsby or Wigan as it is by traditional attractions of the urban fringe. The city nevertheless continues to exercise a high degree of control over the agricultural land use of the fringe. The resultant pattern is, however, very different from that envisaged in von Thünen's Isolated State, and on the basis of experience in the American Mid-West, Sinclair (1967) put forward a model which in some respects may be described as 'reversed-Thünen' (Fig. 68).

Farming on the edge of the city is beset by many problems of which vandalism in a variety of forms is one of the greatest. Farms are divided by new road construction and become less viable units as individual fields are lost to housing or other urban uses. The response, according to Sinclair, is 'urban farming'. Activities most likely to survive are those which are carried on in buildings under conditions approaching those of the factory. Intensive poultry production, mushroom-growing, and the forcing of rhubarb, which takes place in long, low sheds in the West Yorkshire conurbation, are all of this type. Dry-lot dairying is found on the edge of

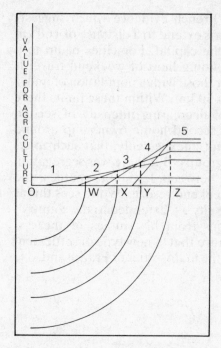
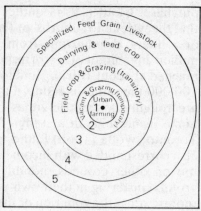

68 Theoretical sequence of land uses around an expanding city in the American Mid-West. After Sinclair, 1967. (Reproduced by permission from the *Annals of the Association of American Geographers,* vol. 57, 1967)

American cities, especially in the West, and Gregor (1963) describes a similar phenomenon in Tokyo and on the fringe of the largest cities in India.

Beyond the zone of urban farming is one in which land is either awaiting development (Sinclair's 'vacant land') or, if it is still in agricultural use, is farmed only at low intensity. Land is often held by speculators or by farmers whose intention it is to sell as soon as a favourable offer can be obtained. Reference was made in Chapter 1 to the speculative subdivision that often precedes sale of actual building plots in the United States. Meanwhile land is likely to be in temporary use, perhaps grazing a few stock, before they proceed to the town abattoir, even leased to some organization for recreational use. Here, and even more typically in Sinclair's third zone (Fields Crops and Grazing), there is no incentive to improve the land. The American situation is well illustrated by a description of farming on the Indiana fringe of Chicago quoted by Hoover (1948): 'As the city limits of the different cities have opened out farther and farther, efficiency of farm production has been reduced in the areas immediately surrounding the cities. When one farmer in a community sells his land for subdivision . . . many other farmers in the community hope that they may soon be able to sell their farms . . . Examples are numerous where farm operators are delaying liming, deferring building a chicken house, refraining from improving the dairy barn . . . because there is at least a remote possibility that the farm may be sold. When it is sold for subdivision purposes it will bring no higher price if it is well limed, has a new poultry house or if the dairy barn is in better condition. As the cities become larger, the zone of "watchful waiting" widens.' Green belt and other legislation lessens the degree of speculation in farm land in the United Kingdom but does not eliminate it (Munton,1974). It is not uncommon for fragmented holdings on the edge of cities to be leased for crops of hay or cereals by 'absentee' farmers whose own units are at some distance from the city. The standard of farming under such conditions is rarely very high and gradual deterioration in the quality of the land makes it vulnerable to various urban pressures even when it is part of a designated green belt.

Sinclair's third zone is also characterized by the presence of part-time farmers, city workers who farm as a source of extra income or as a hobby. In a study carried out in South-East England, Gasson (1966) found that part-time farming was 'commonplace up to 50 miles (80 km) from London'. At 30 km from London the proportion of part-time to full-time farmers was as high as 60 per cent; it was still over 20 per cent at 100 km. Closest to London, part-time farming is principally the concern of manual workers who operate a small holding in their spare time. They are most likely to produce market garden items for sale in the city, perhaps from street markets. Further out, part-time farmers are mostly professional people, the salariat, who, on the whole, are more concerned with the satisfaction that is to be gained from farming than with profit. Since the time they can devote to their farms is limited, they are likely to opt for the simpler and least time-consuming forms of agriculture, preferring cereals or beef production, for example, to mixed farming or dairying. They are less likely to seek to enlarge their holdings than are full-time farmers, and Gasson sees their presence as a restraining influence on farm-size structure in the fringe.

Studies of agricultural land use support the concept of the fringe as a zone over which urban influences are clearly at work. Since it can be demonstrated that certain types of farm are more vulnerable to urban pressures than others — the part-time farm, that owned by an absentee or retired farmer, the farm that has already suffered some loss of territory — the study of agriculture in the fringe also provides clues to the directions of future urban growth and thereby assists the planner whose responsibility it is to anticipate these pressures.

Modelling the urban system

Gottmann described Megalopolis as the cradle of a new order, but one that was still far from orderly. Order cannot be achieved without an understanding of the processes that are at work shaping both the city and the wider urban region. In the introduction to a study of the South-East Lancashire conurbation, L. P. Green (1959) observed that 'The concept of the metropolitan region defines a method of approach to the study of great cities and their problems, and indicates what kind of facts are relevant. We need in addition techniques by which to uncover and present the facts relevant in any given metropolitan field, and much depends on the adequacy of these tools. But the techniques of metropolitan regional analysis are relatively unexplored . . . ' Much progress has been made in the search for these techniques since Green's book was written. Publication of Lowry's model in 1964 was a stimulus to further research, and the 1970s have seen the application of sophisticated mathematical methods to both urban and regional modelling (Wilson, 1974; Batty, 1976). In addition, a systems approach has been applied to plan-making (McLoughlin, 1969). A consequence of the refinement of these techniques has been a better understanding of how the city has come to acquire its present form, and greater skill in both forecasting and directing future developments. But the future city, or metropolitan region, will not be fashioned only by the planner. Politicians are able to influence patterns of urban growth, as are many kinds of public and private organizations and, one hopes, the individual. The thread of idealism that has run through the history of town building will continue to play some part in the decision-making process, but future urban forms are likely to be affected far more by the search for solutions to contemporary urban problems whether this be in the developed or the developing world The nature of these solutions will, in turn, be related to prevailing social attitudes and to the policies that are based on them. Throughout history the city has been a symbol of civilization. Its future continues to depend on man's attitude to his neighbour.

Bibliography of Works Cited

ABEGGLEN, J. C. (1958): *The Japanese factory: aspects of its social organization*, New York, The Free Press. Extracts reproduced as 'Continuity and change in Japanese industry', in Fava, S. F. (ed.), *Urbanism in world perspective: a reader*, New York, Crowell, 1968, 287-96.

ABU-LUGHOD, J. L. (1961): 'Migrant adjustment to city life: the Egyptian case', *American Journal of Sociology*, vol.67, 22-32.

ABU-LUGHOD, J. L. (1966): *The ecology of Cairo, Egypt: a comparative study using factor analysis*, Ph.D. thesis, University of Massachusetts, Amherst.

ABU-LUGHOD, J. L. (1969 a): 'Varieties of urban experience: contrast, coexistence and coalescence in Cairo', in Lapidus, I. M. (ed.), *Middle Eastern cities: a symposium on ancient, Islamic, and contemporary Middle Eastern urbanism*, Berkeley, University of California Press, 159-87.

ABU-LUGHOD, J. L. (1969 b): 'Testing the theory of social area analysis: the ecology of Cairo, Egypt', *American Sociological Review*, vol.34, 198-212.

ABU-LUGHOD, J. L. (1973): 'Cairo: perspective and prospectus', in Brown, L. C. (ed.), *From madina to metropolis*, Princeton, Darwin Press, 95-113.

ABU-LUGHOD, J. L. and FOLEY, M. M. (1960): 'Consumer differences', in Foote, N. N. et al., *Housing choices and constraints*, New York, 95-133.

ADAMS, J. S. (1969): 'Directional bias in intra-urban migration', *Economic Geography*, vol.45, 302-23.

ALAM, S. M. and KHAN, W. (1972): *Metropolitan Hyderabad and its region: a strategy for development*, London, Asia Publishing House.

ALDOUS, J. (1962): 'Urbanization, the extended family, and kinship ties in West Africa', *Social Forces*, vol.41, 6-12.

ALLPASS, J. et al. (1967): 'Urban centres and changes in the centre structure', in University of Amsterdam, *Urban core and inner city,* Leiden, E. J. Brill, 103-17.

ALONSO, W. (1964): *Location and land use,* Cambridge, Mass., Harvard University Press.

AMATO, P. W. (1968): *An analysis of the changing patterns of elite residential areas in Bogota, Colombia,* Latin American Studies Doctoral Dissertation Series, Cornell University.

AMATO, P. W. (1970 a): 'Elitism and settlement patterns in the Latin American city', *Journal of the American Institute of Planners,* vol.36, 96-105.

AMATO, P. W. (1970 b): 'A comparison: population densities, land values and socio-economic class in four Latin American cities', *Land Economics,* vol.46, 447-55.

AMBROSE, P. J. (1968): 'An analysis of intra-urban shopping patterns', *Town Planning Review,* vol.38, 327-34.

APPLETON, J. H. (1968): 'Railways and the morphology of British towns', in Beckinsale, R. P. and Houston, J. M. (eds.), *Urbanization and its problems: essays presented to E. W. Gilbert,* Oxford, Blackwell, 92-118.

BALE, J. R. (1974): 'Towards a definition of the industrial estate: a note on a neglected aspect of urban geography', *Geography,* vol. 59, 31-4.

BANTON, M. (1973): 'Urbanization and role analysis', in Southall, A. (ed.), *Urban anthropology: cross-cultural studies of urbanization,* Oxford, Oxford University Press.

BASCOM, W. (1963): 'The urban African and his world', *Cahiers d'Etudes Africaines,* 163-83, reproduced in Fava, S. F. (ed.), *Urbanism in world perspective,* New York, Crowell, 81-93.

BATTY, M. (1976): *Urban modelling,* Cambridge, Cambridge University Press.

BEAVON, K. S. O. (1974): *A model of the location of intra-metropolitan tertiary activity,* unpublished Ph.D. thesis, University of Witwatersrand.

BEDARIDA, F. (1968): Discussion of L. F. Schnore's 'Problems in the quantitative study of urban history', in Dyos, H. J. (ed.), *The study of urban history,* London, Edward Arnold, 212-3.

BELL, W. (1958): 'Social choice, life styles and suburban residence', in Dobriner, W. (ed.), *The suburban community,* New York, Geo. Putnam, 225-47.

BERESFORD, M. (1967): *New towns of the Middle Ages,* London, Lutterworth Press.

BERRY, B. J. L. (1962): *The commercial structure of American cities: a review,* Chicago, Community Renewal Program.

BERRY, B. J. L. (1963): *Commercial structure and commercial blight,* Research Paper No.85, Department of Geography, University of Chicago.

BERRY, B. J. L. (1971): 'Comparative factorial ecology', Berry, B. J. L. (ed.), *Economic Geography,* vol.47, supplement, 209-367.

BERRY, B. J. L. (1973): *The human consequences of urbanization,* New York, St. Martin's Press.

BERRY, B. J. L. and GARRISON, W. L. (1958): 'Recent developments of central place theory', *Papers and Proceedings of the Regional Science Association,* vol.4, 107-20.

BERRY, B. J. L., and HORTON, F. E. (1970): *Geographic perspectives on urban systems,* Englewood Cliffs, Prentice-Hall.

BERRY, B. J. L. and REES, P. H. (1968-69): 'The factorial ecology of Calcutta', *American Journal of Sociology,* vol.74, 445-91.

BERRY, B. J. L., SIMMONS, J. W. and TENNANT, R. J. (1963): 'Urban population densities: structure and change', *Geographical Review,* vol.53, 389-405.

BERRY, B. J. L. and SPODEK, H. (1971): 'Comparative ecologies of large Indian cities', *Economic Geography,* vol.47, 266-85.

BEYER, G. H. (1967): 'Résumé', in Beyer, G. H. (ed.), *The urban explosion in Latin America,* Ithaca, Cornell University Press, 302-35.

BLIJ, H. J. de, (1962): 'The functional structure and central business district of Lourenço Marques, Mocambique', *Economic Geography,* vol.38, 56-77.

BLUMENFELD, H. (1954): 'The tidal wave of metropolitan expansion', *Journal of the American Institute of Planners,* vol.20, 3-14.

BOAL, F. W. (1969). 'Territoriality on the Shankill-Falls divide, Belfast', *Irish Geographer,* vol.6, 33-4.

BOAL, F. W. (1970): 'Social space in the Belfast urban area', in Stephens, N. and Glasscock, R. (eds.), *Irish geographical studies in honour of E. E. Evans,* Department of Geography, The Queen's University of Belfast.

BOAL, F. W. (1972): 'The urban residential sub-community — a conflict interpretation', *Area,* vol.4, 164-8.

BOAL, F. W. and JOHNSON, D. B. (1965): 'The functions of retail and service establishments on commercial ribbons', *The Canadian Geographer,* vol.9, 154-69.

BODDY, M. J. (1976): 'The structure of mortgage finance: building societies and the British social formation', *Transactions of the Institute of British Geographers,* New Series, vol.1, 58-71.

BOGUE, D. J. and ZACHARIAH, K. C. (1962): 'Urbanization and migration in India', in Turner, R. (ed.), *India's urban future,* Berkeley, University of California Press, 27-54.

BONILLA, F. (1961): *Rio's favelas: the rural slum within the city,* American Universities Field Staff Reports Service, East Coast South American Series, vol.8, no.3.

BOSE, A. (1973): *Studies in India's urbanization,* 1901-1971, Delhi, Tata McGraw-Hill.

BOURNE, L. S. (1968): 'Comments on the transition zone concept', *The Professional Geographer,* vol.20, 313-6.

BOURNE, L. S. (1975): *Urban systems: strategies for regulation,* Oxford, Oxford University Press.

BOWDEN, M. J. (1971): 'Downtown through time: delimitation, expansion, and internal growth', *Economic Geography,* vol.47, 121-35.

BREESE, G. (1966): 'A case study of Delhi-New Delhi, India', in Breese, G., *Urbanization in newly developing countries,* Englewood Cliffs, Prentice-Hall, 55-72.

BRIGHAM, E. F. (1965): 'The determinants of residential land values', *Land Economics,* vol.41, 325-34.

BROMLEY, R. J. (1974): 'The organization of Quito's urban markets: towards a reinterpretation of periodic central places', *Transactions of the Institute of British Geographers,* no.62, 45-70.

BROOKS, E., HERBERT, D. T. and PEACH, G. C. K. (1975): 'Spatial social constraints in the inner city', *Geographical Journal,* vol.141, 355-87.

BROWN, L. C. (ed.) (1973): *From madina to metropolis: heritage and change in the Near Eastern city,* Princeton, The Darwin Press.

BROWN, W. R. Jr. (1972): 'Access to housing: the role of the real estate industry', *Economic Geography,* vol.48, 66-78.

BRUSH, J. E. (1962): 'The morphology of Indian cities', in Turner, R. (ed.), *India's urban future,* Berkeley, University California Press, 57-70.

BRUSH, J. E. (1968): 'Spatial patterns of population in Indian cities', *Geographical Review,* vol.58, 362-91.

BUISSINK, J. D. and WIDT, D. J. DE (1967): 'Some aspects of the development of the shopping centre of the city of Utrecht', in University of Amsterdam, *Urban core and inner city,* Leiden, E. J. Brill, 237-55.

BULSARA, J. F. (1970): *Patterns of social life in metropolitan areas, with particular reference to Greater Bombay,* Bombay, Research Programmes Committee of the Indian Planning Commission.

BURGESS, E. W. (1929): 'Urban areas', in Smith, T. U. and White, L. D. (eds.), *Chicago: an experiment in social science research,*

Chicago, University of Chicago Press, 114-23.

BURKE, G. (1971): *Towns in the making,* London, Edward Arnold.

BURNS, W. (1959): *British shopping centres,* London.

BURTON, I. (1963): 'A restatement of the dispersed city hypothesis', *Annals of the Association of American Geographers,* vol.53, 285-9.

BUSTEED, M. A. (1972): *Northern Ireland: geographical aspects of a crisis,* Research Paper No. 3, School of Geography, University of Oxford.

BUSTEED, M. A. (1974): *Northern Ireland,* Scargill, D. I. (ed.), Problem Regions of Europe, Oxford, Oxford University Press.

CANOYER, H. G. (1946): *Selecting a store location,* Economic Series 56, United States Bureau of Foreign and Domestic Commerce, Washington, Government Printing Office.

CARALP, R. (1972): 'Les villes de la plaine du Gange', *L'Information Géographique,* vol.36, 11-22.

CAROL, H. (1960): 'The hierarchy of central functions within the city', *Annals of the Association of American Geographers,* vol.50, 419-38.

CARR, S. (1970): 'The city of the mind', in Proshansky et al., *Environmental Psychology,* New York, Rinehart and Winston.

CARRUTHERS, W. I. (1962): 'Service centres in Greater London', *Town Planning Review,* vol.33, 5-21.

CARTER, F. W. (1975): 'Bulgaria's new towns', *Geography,* vol.60, 133-6.

CARTER, H. (1972): *The Study of Urban Geography,* London, Edward Arnold.

CARTER, H. and ROWLEY, G. (1966): 'The morphology of the central business district of Cardiff', *Transactions of the Institute of British Geographers,* no.38, 119-34.

CHERRY, G. E. (1972): *Urban change and planning: a history of urban development in Britain since 1750,* Henley-on-Thames, G. T. Foulis.

CHINITZ, B. (1960): *Freight and the metropolis,* Cambridge Mass., Harvard University Press.

CLARK, B. D. and COSTELLO, V. (1973): 'The urban system and social patterns in Iranian cities', *Transactions of the Institute of British Geographers,* no.59, 99-128.

CLARK, C. (1951): 'Urban population densities', *Journal of Royal Statistical Society,* series A, vol.114, 490-6.

CLARK, W. A. V. (1968): 'Consumer travel patterns and the concept of range', *Annals of the Association of American Geog-*

raphers, vol.58, 386-96.

CLARKE, C. G. (1974): 'Urbanization in the Caribbean', *Geography,* vol.59, 223-32.

CLARKE, J. I. (1963): *The Iranian city of Shiraz,* Research Paper Series No.7, Department of Geography, University of Durham.

CLINARD, M. B. and CHATTERJEE, B. (1962): 'Urban community development in India: the Delhi pilot project', in Turner, R. (ed.), *India's urban future,* Berkeley, University of California Press, 71-93.

CLOUT, H. D. (1974): 'The growth of second-home ownership: an example of seasonal suburbanization', in Johnson, J. H. (ed.), *Suburban Growth,* London, John Wiley, 101-27.

COHEN, S. B. and LEWIS, G. K. (1967): 'Form and function in the geography of retailing', *Economic Geography,* vol.43, 1-42.

COLLINS, M. P. (1965): 'Field work in urban areas', in Chorley, R. J. and Haggett, P. (eds.), *Frontiers in geographical teaching,* London, Methuen, 215-38.

COLLISON, P. (1963): *The Cutteslowe walls: a study in social class,* London, Faber and Faber.

COLLISON, P. and MOGEY, J. (1959): 'Residence and social class in Oxford', *American Journal of Sociology,* vol.54, 599-605.

CONNELL, J. (1973): 'Social networks in urban society', in Clark, B. D. and Gleave, M. B. (eds.) *Social patterns in cities,* 41-52.

CONZEN, M. R. G. (1958): 'The growth and character of Whitby', in Daysh, G. H. J. (ed.), *A survey of Whitby and the surrounding area,* Windsor, Shakespeare Head Press, 48-89.

COX, O. C. (1964): 'The preindustrial city reconsidered', *The Sociological Quarterly,* vol.5, 133-44.

CURRY, L. (1962): 'The geography of service centres within towns: the elements of an operational approach', in Norborg, K. (ed.), *The IGU symposium in urban geography, Lund 1960,* 31-53.

DANIELS, P. W. (1974): 'New offices in the suburbs', in Johnson, J. H. (ed.), *Suburban growth,* London, John Wiley, 177-200.

DANIELS, P. W. (1975): *Office location: an urban and regional geography,* London, Bell.

DAVIES, D. H. (1959): 'Boundary study as a tool in CBD analysis: an interpretation of certain aspects of the boundary of Cape Town's central business district', *Economic Geography,* vol.35, 322-45.

DAVIES, D. H. (1960): 'The hard core of Cape Town's central business district: an attempt at delimitation', *Economic Geography,* vol.36, 53-69.

DAVIES, R. J. (1963): 'The growth of the Durban metropolitan area', *South African Geographical Journal,* vol.45, 15-43.

DAVIES, R. J. (1964): 'Social distance and the distribution of occupational categories in Johannesburg and Pretoria', *South African Geographical Journal,* vol.46, 24-39.

DAVIES, R. J. and RAJAH, D. S. (1965): 'The Durban CBD: boundary delimitation and racial dualism', *South African Geographical Journal,* vol.47, 45-58.

DAVIES, R. L. (1968): 'Effects of consumer income differences on the business provisions of small shopping centres', *Urban Studies,* vol.5, 144-64.

DAVIES, R. L. (1969): 'Effects of consumer income differences on shopping movement behaviour', *Tijdschrift voor Economische en Sociale Geografie,* vol.60, 111-21.

DAVIES, R. L. (1972 a): 'The retail pattern of the central area in Coventry', in *The retail structure of cities,* Occasional Publications No.1, Urban Study Group of the Institute of British Geographers, London, 1-32.

DAVIES R. L. (1972 b): 'Structural models of retail provision', *Transactions of the Institute of British Geographers,* no.57, 59-82.

DAVIES, W. K. D. (1966): 'The ranking of service centres: a critical review', *Transactions of the Institute of British Geographers,* no.40, 51-65.

DAVIS, J. T. (1965): 'Middle class housing in the central city', *Economic Geography,* vol. 41, 238-51.

DAWSON, A. H. (1971): 'Warsaw: an example of city structure in free-market amd planned socialist environments', *Tijdschrift voor Economische en Sociale Geografie,* vol.62, 104-13.

DAWSON, J. A. (1974): 'The suburbanization of retail activity', in Johnson, J. H. (ed.), *Suburban growth,* London, John Wiley, 155-75.

DE MEIRLIER, M. J. (1950): *Manufactural occupance in the West Central area of Chicago,* Chicago.

DENHAM, D. and CLAPPERTON, H. (1826): *Narrative of travels and discoveries in Northern and Central Africa, 1822, 1823 and 1824,* London. Extracts reproduced in Howard, C. (ed.), *West African Explorers,* Oxford, Oxford University Press, 1951.

DETHIER, J. (1973): 'Evolution of concepts of housing, urbanism and country planning in a developing country: Morocco, 1900 — 1972', in Brown, L. C. (ed.) *From madina to metropolis: heritage and change in the Near Eastern city,* Princeton, Darwin Press, 197-243.

DIAMOND, D. R. (1962): 'The central business district of Glasgow', in Norborg, K. (ed.), *Proceedings of the IGU symposium in urban geography, Lund 1960,* Lund, 525-34.

DORE, R. P. (1958): *City life in Japan,* Berkeley and Los Angeles, University of California Press.

DUNCAN, S. S. (1976): 'Research directions in social geography: housing opportunities and constraints', *Transactions of the Institute of British Geographers,* New Series, vol.1, 10-19.

DUNNING, J. H. (1969): 'The City of London: a case study in urban economics', *Town Planning Review,* vol.40, 207-32.

DWYER, D. J. (1968): *The city in the Developing World and the example of South-East Asia,* Inaugural Lecture from the Chair of Geography, University of Hong Kong, Supplement to the Gazette, vol.15, no.6.

DWYER, D. J. (1975): *People and housing in Third World cities: perspectives on the problem of spontaneous settlements,* London, Longman.

DYOS, H. J. (1961): *Victorian suburb: a study of the growth of Camberwell,* Leicester, Leicester University Press.

EMERY, F. V. (1974): *The Oxfordshire landscape,* London, Hodder and Stoughton.

ENGLES, F. (1845): *The condition of the working class in England,* Leipzig.

ENGLISH, P. (1973): 'The traditional city of Herat, Afghanistan', in Brown, L. C. (ed.), *From madina to metropolis: heritage and change in the Near Eastern city,* Princeton, Darwin Press, 73-90.

ETTINGHAUSEN, R. (1973): 'Muslim cities: old and new', in Brown, L. C. (ed.), *From madina to metropolis: heritage and change in the Near Eastern city,* Princeton, Darwin Press.

EVANS, H. (ed.) (1972): *New towns: the British experience,* London, Charles Knight for the Town and Country Planning Association.

EYRE, L. A. (1972): 'The shanty towns of Montego Bay, Jamaica', *Geographical Review,* vol.62, 394-413.

FATHY, H. (1973): 'Constancy, transposition and change in the Arab city', in Brown, L. C. (ed.), *From madina to metropolis: heritage and change in the Near Eastern city,* Princeton, Darwin Press, 319-33.

FELLMANN, J. D. (1957): 'Pre-building growth patterns of Chicago', *Annals of the Association of American Geographers,* vol.47, 59-82.

FERNEA, R. A. (1969): Discussion following J. L. Abu-Lughod's paper, 'Varieties of urban experience: contrast, coexistence and coalescence in Cairo', in Lapidus, I.M. (ed.), *Middle Eastern Cities,* Berkeley, University of California Press, 184.

FIREY, W. (1947): *Land use in Central Boston,* Cambridge Mass., Harvard University Press.

FISHER, J. C. (1963): 'Urban analysis: a case study of Zagreb, Yugoslavia', *Annals of the Association of American Geographers,* vol.53, 266-84.

FLORENCE, S. (1948): *Investment, location and size of plant,* Cambridge, Cambridge University Press.

FORD, L. R. (1973): 'Individual decisions in the creation of the American downtown', *Geography,* vol.58, 324-7.

FORD, L. and FITZSIMONS, D. (1974): 'Economic man and the city of the mind: comments on perception and the sense of place', *Antipode,* vol.6, 80-5.

FOX, D. J. (1963): 'Odessa', *Scottish Geographical Magazine,* vol.79, 5-22.

FOX, D. J. (1969): 'Urbanization and economic development in Mexico', in *Cities in a changing Latin America,* London, Latin American Publications Fund.

FRANKENBERG, R. (1966): *Communities in Britain: social life in town and country,* London, Penguin.

FRIEDMANN, J. and MILLER, J. (1965): 'The urban field', *Journal of the American Institute of Planners,* vol.31. Reproduced in Blowers, A. et al. (eds.) (1974), *The future of cities,* London, Hutchinson Educational, 152-66.

FROLIC, B. M. (1963-4): 'The Soviet city', *Town Planning Review,* vol.34, 285-306.

GANS, H. J. (1962): *The urban villagers: group and class in the life of Italian-Americans,* New York, The Free Press.

GANS, H. J. (1968): 'Urbanism and suburbanism as ways of life', in Pahl, R. E. (ed.), *Readings in urban sociology,* Oxford, Pergamon Press, 95-118. Also in Rose, A. M. (ed.), *Human behaviour and social processes,* Routledge and Kegan Paul.

GARNER, B. J. (1966): *The internal structure of retail nucleations,* Evanston, Northwestern University Press.

GARRISON, W. L. et al. (1959): *Studies of highway development and geographic change,* Seattle, University of Washington Press.

GASSON, R. M. (1966): *The influence of urbanization on farm ownership and practice,* Studies in Rural Land Use No.7, Wye College, Ashford.

GEDDES, P. (1915): *Cities in evolution,* London, Williams and Norgate.

GETIS, A. (1968): 'Retail store spatial affinities', *Urban Studies,* vol.5, 317-32.

GIGGS, J. A. (1972): 'Retail change and decentralization in the Nottingham metropolitan community', in Dziewonski, Osborne and Korcelli (eds.), *Geographical aspects of rural-urban interaction*, Proceedings of the Fourth Anglo-Polish Geographical Seminar, Warsaw, Polish Scientific Publishers, 173-88.

GINSBURG, N. P. (1965): 'Urban geography and "non-western" areas', in Hauser, P. M. and Schnore, L. F. (eds.), *The study of urbanization*, New York, John Wiley, 311-46.

GIST, N. P. (1957): 'The ecology of Bangalore: an east-west comparison', *Social Forces*, vol.35, 356-65.

GLASS, R. and FRENKEL, M. (1946): How they live at Bethnal Green', in *Contact: Britain between west and east*, London, Contact Books.

GLAZER, N. (1975): 'Ethnicity: a world phenomenon', *Dialogue*, United States Information Agency , vol.8, 34-46.

GLAZER, N. and MOYNIHAN, D. P. (1964): *Beyond the melting pot*, Cambridge Mass., M.I.T. Press.

GODDARD, J. B. (1967): 'The internal structure of London's central area', in University of Amsterdam, *Urban core and inner city*, Leiden, E. J. Brill, 118-40.

GODDARD, J. B. (1968): 'Multivariate analysis of office location patterns in a city centre: a London example', *Regional Studies*, vol.2, 69-85.

GODDARD, J. B. (1970): 'Functional regions within the city centre: a study by factor analysis of taxi flows in central London', *Transactions of the Institute of British Geographers*, no.49, 161-82.

GODDARD, J. B. (1973): *Office linkages and location*, Progress in Planning, vol.1 no.1, Oxford, Pergamon Press.

GODDARD, J. B. (1975): *Office location in urban and regional development*, Theory and Practice in Geography, Oxford, Oxford University Press.

GOLLEDGE, R. G., Rushton, G. and Clark, W. A. V. (1966): 'Some spatial characteristics of Iowa's dispersed farm population and their implications for the grouping of central place functions', *Economic Geography*, vol.42, 261-72.

GOODALL B. (1972): *The economics of urban areas*, Oxford, Pergamon Press.

GOTTMANN, J. (1961): *Megalopolis: the urbanized northeastern seaboard of the United States*, New York, The Twentieth Century Fund.

GOTTMANN, J. (1966): 'Why the skyscraper?', *Geographical*

Review, vol.56, 190-212.

GOTTMANN, J. (1970): 'Urban centrality and the interweaving of quaternary activities', *Ekistics,* vol.29, 322-31.

GOULD, P. R. and WHITE, R. R. (1974): *Mental maps,* Harmondsworth, Penguin Books.

GRABAR, O. (1969): 'The architecture of the Middle Eastern city from past to present: the case of the mosque', in Lapidus I. M. (ed.), *Middle Eastern cities,* Berkeley, University of California Press, 26-46.

GRAY, F. (1976): 'Selection and allocation in council housing', *Transactions of the Institute of British Geographers,* New Series, vol.1 34-46.

GREEN, L. P. (1959): *Provincial metropolis: the future of local government in South-East Lancashire,* London, Geo. Allen and Unwin.

GREGOR, E. G. (1963): 'Industrialized drylot dairying: an overview', *Economic Geography,* vol.39, 299-318.

GRIFFIN, D. W. and PRESTON, R. E. (1966): 'A restatement of the "transition zone" concept', *Annals of the Association of American Geographers,* vol.56, 339-50.

GRIFFIN, D. W. and PRESTON, R. E. (1969): 'A reply to "Comments on the transition zone concept".' *The Professional Geographer,* vol.21, 232-7.

GROVES, P. A. (1971): *Towards a typology of intrametropolitan manufacturing location: a case study of the San Francisco Bay area,* Occasional Papers in Geography No.16, University of Hull.

GUEST, A. M. (1972): 'Urban history, population densities, and higher status residential location', *Economic Geography,* vol.48, 375-87.

GULICK, J. (1967): *Tripoli (Lebanon): a modern Arab city,* Cambridge Mass.

GULICK, J. (1969): 'Village and city: cultural continuities in twentieth century Middle Eastern cultures', in Lapidus, I. M. (ed.), *Middle Eastern cities,* Berkeley, University of California Press, 122-58.

HALL, P. G. (1962): *The industries of London since 1861,* London, Hutchinson University Library.

HALL, P. G. (1975): *Urban and regional planning,* Newton Abbot, David and Charles.

HAMILTON, F. E. I. (1967): 'Models of industrial location', in Chorley, R. J. and Haggett, P. (eds.) *Models in geography,* London, Methuen, 361-424.

HAMILTON, F. E. I. (1973): 'Muscovites move away from the centre', *The Geographical Magazine*, vol.45, 451-9.

HAMILTON, F. E. I. (1976): *The Moscow City region*, Scargill, D. I. (ed.), Problem Regions of Europe, Oxford, Oxford University Press.

HANNERZ, U. (1969): *Soulside: an inquiry into ghetto culture*, New York, Columbia University Press.

HARRIS, C. D. and ULLMAN, E. L. (1945): 'The nature of cities', *Annals of the American Academy of Political Science*, no.242, 7-17.

HARRISON, R. S. (1967): 'Migrants in the city of Tripoli, Libya', *Geographical Review*, vol.57, 397-423.

HARTLEY, G. and SMAILES, A. E. (1961): 'Shopping centres in the Greater London area', *Transactions of the Institute of British Geographers*, no.29, 201-13.

HARTMAN, C. W. (1963): 'The limitations of public housing', *Journal of the American Institute of Planners*, vol.29, 283-96.

HARTMAN, G. W. (1950): 'Central business district, a study in urban geography', *Economic Geography'*, vol.26, 237-44.

HARVEY, D. (1975): Review of B. J. L. Berry's The Human Consequences of Urbanization, *Annals of the Association of American Geographers*, vol.65, 99-103.

HAUGHTON, J. P. (1949): 'The social geography of Dublin', *Geographical Review*, vol.39, 257-77.

HEAP, SIR DESMOND (1975): Extracts from Hamlyn Lecture at the Law Society Hall, reported in *The Times*, 5 November.

HERBERT, D. T. (1967): 'Social area analysis: a British study', *Urban Studies*, vol.4, 41-60.

HERBERT, D. T. (1972): *Urban geography: a social perspective*, Newton Abbot, David and Charles.

HINTON, D. A. (1974): 'An early garden suburb: North Oxford in the nineteenth century', *Country Life*, vol.156, 844-6

HIORNS, F. R. (1956): *Town-building in history*, London, Geo. Harrap.

HODDER, B. W. (1953): 'Racial groupings in Singapore', *Malayan Journal of Tropical Geography*, vol.1, 25-36.

HOLZNER, L. (1967): 'World regions in urban geography', *Annals of the Association of American Geographers*, vol.57, 704-12.

HOOVER, E. M. (1948): *The location of economic activity*, New York, McGraw-Hill.

HORTON, F. E. and REYNOLDS, D. R. (1971): 'Effects of urban spatial structure on individual behaviour', *Economic Geography*, vol.47, 36-48.

HORWOOD, E. M. and BOYCE, R. R. (1959): 'The CBD core-frame concept', in Horwood and Boyce, *Studies of the central business district and urban freeway development,* Seattle, University of Washington Press.

HOSELITZ, B. F. (1959): 'The cities of India and their problems', *Annals of the Association of American Geographers,* vol.59, 223-31.

HOSKINS, W. G. (1955): *The making of the English landscape,* London, Hodder and Stoughton.

HOURANI, A. H. (1970): 'The Islamic city in the light of recent research', in Hourani, A. H. and Stern, S. M. (eds.), *The Islamic city,* Oxford, Bruno Cassirer, 9-24.

HOUSTON, J. M. (1968): 'The foundation of colonial towns in Hispanic America', in Beckinsale, R. P. and Houston, J. M. (eds.), *Urbanization and its problems: essays presented to E. W. Gilbert,* Oxford, Blackwell, 352-90.

HOYT, H. (1939): *The structure and growth of residential neighbourhoods in American cities,* Washington, Federal Housing Administration.

HOYT, H. (1964): 'Recent distortions of the classical models of urban structure', *Land Economics,* vol.40, 199-212.

HUFF, D. L. (1960): 'A topographical model of consumer space preferences', *Papers and Proceedings of the Regional Science Association,* vol.6, 159-73.

JACKLE, J. A. and WHEELER, J. O. (1969): 'The changing residential structure of the Dutch population in Kalamazoo, Michigan', *Annals of the Association of American Geographers,* vol.59, 441-60.

JACKSON, J. C. (1974): 'Urban squatters in Southeast Asia', *Geography,* vol.59, 24-30.

JACOBS, J. (1969): *The economy of cities,* published as a Pelican Book, London, 1972.

JANSON, C-G. (1971): 'A preliminary report on Swedish urban spatial structure', *Economic Geography,* vol.47, 249-57.

JAY, L. S. and HIRSCH, G. P. (1960): 'The comparative analysis of settlements', *Sociologia Ruralis,* vol.1, 51-65.

JOHNSON, J. H. (1974): 'Geographical processes at the edge of the city', in Johnson, J. H. (ed.), *Suburban growth,* London, John Wiley, 1-16.

JOHNSTON, R. J. (1966): 'The distribution of an intra-metropolitan central place hierarchy', *Australian Geographical Studies,* vol.4, 19-33.

JOHNSTON, R. J. (1969): 'Towards an analytical study of the townscape: the residential building fabric', *Geografiska Annaler*, Series B, vol.51, 20-32.

JOHNSTON, R. J. (1971): *Urban residential patterns: an introductory review*, London, Bell.

JOHNSTON, R. J. (1972 a): 'Activity spaces and residential preferences: some tests of the hypothesis of sectoral mental maps', *Economic Geography*, vol.48, 199-211.

JOHNSTON, R. J. (1972 b): 'Towards a general model of intraurban residential patterns: some cross-cultural observations', in Board, C. et al. (eds.), *Progress in Geography*, vol.4, 83-124.

JONES, E. (1960): *A social geography of Belfast*, London, Oxford University Press.

JONES, E. (1975): *Readings in social geography*, Oxford, Oxford University Press.

JONES, P. N. (1967): *The segregation of immigrant communities in the city of Birmingham, 1961*, Occasional Papers in Geography No.7, University of Hull.

JONES, P. N. (1970): 'Some aspects of the changing distribution of coloured immigrants in Birmingham, 1961-1966', *Transactions of the Institute of British Geographers*, no.50, 199-219.

JONES, P. N. (1976): 'Coloured minorities in Birmingham, England', *Annals of the Association of American Geographers*, vol.66, 89-103.

JONES, R. (1975): *Essays on world urbanization*, London, Geo. Philip.

KAYE, B. (1960): *Upper Nankin Street, Singapore: a sociological study of Chinese households living in a densely populated area*, Singapore, University of Malaya Press.

KEEBLE, D. E. (1969): 'Local industrial linkage and manufacturing growth in outer London', *Town Planning Review*, vol.40, 163-88.

KELLETT, J. R. (1969): *The impact of railways on Victorian cities*, London. Routledge and Kegan Paul.

KELLEY, E. J. (1955): 'Retail structure of urban economy', *Traffic Quarterly*, vol.9, 411-30.

KENYON, J. B. (1964): 'The industrial structure of the New York garment center', in Thoman, R. S. and Patton, D. J. (eds.), *Focus on geographic activity*, New York, McGraw-Hill, 159-66.

KHALAF, S. and KONGSTAD, P. (1973): 'Urbanization and urbanism in Beirut: some preliminary results', in Brown, L. C. (ed.), *From madina to metropolis: heritage amd change in the Near Eastern city*, Princeton, Darwin Press.

KORNHAUSER, D. (1976): *Urban Japan: its foundations and*

growth, The World's Landscapes, London, Longman.

LANDAY, S. (1971): 'The ecology of Islamic cities: the case for the ethnocity', *Economic Geography,* vol.47, 303-13.

LANGTON, J. (1975): 'Residential patterns in pre-industrial cities: some case studies from seventeenth-century Britain', *Transactions of the Institute of British Geographers,* no.65, 1-27.

LAPIDUS, I. M. (1969): 'Muslim cities and Islamic societies', in Lapidus, I. M. (ed.), *Middle Eastern cities,* Berkeley, University of California Press, 47-79.

LAPIDUS, I. M. (1973): 'Traditional Muslim cities: structure and change', in Brown, L. C. (ed.), *From madina to metropolis: heritage and change in the Near Eastern city,* Princeton, Darwin Press, 51-69.

LASSERRE, G. (1958): *Libreville, la ville et sa région,* Cahiers de la Fondation Nationale des Sciences Politiques, Paris, Armand Colin.

LEEMING, F. A. (1959): 'An experimental survey of retail shopping and service facilities in part of North Leeds', *Transactions of the Institute of British Geographers,* no.26, 133-52.

LEMON, A. (1976): *Apartheid: a geographical perspective,* London, Saxon House.

LENCZOWSKI, G. (1969): Discussion following the paper by J. Gulick, 'Village and city', in Lapidus, I. M. (ed.), *Middle Eastern cities,* Berkeley, University of California Press, 156.

LEVER, W. F. (1972): 'The intra-urban movement of manufacturing: a Markov approach', *Transactions of the Institute of British Geographers,* no.56, 21-38.

LEVINE R. A., KLEIN N. H. and OWEN, C. R. (1967): 'Father-child relationships and changing life-styles in Ibadan, Nigeria', in Miner, H. (ed.), *The city in modern Africa,* London, Pall Mall Press, 215-55.

LLOYD, P. C. (1973): 'The Yoruba: an urban people?', in Southall, A. (ed.), *Urban anthropology: cross-cultural studies of urbanization,* Oxford, Oxford University Press, 107-23.

LOEWENSTEIN, L. K. (1963): 'The location of urban land uses', *Land Economics,* vol.39, 407-20.

LOGAN, M. I. (1966 a): 'Locational behaviour of manufacturing firms in urban areas', *Annals of the Association of American Geographers,* vol.56, 451-66.

LOGAN, M. I. (1966 b): 'Capital city manufacturing in Australia', *Economic Geography,* vol.42, 139-51.

LOWENTHAL, D. (1972): *Publications in environmental perception,* No.8, New York, American Geographical Society.

LYNCH, K. (1960): *The image of the city,* Cambridge Mass., M. I. T. Press.

LYNCH, K. (1974): 'The pattern of the metropolis', in Blowers, A. et al. (eds.), *The future of cities,* London, Hutchinson Educational.

MABOGUNJE, A. L. (1962): *Yoruba towns,* Ibadan, Ibadan University Press.

MABOGUNJE, A. L. (1967): 'The morphology of Ibadan', in Lloyd, P. C., Mabogunje, A. L. and Awe, B. (eds.), *The city of Ibadan,* London, Cambridge University Press, 35-56.

MABOGUNJE, A. L. (1968): *Urbanization in Nigeria,* London, University of London Press.

MCCULLOCH, F. J. et al. (1965): *Land use in an urban environment,* Liverpool, Liverpool University Press.

MCELRATH, D. C. (1962): 'The social areas of Rome: a comparative study', *American Sociological Review,* vol.27, 376-91.

MCEVOY, D. (1967): 'Alternative methods of ranking shopping centres: a study from the Manchester conurbation', *Tijdschrift voor Economische en Sociale Geografie,* vol.58, 211-7.

MCGEE, T. G. (1967): *The Southeast Asian city,* London, Bell.

MCGEE, T. G. (1971): *The urbanization process in the Third World,* London, Bell.

MACKINDER, H. J. (1902): *Britain and the British seas,* Oxford, Oxford University Press.

MCLOUGHLIN, J. B. (1969): *Urban and regional planning: a systems approach,* London, Faber and Faber.

MANGIN, W. (1967): 'Latin American squatter settlements: a problem and a solution', *Latin American Research Review,* vol.2, 65-98.

MANN, P. H. (1965): *An approach to urban sociology,* London, Routledge and Kegan Paul.

MARRIS, P. (1960): 'Slum clearance and family life in Lagos', *Human Organization,* vol.19, 123-8.

MARSHALL, J. D. (1968): 'Colonisation as a factor in the planting of towns in north-west England', in Dyos, H. J. (ed.), *The study of urban history,* London, Edward Arnold, 215-30.

MARTIN, J. E. (1964): 'The industrial geography of Greater London', in Clayton, R. (ed.), *The geography of Greater London,* London, Geo. Philip, 111-42.

MARTIN, J. E. (1966): *Greater London: an industrial geography,* London, Bell.

MARTINDALE, D. (1958): 'Prefatory remarks: the theory of the city', introduction to Weber, Max, *The city,* New York, Free

Press of Glencoe, 9-67.

MASAI, Y. (1970): 'The contemporary Japanese townscape', in *Japanese cities: a geographical approach,* Tokyo, Association of Japanese Geographers, 97-108.

MATTINGLY, P. F. (1964): 'Delimitation and movement of CBD boundaries through time: the Harrisburg example', *The Professional Geographer,* vol.16, 9-13.

MAYER, H. M. (1964): Centex industrial park: an organized industrial district', in Thoman, R. S. and Patton, D. J. (eds.), *Focus on geographic activity,* New York, McGraw-Hill, 135-45.

MAYER, P. (1962): *Townsmen or tribesmen,* Cape Town, Oxford University Press.

MEIER, R. L. (1962): *A communication theory of urban growth,* Cambridge Mass., Harvard University Press.

MERLIN, P. (1969): *Les villes nouvelles,* Paris, Presses Universitaires de France. English language edition 1971, London, Methuen.

MITCHELL, J. C. (1961): 'Wage labour and African population movements in Central Africa', in Barbour, K. M. and Prothero, R. M. (eds.), *Essays on African population,* London, Routledge and Kegan Paul, 193-248.

MITCHELL, J. C. (1967): 'Africans in industrial towns in Northern Rhodesia', in H.R.H. The Duke of Edinburgh's Study Conference No.1, p.5. Quoted by Hanna, W. J. and Hanna, J. L. in Miner, H. M., *The city in modern Africa,* London, Pall Mall Press, 155.

MITCHELL, J. C. (1973): 'Distance, transportation and urban involvement in Zambia', in Southall, A. (ed.), *Urban anthropology: cross-cultural studies of urbanization,* Oxford, Oxford University Press, 287-314.

MORGAN, B. S. (1976): 'The bases of family status segregation: a case study in Exeter', *Transactions of the Institute of British Geographers,* New Series, vol.1, 83-107.

MORGAN, W. T. W. (1961 a): 'The two office districts of Central London', *Journal of the Town Planning Institute,* vol.47, 161-6.

MORGAN, W. T. W. (1961 b): 'A functional approach to the study of office distribution', *Tidjschrift voor Economische en Sociale Geografie,* vol.52, 207-10.

MORRILL, R. L. (1965): 'The negro ghetto: problems and alternatives', *Geographical Review,* vol.55, 339-61.

MORRILL, R. L. (1968): 'Waves of spatial diffusion', *Journal of Regional Science,* vol.8, 2.

MORRIS, A. E. J. (1972): *History of urban form,* London, Geo.

Godwin.

MORRIS, F. B. and PYLE, G. F. (1971): 'The social environment of Rio de Janeiro', *Economic Geography,* vol.47, 286-99.

MORSE, R. M. (1971): 'Trends and issues in Latin American urban research, 1965-1970, Part 1', *Latin American Research Review,* vol.6, 3-52.

MORTIMORE, M. J. (1969): 'Landownership and urban growth in Bradford and its environs in the West Riding conurbation, 1850-1950', *Transactions of the Institute of British Geographers,* no.46, 105-19.

MOSES, L. and WILLIAMSON, H. F. (1967): 'The location of economic activity in cities', *American Economic Review,* vol.57, 211-22.

MUNTON, R. J. C. (1974): 'Farming on the urban fringe', in Johnson, J. H. (ed.), *Suburban growth,* London, John Wiley, 201-23.

MURIE, A. (1974): *Household movement and housing choice,* Occasional Paper No.28, Centre for Urban and Regional Studies, University of Birmingham.

MURPHY, R. E. (1966): *The American city: an urban geography,* New York, McGraw-Hill.

MURPHY, R. E. (1971): *The central business district,* London, Longman.

MURPHY, R. E. and VANCE, J. E. (1954 a): 'Delimiting the CBD', *Economic Geography,* vol.30, 189-222.

MURPHY, R. E., and VANCE, J. E. (1954 b): 'A comparative study of nine central business districts', *Economic Geography,* vol.30, 301-36.

MURPHY, R. E. VANCE, J. E. and EPSTEIN, B. J. (1955): 'Internal structure of the CBD', *Economic Geography,* vol.31, 21-46.

MUSIL, J. (1968): 'The development of Prague's ecological structure', in Pahl, R. E. (ed.), *Readings in urban sociology,* Oxford, Pergamon, 232-59.

MUTH, R. F. (1969): *Cities and housing,* Chicago, University of Chicago Press.

NADER, G. A. (1968): 'Private housing estates: the effect of previous residence on workplace and shopping activities', *Town Planning Review,* vol.39, 65-74.

NADER, G. A. (1969): 'Socio-economic status and consumer behaviour', *Urban Studies,* vol.6, 235-45.

NAKAMURA, H. (1968): 'Urban ward associations in Japan', in Pahl, R. E. (ed.), *Readings in urban sociology,* Oxford, Pergamon, 186-208.

NATIONAL ECONOMIC DEVELOPMENT OFFICE (1971): *The future pattern of shopping*, London, H.M.S.O.

NATOLI, S. J. (1971): 'Zoning and the development of urban land use patterns', *Economic Geography*, vol.47, 171-84.

NEWLING, B. E. (1966): 'Urban growth and spatial structure: mathematical models and empirical evidence', *Geographical Review*, vol.56, 213-25.

NEWLING, B. E. (1969): 'The spatial variation of urban population densities', *Geographical Review*, vol.59, 242-52.

NORTHAM, R. M. (1975): *Urban geography*, New York, John Wiley.

ODELL, P. R. and PRESTON, D. A. (1973): *Economies and societies in Latin America: a geographical interpretation*, New York, John Wiley.

OGDEN, P. E. and WINCHESTER, S. W. C. (1975): 'The residential segregation of provincial migrants in Paris in 1911', *Transactions of the Institute of British Geographers*, no.65, 29-44.

OSBORN, R. J. (1966): 'How the Russians plan their cities', *Trans-Action Magazine*, pp.25-30. Reproduced in Fava, S. F. (ed.), *Urbanism in world perspective*, New York, Crowell, 556-63.

PAHL, R. E. (1968): 'The rural-urban continuum', in Pahl, R. E. (ed.), *Readings in urban sociology*, Oxford, Pergamon, 263-97.

PAHL, R. E. (1970): *Patterns of urban life*, London, Longman.

PALM, R. (1976): 'Real estate agents and geographical information', *Geographical Review*, vol.66, 266-80.

PARK, R. E. BURGESS, E. W. and MCKENZIE, R. D. (1925): *The city*, Chicago, University of Chicago Press.

PEACH, G. C. K. (1975): *Urban social segregation*, London, Longman.

PERRY, C. A. (1929): 'The neighbourhood unit: a scheme of arrangement for the family life community', *Regional Survey of New York and its Environs*, vol.7, New York.

PETERSON, J. (1916): 'Illusions of direction orientation', *Journal of Philosophy, Psychology and Scientific Methods*, vol.13, 225-36.

PHILLIPS, D. G. (1958): 'Rural-to-urban migration in Iraq', *Economic Development and Cultural Change*, vol.7, 405-21.

POLLOCK, N. C. (1968): 'The development of urbanization in Southern Africa', in Beckinsale, R. P. and Houston, J. M. (eds.), *Urbanization and its problems: essays presented to E. W. Gilbert*, Oxford, Blackwell, 304-29.

POOLE, M. A. and BOAL, F. W. (1973): 'Religious residential

segregation in Belfast in mid-1969: a multi-level analysis', in Clark, B. D. and Gleave, M. B. (eds.), *Social patterns in cities,* Special Publication No.5, Institute of British Geographers, 1-40.

PORTEOUS, J. D. (1970): 'The nature of the company town', *Transactions of the Institute of British Geographers,* no.51, 127-42.

PRED, A. R. (1964): 'The intrametropolitan location of American manufacturing', *Annals of the Association of American Geographers,* vol.54, 165-80.

PRED, A. R. (1967): *Behaviour and location,* Part I, Lund Studies in Geography, Series B, Human Geography, No.27, Department of Geography, Royal University of Lund.

PRITCHARD, R. M. (1976): *Housing and the spatial structure of the city,* Cambridge, Cambridge University Press.

PROTHERO, R. M. (1964): 'Continuity and change in African population mobility', in Steel, R. W. and Prothero, R. M. (eds.), *Geographers and the Tropics: Liverpool essays,* London, Longman, 189-214.

PROUDFOOT, M. J. (1937): 'City retail structure', *Economic Geography,* vol.13, 425-8.

RANNELLS, J. (1956): *The core of the city : a pilot study of changing land uses in central business districts,* New York, Columbia University Press.

RATCLIFF, R. U. (1939): *The problem of retail site selection,* Michigan Business Studies, vol.9, no.1, Ann Arbor, University of Michigan School of Business Administration.

RATCLIFF, R. U. (1953): *The Madison central business area: a case study of functional change,* Wisconsin Commerce Papers, vol.1, no.5, University of Wisconsin.

REDFIELD, R. and SINGER, M. B. (1954): 'The cultural role of cities', *Economic Development and Cultural Change,* vol.3, 53-73.

REES, P. H. (1971): 'Factorial ecology: an extended definition, survey and critique of the field', *Economic Geography,* vol.47, 220-33.

REX, J. and MOORE, R. (1967): *Race, community and conflict: a study of Sparkbrook,* London.

RICHARDSON, H. W. (1971): *Urban economics,* Harmondsworth, Penguin Books.

ROBSON, B. T. (1968): 'New techniques in urban analysis', in Bowen, E. G. , Carter, H. and Taylor, J. A. (eds.), *Geography at Aberystwyth,* Cardiff, University of Wales Press.

ROBSON, B. T. (1969): *Urban analysis: a study in city structure,* Cambridge, Cambridge University Press.

ROBSON, B. T. (1975): *Urban social areas,* Oxford, Theory and Practice in Geography, Oxford University Press.

RODGERS, H. B. (1962): 'Victorian Manchester', *Journal of the Manchester Geographical Society,* vol.58, 1-12.

ROLPH, I. K. (1929): *The location structure of retail trade,* Washington, United States Government Printing Office for the Bureau of Commerce.

ROSE, H. M. (1969): *Social processes in the city: race and urban residential choice,* Resource Paper No.6, Association of American Geographers' Commission on College Geography, Washington.

ROSE, H. M. (1970): 'The development of an urban subsystem: the case of the negro ghetto', *Annals of the Association of American Geographers,* vol.60, 1-17.

ROSE, H. M. (1972). 'The spatial development of black residential subsystems', *Economic Geography,* vol.48, 43-65.

ROSSI, P. H. (1955): *Why families move: a study in the social psychology of urban residential mobility,* Glencoe, The Free Press.

ROUCH, J. (1956): 'Migrations au Ghana', *Journal de la Société des Africanistes,* vol.26, 33-196. Quoted by Hanna, W. J. and Hanna, J. L. in Miner, H.M. (ed.), *The city in modern Africa,* London, Pall Mall Press, 155.

ROWE, W. L. (1973): 'Caste, kinship, and association in urban India', in Southall, A. (ed.), *Urban anthropology: cross-cultural studies of urbanization,* Oxford, Oxford University Press, 211-49.

ROWLAND, D. T. (1971): 'Maori migration to Auckland', *New Zealand Geographer,* vol.27, 21-37.

ROWLEY, G. (1972): 'Spatial variations in the prices of central goods: a preliminary investigation', *Tijdschrift voor Economische en Sociale Geografie,* vol.63, 360-8.

SCARGILL, D. I. (1963): 'Factors affecting the location of industry: the example of Halifax', *Geography,* vol.48, 166-74.

SCARGILL, D. I. (1967): 'Metropolitan influences in the Oxford region', *Geography,* vol.62, 157-65.

SCARGILL, D. I. (1968): 'The expanded town in England and Wales', in Beckinsale, R. P. and Houston, J. M. (eds.), *Urbanization and its problems: essays in honour of E. W. Gilbert,* Oxford, Blackwell, 119-42.

SCARGILL, D. I. (1975): 'Urbanization of Oxford's green belt', in

Smith, C. G. and Scargill, D. I. (eds.), *Oxford and its region*, Oxford, Oxford University Press, 77-82.

SCHELL, E. (1964): 'Aspects of central place theory unsubstantiated by store facilities in Boston's retail landscape', *Abstract of Papers, Twentieth International Geographical Congress*, London, 207.

SCHNORE, L. F. (1964): 'Urban structure and suburban selectivity', *Demography*, vol.1, 164-76.

SCHNORE, L. F. (1965 a): *The urban scene*, New York, The Free Press.

SCHNORE, L. F. (1965 b): 'On the spatial structure of cities in the two Americas', in Hauser, P. M. and Schnore, L. F. (eds.), *The study of urbanization*, New York, John Wiley, 347-98.

SCOTT, P. (1959): 'The Australian CBD', *Economic Geography*, vol.35, 290-314.

SCOTT, P. (1970): *Geography and retailing*, London, Hutchinson University Library.

SELF, P. J. O. (1945): 'Voluntary organizations in Bethnal Green', in Bourdillon, A. F. C. (ed.), *Voluntary social services*, London, Methuen, 236.

SENDUT, H. (1965): 'The structure of Kuala Lumpur: Malaysia's capital city', *Town Planning Review*, vol.36, 125-38.

SHACK, W. A. (1973): 'Urban ethnicity and the cultural process of urbanization in Ethiopia', in Southall, A. (ed.), *Urban anthropology: cross-cultural studies of urbanization*, Oxford, Oxford University Press, 251-85.

SHEVKY, E. and BELL, W. (1955): *Social area analysis: theory, illustrative application and computational procedures*, Stanford, Stanford University Press.

SHEVKY, E. and WILLIAMS, M. (1949): *The social areas of Los Angeles: analysis and typology*, Berkeley and Los Angeles, University of California Press.

SIMIRENKO, A. (1964): *Pilgrims, colonists, and frontiersmen*, New York, The Free Press.

SIMMONS, J. W. (1964): *The changing pattern of retail location*, Research Paper No.92, Department of Geography, University of Chicago.

SIMMONS, J. W. (1966): *Toronto's changing retail complex: a study in growth and blight*, Research Paper No.104, Department of Geography, University of Chicago.

SIMMONS, J. W. (1968): 'Changing residence in the city: a review of intra-urban mobility', *Geographical Review*, vol.58, 621-51.

SINCLAIR, R. (1967): 'Von Thünen and urban sprawl', *Annals of the Association of American Geographers,* vol.57, 72-87.

SINGH, R. L. (1964): *Bangalore: an urban survey,* Varanasi, Tara Publications for the National Geographical Society of India.

SJOBERG, G. (1960): *The preindustrial city: past and present,* Glencoe, The Free Press.

SJOBERG, G. (1965): 'Cities in developing and in industrial societies: a cross-cultural analysis', in Hauser, P. M. and Schnore, L. F. (eds.), *The study of urbanization,* New York, John Wiley, 213-63.

SMAILES, A. E. (1955): 'Some reflections on the geographical description and analysis of townscapes', *Transactions of the Institute of British Geographers,* no.21, 99-115.

SMITH, D. M. (1971): *Industrial location: an economic geographical analysis,* New York, John Wiley.

SMITH, L. (1971): 'Space for the CBD's functions', in Bourne, L. S. (ed.), *Internal structure of the city,* New York, Oxford University Press, 352-60.

SOUTHALL, A. (1967): 'Kampala-Mengo', in Miner, H. M. (ed.), *The city in modern Africa,* London, Pall Mall Press, 297-332.

SPATE, O. H. K. and AHMAD, E. (1950): 'Five cities of the Gangetic plain: a cross section of Indian cultural history', *Geographical Review,* vol.40, 260-78.

SPATE, O. H. K. and TRUEBLOOD, L. (1942): 'Rangoon: a study in urban geography', *Geographical Review,* vol.32, 56-73.

SPENGLER, J. J. (1967): 'Africa and the theory of optimum city size', in Miner, H. M. (ed.), *The city in modern Africa,* London, Pall Mall Press, 55-89.

STADEL, C. (1975): 'The structure of squatter settlements in Medellin, Colombia', *Area,* vol.7, 249-54.

STANISLAWSKI, D. (1947): 'Early Spanish town planning in the New World', *Geographical Review,* vol.37, 94-105.

STEIN, C. S. (1964): 'A regional plan for dispersal', *Architectural Record,* vol.136, 205-6.

STERN, S. M. (1970): 'The constitution of the Islamic city', in Hourani, A. H. and Stern, S. M. (eds.), *The Islamic city,* Oxford, Bruno Cassirer, 25-50.

STOKES, C. J. (1962): 'A theory of slums', *Land Economics,* vol.38, 187-97.

TAEUBER, K. E. and TAEUBER, A. F. (1965): *Negroes in cities,* Chicago, Aldine Publishing Company.

TANABE, K. (1970): 'Intra-regional structure of Japanese cities', in *Japanese cities: a geographical approach,* Tokyo, Association of Japanese Geographers, 109-19.

THOMAS, C. J. (1966): 'Some geographical aspects of council

housing in Nottingham', *East Midland Geographer*, vol.4, 88-98.

THOMAS, D. (1970): *London's green belt*, London, Faber and Faber.

THOMAS, R. W. (1972): 'The retail structure of the central area', in *The retail structure of cities*, Occasional Publication No.1, Urban Study Group of the Institute of British Geographers, 69-94.

THOMPSON, D. L. (1966): 'Future directions of retail area research', *Economic Geography*, vol.42, 1-18.

THORNGREN, B. (1967): 'External economies of the urban core', in University of Amsterdam, *Urban core and inner city*, Leiden, E. J. Brill, 413-20.

THORPE, D. and NADER, G. A. (1967): 'Customer movement and shopping centre structure: a study of a central place system in Northern Durham', *Regional Studies*, vol.1, 173-91.

THORPE, D. and RHODES, T. C. (1966): 'The shopping centres of the Tyneside urban region and large scale grocery retailing', *Economic Geography*, vol.42, 52-73.

TIMMS, D. W. G. (1971): *The urban mosaic: towards a theory of residential differentiation*, Cambridge, Cambridge University Press.

TUAN, Y-F. (1968): 'A preface to Chinese cities', in Beckinsale, R. P. and Houston, J. M. (eds.), *Urbanization and its problems: essays presented to E. W. Gilbert*, Oxford, Blackwell, 218-53.

TUAN, Y-F. (1974): *Topophilia: A study of environmental perception, attitudes, and values*, Englewood Cliffs, Prentice-Hall.

TURNER, J. F. C. (1966): *Uncontrolled urban settlement: problems and policies*, Working Paper No.11, Inter-regional Seminar on Development Policies and Planning in Relation to Urbanization, University of Pittsburg. Reproduced in Breese, G. (ed.), *The city in newly developing countries*, Englewood Cliffs, Prentice-Hall , 507-34.

TURNER, J. F. C. (1967): 'Barriers and channels for housing development in modernizing countries', *Journal of the American Institute of Planners*, vol.33, 167-81.

TURNER, J. F. C. (1968): 'Housing priorities, settlement patterns and urban development in modernizing countries', *Journal of the American Institute of Planners*, vol.34, 354-63.

TURNOCK, D. (1974): 'Urban development in a socialist city: Bucureşti', *Geography*, vol.59, 344-8.

VAN ARSDOL, M. D., CAMILLERI, S. F. and SCHMID, C. F. (1958): 'The generality of urban social area indices', *American Sociological Review*, vol.23, 227-84.

VANCE, J. E. (1962): 'Emerging patterns of commercial structure in American cities', in Norborg, K. (ed.), *The IGU symposium in urban geography, Lund 1960,* 485-518.

VANCE, J. E. (1966): 'Housing the worker: the employment linkage as a force in urban structure', *Economic Geography,* vol.42, 294-325.

VANCE, J. E. (1971 a): 'Focus on downtown', in Bourne, L. S. (ed.), *Internal structure of the city,* New York, Oxford University Press, 112-20.

VANCE, J. E. (1971 b): 'Land assignment in the precapitalist, capitalist, and postcapitalist city', *Economic Geography,* vol.47, 101-20.

VAN HULTEN, M. (1967): 'In search of the urban core of Amsterdam', in University of Amsterdam, *Urban core and inner city,* Leiden, E. J. Brill, 183-200.

VAUGHAN, D. R. (1970): *The spatial distribution of initial residence and post arrival residential mobility of migrants to Monterrey, Mexico,* Unpublished M.A. thesis, University of Texas at Austin.

VON GRUNEBAUM, G. E. (1961): 'The structure of the Muslim town', in Von Grunebaum, G. E. (ed.), *Islam and the growth of a cultural tradition,* London, Routledge and Kegan Paul, 141-58.

VON THÜNEN J. H. (1826): *Der isolierte staat in beziehung auf landwirtschaft und nationalökonomie,* Hamburg, Perthes.

WARD, D. (1962): 'The pre-urban cadaster and the urban pattern of Leeds', *Annals of the Association of American Geographers,* vol.52, 150-66.

WARD, D. (1966): 'The industrial revolution and the emergence of Boston's central business district', *Economic Geography,* vol.42, 152-71.

WARD, D. (1968): 'The emergence of central immigrant ghettoes in American cities 1840-1920', *Annals of the Association of American Geographers,* vol.58, 343-59.

WARD, D. (1971): *Cities and immigrants: a geography of change in Nineteenth Century America,* New York, Oxford University Press.

WEBBER, M. M. (1964): 'The urban place and the nonplace urban realm', in Webber, M. M. et al. (eds.), *Explorations into urban structure,* University of Pennsylvania Press, 79-153.

WEBER, M. (1962): *The city,* translated by Martindale, D. and Neuwirth, G., New York, Collier Books.

WEEKLEY, I. G. (1956): 'Service centres in Nottingham: a concept in urban analysis', *East Midland Geographer,* vol.6, 41-6.

WEISS, S. F., KENNEY, K. B. and STEFFENS, P. C. (1966): 'Consumer preferences in residential location: a preliminary investigation of the house purchase decision', *University of California Research Reviews,* vol.13, 1-32.

WEITZ, R. (1973): *Urbanization and the developing countries,* New York, Praeger.

WHEATLEY, P. (1963): 'What the greatness of the city is said to be: reflections on Sjoberg', *Pacific Viewpoint,* vol.4, 163.

WHEATLEY, P. (1971): *The pivot of the four quarters: a preliminary enquiry into the origins and character of the ancient Chinese city,* Edinburgh, Edinburgh University Press.

WHITEHAND, J. W. R. (1967): 'Fringe belts: a neglected aspect of urban geography', *Transactions of the Institute of British Geographers,* no.41, 223-33.

WHITEHAND, J. W. R. (1974): 'The changing nature of the urban fringe: a time perspective', in Johnson, J. H. (ed.), *Suburban growth,* London, John Wiley, 31-52.

WILLIAM-OLSSON, W. (1940): 'Stockholm: its structure and development', *Geographical Review,* vol.30, 420-38.

WILLIAMS, P. R. (1976): 'The role of institutions in the inner London housing market: the case of Islington', *Transactions of the Institute of British Geographers,* New Series, vol.1, 72-82.

WILLMOTT, P. (1963): *The evolution of a community,* London, Routledge and Kegan Paul.

WILSON, A. G. (1974): *Urban and regional models in geography and planning,* London, John Wiley.

WINCHESTER, S. W. C. (1975): *Spatial structure and social activity: a social geography of Coventry,* Unpublished D.Phil. thesis, University of Oxford.

WIRTH, L. (1938): 'Urbanism as a way of life', *American Journal of Sociology,* vol.44, 1-24.

WISE, M. J. (1949): 'On the evolution of the jewellery and gun quarters in Birmingham', *Transactions of the Institute of British Geographers,* no.15, 57-72.

WOLFE, R. I. (1966): 'Recreational travel: the new migration', *Canadian Geographer,* vol.10, 1-14.

WOOD, P. A. (1969): 'Industrial location and linkage', *Area,* vol.1, 32-9.

WOOD, P. A. (1974): 'Urban manufacturing: a view from the fringe', in Johnson, J. H. (ed.), *Suburban growth,* London, John Wiley, 129-54.

WRIGHT, F. L. (1958): *The living city,* New York, Horizon Press.

YAMORI, K. (1970): 'On the regional structure of Japanese castle towns', in Association of Japanese Geographers, *Japanese cities:*

a geographical approach, Tokyo, 17-21.

YAZAKI, T. (1963): *The Japanese city: a sociological analysis,* Tokyo, Japan Publications Trading Company.

YAZAKI, T. (1973): 'The history of urbanization in Japan', in Southall, A. (ed.), *Urban anthropology: cross-cultural studies of urbanization,* New York, Oxford University Press, 139-61.

YOUNG, B. S. (1961): 'Aspects of the central business district of Port Elizabeth, Cape Province', *Journal for Social Research,* vol.12, 27-48.

YOUNG, M. and WILLMOTT, P. (1957): *Family and kinship in East London,* Harmondsworth, Penguin Books.

ZIPF, G. W. (1941): *National unity and disunity,* Bloomington Illinois.

ZWINGLI, U. (1967): 'Criteria for delimitation of urban zones, particularly the town centre, and their application to the city of Zurich', in University of Amsterdam, *Urban core and inner city,* Leiden, E. J. Brill, 441-67.

Index